S0-BVP-279

11-20-73

A NATION WRIT LARGE?

A NATION WRIT LARGE?

Foreign-Policy Problems before the European Community

Edited by

MAX KOHNSTAMM

and

WOLFGANG HAGER

A HALSTED PRESS BOOK

JOHN WILEY & SONS
New York – Toronto

© Institut de la Communauté Européenne pour les
Études Universitaires 1973

First published in the United Kingdom 1973 by
The Macmillan Press Ltd

Published in the U.S.A. and
Canada by Halsted Press, a
Division of John Wiley & Sons, Inc.,
New York

Printed in Great Britain

Library of Congress Cataloging in Publication Data

Kohnstamm, Max, 1914–
    A nation writ large?

    "A Halsted Press book."
    Survey of the European community initiated by the
European Community Institute for University Studies.
    1. European Economic Community—Addresses, essays,
lectures. 2. European Economic Community countries—
Foreign relations—Addresses, essays, lectures.
I. Hager, Wolfgang, joint author. II. European
Community Institute for University Studies. III. Title.
HC241.2.K574   382′.9142   73–6817
ISBN 0–470–49795–5

Contents

1785251

Preface

The European Community Institute for University Studies presents in this volume a survey of the main problems in the realm of foreign policy which confront the nations now forming the European Community. Although its authors hope that within the present decade it will be possible to speak of the foreign policy of the European Community, they are under no illusion concerning the difficulties that have to be overcome before this can be the case.

But it seems to them that the Community cannot choose not to have a common foreign policy. As many chapters of this volume show, the distinction between internal and foreign affairs is becoming blurred. For this reason the internal progress of the Community, especially towards economic and monetary union – an objective accepted by all member states – will only be possible if progress is made at the same time towards common positions, and common policies, in what we still call 'foreign affairs'.

Such progress cannot and should not be made without a public debate. For the past twenty years important decisions have been taken by the European Community without much debate outside the charmed circle of its institutions. This volume is intended as a contribution to what must become a continuous, informed, Community-wide debate on foreign policy issues which, however disguised in technicalities, involve fundamental political choices.

Our method of work reflects our interest in the process, the debate, as well as the product, the insights which resulted from it. The authors of the chapters, originating from different member states, had occasion to discuss successive drafts with equally multi-national discussion groups. The names of the participants can be found on p. 257. We are deeply grateful for the time and expertise they have contributed to this effort.

We did not, however, wish to produce a series of reports

reflecting a colourless consensus: the final responsibility for each chapter rests with its author.

One great advantage of the long preparation of each chapter in discussion groups was the opportunity it gave for confronting relevant chapters with each other, letting members of one discussion group take part in the discussion of another, etc. The result, we feel, is a unity of conception otherwise difficult to achieve in a work with several contributors. This unity was greatly helped by the fact that the discussions on the introductory chapter preceded most of the others.

To apply the method of international group discussion with different authors on this scale is relatively complicated and expensive. Only the very generous financial aid of the Volkswagen, Agnelli and Ford Foundations and the Royal Dutch Shell Group made possible the process of which this volume is the result. Needless to say, these donors are in no way responsible for its contents. That the effort could be made, however, was only possible thanks to their backing. Without the devotion of the small staff of the European Community Institute for University Studies this project would never have been carried out. To all of them, thanks.

Special thanks are also due to Richard Mayne, whose help and great experience were invaluable during the final review of the text.

The structure of this volume speaks for itself. The first chapter attempts to describe the general political framework in which the Community must operate and decide on its policy-choices. The second chapter does the same for the international economic context. Chapters 3–6 throw light on different aspects of the Community's foreign policy; they take a functional look at the problem. Chapters 7–10 bring the different aspects together in looking at countries and regions which are of special importance to the Community.

It would have been tempting to include chapters concerning Japan, China, India and Latin America in this book. However, a choice had to be made and the present one seemed the most relevant to Europe's present situation.

Finally a word about the European Community Institute for University Studies which took the initiative for the project.

The Institute is an independent organisation founded in 1958 and aimed originally at furthering university studies relating to the economic, social, political and legal aspects of European integration. During the first decade of its existence it assisted in the establishment of several university centres for European studies, and fostered contacts between those engaged in such studies through meetings and seminars and through the regular publication of bulletins concerning university research, courses and doctoral theses on various aspects of European integration.

After the Summit conference at The Hague, it was felt that new efforts were necessary to stimulate a Europe-wide debate on the many problems that must be solved to attain the objectives agreed upon on that occasion, a debate not confined to governments and civil servants, but involving men and women of different disciplines and walks of life.

In the United States, such debate is nourished and organised not only by many universities but also by many other independent institutes. These organisations all have one common characteristic: they take a continent-wide view of the question and they help, through research and public debate, to establish a basis for government action.

To stimulate such a continent-wide debate in the Community, Europe needs similar institutions. Those who are already studying and discussing European matters need better opportunities for regular and sustained work together.

In 1970, the European Community Institute for University Studies therefore decided to extend its activities and to develop gradually into an institute for European policy planning. The present volume is the result of the first major project undertaken by the Institute in this field.

MAX KOHNSTAMM
President of the
European Community Institute
for University Studies

Brussels
December 1972

1 The European Community and the Uncertainties of Interdependence

François Duchêne

The enlargement of the European Community from six countries to nine, including Britain, comes at a time when the whole world system appears to be in flux. In Europe, a series of agreements culminating in the codification of the status of West Berlin is virtually closing that phase of history associated with the phrase 'the cold war', though they do not settle the ambiguities of the long-term balance between the Eurasian super-power, the Soviet Union, and the rest of the European peninsula, especially if, as it now seems, the position of the United States is to be uncertain. While Europe seems to be settling down, in the Far East new stars of the first magnitude, China and Japan, are coming to the fore on a scale comparable almost with the super-powers themselves. The Sino-Soviet quarrel, the American recognition of Mao's China, and the latter's triumphant entry into the United Nations, mark the coming of age of the Far East as the major centre of the world balance. These changes accompany a major modulation in relations between the super-powers themselves. America, disillusioned with the notion of policing the world, seems potentially to be consummating the retreat of the West begun with the collapse of the great European empires after the war. The Soviet Union is coming out for the first time from its North Eurasian glacis and claiming all the perquisites of global power. At the same time, in the West (if that term is taken to include the easternmost state of Asia, Japan), the smooth surface of post-war economic co-operation, so long suggestive of a new, contractual, and more civilised form of relations between states, has been broken by uncouth sounds of rising competition between a hitherto invulnerable United States and hitherto outclassed Western Europe and Japan. Charges of protectionism, forcing bids in international bargaining and threats of breakdown in common institutions have rent the air. All these developments have been far from a representative vision of the future ten years ago, such as President Kennedy's notion of an 'Atlantic partnership' enunciated in 1962: a United States of America and a uniting states of Europe together would negotiate peace with the Soviet Union and along with Japan organise the capitalist world economy and help the developing countries, in the hope that prosperity and peace would broadly go forward hand-in-hand to a better world. Instead, both in fact and in mood, the world seems to be moving away from ideologies of Eldorados, revolutionary or reformist, such as the Marxist 'East' and the liberal 'West' cherished in the cold war, towards an increasing emphasis on power relations between states and even subnational groups or classes. A new balance of great powers, spreading this time virtually right across the industrialised northern hemisphere, seems to be emerging. Such a world seems radically different from the assumptions of the founding fathers of the European Community.

The consensus of the founding fathers was grounded in two experiences. One was that the whole Western leadership, having lived through the disastrous 1930s, associated national-ism and economic restriction with Depression and Fascism culminating in war. International co-operation in their eyes of itself constituted a root-and-branch reform of the bad old system of rivalries between states. However, the quarrels between East and West showed that the United Nations could not be a practical regulator of the international system. Narrower but more concrete goals were necessary. This con-verged with the second experience, the sickening tension of cold war which took over almost where hot war left off. The power of Russia in Europe could only be met by collective defence and the threat of Communism by an *idée force* with comparable energy.

The ideal of unity, even limited at first to the six initial members of the European Community, met all these requirements. Behind these assumptions lay a third, less visible, but rock-like reality: this was the backing of the United States, which was so much more powerful than Western Europe and Japan that it could afford to sustain collective defence and international economic co-operation virtually single-handed. American power after the war gave a natural unity to Western policies.

All this has gradually changed in the last decade. Collective Western defence and the Western economic 'miracles', belying prophecies of capitalist doom, have gradually reduced the fear of Soviet power. The ideological attraction of Communism, itself riven by schisms, has declined. At the same time, the price of rapid economic growth, desired by all in a context of poverty, has become more and more obtrusive in a world of emerging affluence. The costs of sections of society going to the wall, like small peasants or drop-outs, have occupied much of politics; even more has been taken up with the demands of constituencies whose power has been growing such as Blacks, students and technological workers. Most striking of all has been a new attitude which is more aloof from, and even hostile to, material progress alone and increasingly preoccupied with spiritual values, the quality of living, feelings, the environment, anything which takes society from the all-embracing productive machine back to men as the measure of things. This *crise de civilisation* makes governments of rich nations more introspective and less responsive to the needs of neighbours. The spectacular growth of interdependence between societies, at least in the West, has added to the strains. To the extent that countries are more intimately affected by each other's economic and political affairs, but not collectively responsible for meeting the consequences of them, they are also more subject to the tensions and vagaries of each other's societies. This leads to a phenomenon of attraction–repulsion. Paradoxically, societies where nationalism is ideologically under attack are becoming more truculent towards one another.

As a result the international economic system has lost the fine simplicity it derived from the immediate post-war consensus on the need to maximise growth and on the policies to achieve it. So has the international security system, as 'cold

war' gradually fades without all of its underlying problems
necessarily disappearing. The tendency of the United States to
withdraw from direct involvement in Eurasia; détente, with
the effect relatively loose East–West co-operation might have
in diluting Western integration; social instabilities in both East
and West Europe; and the partial shift from Europe as the
former centre of world politics to a global stage where the Far
East may matter more; all raise new question marks and tend
to diversify the ways in which nations, even inside the European Community, see their interests. The result is not necessarily to dissolve the achievements of internationalism, though
in some cases they do seem watered down. But the climate in
which the newly extended European Community defines and
pursues its internal and external purposes will, at least superficially, be utterly different from that in which European unity
was launched by the core of the Six in the 1950s in full 'cold
war'.

Appearances, however, can be deceptive. The contrast
between the dominance of the two super-powers and their
alliance system during the 'cold war' and the worldwide
balance of major powers which seems to be emerging is so
riveting that it may mislead one into underemphasising the
striking continuity of functions in the post-war system, then
and now. If there is one development which has changed the
'cold war' more than others, this is the nuclear inhibition on
the traditional advantages conferred by military power. The
fear of 'another Cuba' has impelled both super-powers to
avoid confrontation at any military levels and to enter into
more and more negotiations such as the Strategic Arms Limitation Talks (SALT). Though the formal restraints in the
'limited adversary relationship' are far from absolute, and one
could even conceive the informal ones being less constraining
than is now assumed, they are nevertheless so powerful as to
lead to a quasi-contractual relationship between the US and
USSR. They have been forced to move from conflict to an
'interdependence' of sorts. It may seem that elsewhere
developments point the other way. The recriminatory style of
the great international economic negotiations of the past
decade, the Kennedy Round to cut obstacles to trade and
even more the dollar crisis of 1971, have suggested the end of

the old harmony between the United States and its European and Japanese proteges now they have become more nearly its equals in this field. Yet the outcomes of these negotiations, which have been far less spectacular because they have fitted in better with the now normal preconceptions of collective action, have probably reinforced the common Western economic system. They have shown that when faced with a breakdown the partners dare not play fast and loose with the joint arrangements which buttress their collective employment and growth. Conflict is played out within a common framework. Even the revived social violence which rocked society in 1968, is perhaps more ambiguous than it seems. Since it appears to affect the West more than the East it might affect the balance of power between diverse Western societies, which are becoming increasingly civilian in outlook, and the Soviet state which can more easily manipulate its less assertive public opinion. But, elsewhere, especially in the Third World, the rise in individual and collective self-assertion, of which nationalism is an early expression, undoubtedly limits the ability of great powers to bully small ones. This may even prove in the 1970s to have made an anachronism of subversion, as Latin America to some extent already suggests. Here again, the evolution of the world places new limits on the abuse of power.

At all these diverse levels, nuclear, economic and sociocultural, one finds a balance between conflict on the one hand and a willed or unwilled recognition of limits and contract on the other. In fact, conflicts not only operate within this framework of interdependence: they tend sometimes to assume and even to arise from it. It is often suggested of the Nixon Doctrine, and especially of Dr Kissinger, that Western internationalism has foundered in a revival of Metternich and the nineteenth-century notion of the balance of power. There are certainly overtones of this in the scholaticism of bargaining, 'zero-sum games', and adversary relationships which has produced its hundred flowers at Harvard in the past decade. Yet when one actually reads President Nixon's major Foreign Policy messages, one finds in them an assumption of interdependence which is more than merely rhetorical since it helps to give intellectual shape to national choices, precisely in the nuclear, economic and social fields.

Much of the revival of conflict in the world seems, then, to be a consequence of new problems born of increasing inter-dependence itself. From this standpoint, the superficial anti-thesis between the desire for unity and reconciliation of the founding fathers of the European Community and the present realities of the balance of power tends to disappear. On the contrary, what the founding fathers may have helped to create was an instrument and a method useful precisely in dealing with the conflicts of interdependence.

The ambivalence of Europe

This does not of itself eliminate the ambiguities of the Euro-pean Community's situation, of its potential or indeed of its tradition. There has from the beginning been a dualism in the support for West European integration. This dualism has been a matter not only of the reasons why different people or groups gave it their backing. It has been implicit in the idea itself and present, in different mixtures, in all supporters. On the one hand, there has been the stated aim of the founding fathers, the one of which they were most proud: the con-tribution of unity to reconciling former enemies, creating equality between them, spreading the area of peace, not only within the confines of the Community but also, at least in aspiration, with the outside world.[1] This has represented the application of the reforming liberal spirit to a subcontinent; even for conservatives, particularly in Germany, it has meant the triumph between nations as well as within them of the *Rechtstaat*, the rule of law, violated by all of Europe's would-be conquerors down to Hitler. On the other hand, there has been a strand of ambition for power from the very beginning in the European ideal. This too has taken different forms. In the statements of Jean Monnet, it has always been pre-sented as the necessary means to co-operation with one super-power, the United States, and to peace with the other, the Soviet Union: it has amounted to an assertion of the need for countervailing powers as the basis of equitable inter-

---

[1] The opening words of the Schuman declaration of 9 May 1950 are: 'World peace can only be preserved by creative efforts which match the dangers that threaten it.'

dependence and effective common action. In the speeches of many other West European politicians, the outstanding one being Charles de Gaulle, it has echoed and amplified the nationalist traditions of the European continent, implying adversary relations with the United States, the Soviet Union or both.

There is little doubt that the success of the European idea as a political catchment area has been bound up with this necessary ambiguity about its ultimate purposes. It has appealed, like all *idées force*, to widely differing and even radically opposed political temperaments. Hitherto, this many-sidedness has been interesting but to some extent academic. Today, however, it becomes more urgent to discuss its implications. Britain's entry into the European Community gives it a new potential, because it ends the schism in Western Europe of the past twenty years. This coincides with the sense within its present membership that the end of the road for stealthy economic functionalism has come in sight. Henceforth, there will be both a need and an opportunity to go beyond the common market to a political and economic union which is a new force in the world. This has been stressed in the speeches of Chancellor Brandt, Prime Minister Heath and above all President Pompidou in the past eighteen months.

From 1973 onwards, the moment to build on the new aspiration to political association in Western Europe has arrived and what should and can be done will have to be defined, agreed and acted upon. Moreover, this comes at a time when the context is itself changing. Increasing competition with the United States will cast doubt on the permanence of Europe's 'free ride' of the past generation. More normal relations with the Soviet Union will raise questions as to what a political European Community stands for. It will be necessary to choose between the various possibilities open to a European Community. At this turning point in the history not only of the Community but of Europe and even the wider world any policy – and *a fortiori* any policy publication like this – must examine the alternatives and declare its viewpoint and its interest.

A European super-power?

Nationalism writ large on the European scale is one such choice. In a world of super-powers, a uniting Western Europe might become one of the governors of the age, just as in the previous era its 'great powers' ruled the world. President Nixon himself has given currency to this notion by speaking of the 'five powers' which will dominate the seventies, including Europe among them. It is natural that this should have attractions for at least some elements in societies which only half a century ago lorded it on the centre of the political stage. Even now the hope can be buttressed by impressive statistics. The enlarged European Community will represent nearly ten per cent of the population and arms budgets, over twenty per cent of the annual output, thirty per cent of the trade and forty per cent of the money reserves, of the world. These are figures with bottom, even by super-power standards. Though West European social structures and political attitudes have changed in many ways, not least as the result of two ruinous wars, state traditions of power and prestige still live on in the habits of thought, nostalgia and instinctive ambitions, particularly of the bureaucracies of the two nuclear European powers, Britain and France. They even seem reflected in the outlook of Georges Pompidou and Edward Heath, though M. Pompidou would seem more characteristic of widespread attitudes in France than Mr Heath of those in Britain. Moreover, the very difficulties of bringing nine disparate countries together in some kind of cohesive group may require some collective emotional force, which could well be generated in reaction against some third party, most probably one of the super-powers. The theme of opposition to the 'Dual Hegemony' of the two super-powers already surfaced once in de Gaulle's time. In a period when there is less fear of Soviet military domination of Europe and less certainty about the American commitment to the defence of West European interests in the face of the Soviet Union, that is to say, less need but also less expectation of protection, the idea of a European super-power equipped with all the panoply of one could be a natural development.

This would be all the more the case if it was found that

the lack of the accoutrements of a super-power in some way handicapped Western Europe in its relations with the outside world in general. One can well imagine Western Europe's policies on the margins of the continent being extremely cautious, and even castrated, as a result of the likely confrontation at numerous points with a super-nuclear Soviet Union which constitutes the main security concern in Europe itself. This could be true not only, as today, of Eastern Europe (for example, Czechoslovakia after 1968), but of the Mediterranean, Middle East, Africa and even the maritime environment of the North Atlantic. This would be particularly constraining if the American withdrawal from the periphery of Western Eurasia were to continue to a point where the Soviet Union became its uniquely dominant power. In all these areas, Western Europe's ability to pursue politico-military policies is severely circumscribed by its lack of nuclear or indeed of major conventional military power. This situation is unlikely to change if Western Europe continues to lack such power. It is difficult to imagine politicians with ambitions of the kind at which Heath and Pompidou have hinted, living in permanent comfort with such a constraint. The sense of some inferiority to be rectified could even invade the economic field. One of the major factors leading France (and perhaps other West European countries) to enter into trade negotiations with the United States as a result of the dollar crisis of 1971 was a feeling that an economic and commercial rift might hasten the withdrawal of America's security guarantees from Western Europe. In short, for Western Europe as a whole, as already for Germany for many years, there is an emerging sense that it may be necessary to make economic concessions to pay for protection. Should these concessions, as a result of American over-bidding (not to say bullying in Mr Connally's case), begin to seem excessive, aspirations to shake the protectorate might emerge. There might even appear a sense, popularising the gaullist concept of the 'Dual Hegemony' as it could not be popularised in the 1960s, that the super-powers are reaching their accomodations too much at the expense of Europeans. The nationalism which aims at a European super-state could thrive on such frustrations. And yet, even if one looks beyond the timescale of the present study, such an ambition seems to take little account of the diverse aims and concrete possibilities of the members of the enlarged European Community for many years to come. A European super-power, really independent of all the controls of the Dual Hegemony, would have to have its own nuclear weapons. These cannot be provided by Britain or France, separately or in conjunction, because from the point of view of the seven non-nuclear powers in the enlarged European Community, including the German Federal Republic, they are no substitute for the far larger force (nuclear, political and economic) of the United States. Worse, these two powers have shown signs of giving themselves superior political airs as a result of their nuclear status, pretensions which are not popular and are considered largely hollow by their neighbours. The British and French nuclear deterrents do probably play an increasing role in German thinking as a supplementary insurance to the American nuclear guarantee in so far as Germany is anxious about the ultimate American nuclear commitment to Europe. They could become more than that only if the United States were deliberately and clearly to dissociate itself from deterrence in Europe. Even in that case, the Federal Republic and the other non-nuclear states would be much more likely to look for their salvation to a European security system of the kind once sponsored by the Soviet Union and General de Gaulle together than to a wizened continuation of NATO with the British and France playing dwarf Americans to a Soviet giant. All these developments point to the sterilisation of the European Community, its stunting at a primitive commercial level, not to its growth into a super-state. A super-state would require a European force. But this implies a European Federation with a President able to press the button for the whole Community; and this is still a remote prospect. Moreover, there is every probability that the West Germans, aiming at better relations with Eastern Europe, partly because of their desire for at least some of the fruits of the reunification of the two Germanies, even if they cannot unite in a single state, will be at one with the Russians in being determined to avoid the nuclear issue. This is probably the one development which could long postpone all hope of easier relations in Europe. Long before that, in an 'era of negotiation' there would be nothing easier for the Soviet Union than to mobilise West European opinion against an attempt at creating a nuclear power which would be regarded as the wrecker of détente. It is also more than likely that the United States would be torn in such an event between those who condemn a European nuclear force as a violation of the spirit of détente and a potential threat, and those who might favour it because it justifies American isolationism. This in turn would increase West European divisions, within and between countries, because it would point to a period of transition when Western Europe as yet had no nuclear deterrent but risked a major conflict with the Soviet Union about the prospect while America remained neutral or disapproving. This would be a regression from the sense of security not only of the détente but of the 'cold war' as well. Nothing could be more calculated to retard rather than further West European unity.

For all these reasons, any movement by the European Community towards a real European nuclear force (as apart from secondary French or British premiums under the American insurance scheme) seems extremely unlikely in the coming decade. At the very least, enough time would have to pass first to change some of the basic assumptions of the European situation, second to let the political implications sink in and third to exploit the technological consequences in terms of building a force. Experience shows that in Europe such changes do not take place rapidly and may not take place at all.

Without a nuclear focus, it will be well-nigh impossible for a full-fledged European super-state, or the mentality of one, to emerge. 'European gaullism' is a contradiction in terms. While President de Gaulle's speeches and press conferences often invoked a sense of European solidarity against outsiders, his policy choices were based on French nationalism, so that he himself short-circuited the European political emotions to which he appealed. Had he given them a lead, he might have left a different and more potent heritage. All the same, a spirit misnamed 'gaullist' might begin to suffuse European attitudes even if a super-state remained a *vue de l'esprit*. France in Africa, Britain more spasmodically in Africa and the Indian Ocean, have both displayed a desire to prolong their old 'world roles'. It is possible that West Germany which has hitherto been essentially commercial in its foreign policy might give them more backing than now seems likely if it were to find the world environment less accomodating as the United States ceases to shape it so intimately. The United States has tended to preserve the European world system beyond the fall of the European empires by its strategic control of the Eurasian rim and oceans. The Nixon Doctrine may change much of that and face Western Europe for the first time with the consequences of its own self-destruction as a political power in the first half of the century. If so, there may be some support for policies of intervention and control, notably in Africa, of the kind France had sustained during the 1960s. The backing France has obtained from the others of the Six for investment in French-speaking Africa and the 'reverse preferences' which have so incensed the United States administration already provide some precedent for this. West Germany has shown signs of seeking to use what power it had for national purposes – for instance, to prevent the diplomatic recognition of East Germany by third powers. On the other hand, there has been no real collective enthusiasm for neo-colonial French policies in Africa and the entry not only of Britain, with its widely dispersed connections, but also of the Scandinavians with their resolute anti-colonialism, suggests that the obstacles to pursuing really focussed European Community policies overseas are likely to be very great. In any case, it is most unlikely, on the record, that any British or French government can obtain public backing for any 'Vietnam', large or small, so that European involvements are likely to be economic rather than strategic. In such circumstances, any policy of spheres of influence is liable to be economic or rhetorical, too quiet or too loud to be effective in a crisis or against resolute opposition. Even as rhetoric, it is likely to divide the member nations of the European Community rather than unite them. In fact, because they know they are unlikely to obtain whole-hearted support, countries with such ambitions will tend to pursue them *outside* the European Community, unilaterally, bilaterally, or as a group. This will tend, if not overtly to divide the Community, at least to hold up the development of any significant political union. Like the policies of President de Gaulle, its manner of presenting European aspirations in ways which fail to win a consensus will tend to freeze the effective business of cementing the West Europeans together. Far from promoting a European super-state, it will raise extra obstacles against its appearance. It will not help if, unlike de Gaulle, the promoters of a spheres-of-influence policy are subjectively 'good Europeans' seeking to strengthen the institution.

The attitude to common government is not the heart of the conflict here. The core lies in the divisive concept of policy itself. In short, while a collective nationalism will probably be a significant strand of the European mood, its most forthright expression, a policy to found a European super-power, is most unlikely to emerge, because the consensus for it is missing. Vigorous or noisy attempts to raise it from the wrong soil are more likely to make political union impossible, and sterilise the European Community at its present stage as a customs union, than to promote a super-state. The European Community may be one of the five major powers of the 1970s, but if so 'major power' must not be identified with 'super-power' and Europe's leverage cannot be exerted along traditional lines.

A neutral Community?

Could neutrality be a goal for the European Community where assertive nationalism cannot be? Neutralism, the desire to be rid of balance-of-power politics and live free of foreign entanglements has been a constant though never dominant attitude in Europe since the war. It would appeal to some of the left and Scandinavians just as European nationalism would appeal to some of the right and British and French. This in itself would be an obstacle, since on the record it would be very difficult to conceive of neutrality as a policy likely to unite, and therefore to be pursued consistently, by the European Community. This fact could bring out some of the ambiguities in the concept itself. If neutrality is to be construed as *armed* neutrality, in the way the Swiss and Swedes have interpreted it since the Treaty of Vienna, today this must mean the possession of a credible nuclear deterrent. This faces one with all the problems involved in the effort to develop a European nuclear force.

If neutrality is to be construed as the unarmed neutrality of a completed European union this too seems incredible. It is possible to be a neutral if one is small enough to have an almost neutral effect on one's environment. This is not conceivable for an entity which groups, as has been said, ten per cent of the world's population, twenty per cent of its output, thirty per cent of its trade and forty per cent of its monetary reserves. Such a group cannot abstract itself from wider conflicts. In practice, then, neutrality for Europe would have to mean American and Russian guarantees of neutrality for a largely demilitarised Europe (west of Russia) from which American and Russian troops would have withdrawn. Apart from the low likelihood of any such thing in Eastern Europe – the whole thrust of the Soviet Union's policy is in the other direction of confirming its politico-military presence there and the *status quo* – this would militate against the development of any European Community beyond a customs union. The nations of the European Community could not isolate themselves from all conflict with either the Soviet Union or United States and so could not count on their neutrality being permanently guaranteed by either super-power. If (by definition) they were themselves partly, or selectively, demilitarised, the non-nuclear states, including West Germany, would emphasise good neighbour policies with the Soviet Union as their premium for security. The British and French might emphasise their nuclear deterrents. The essence of the situation would be that the security perceptions of the members of the European Community would be fundamentally divergent and each of them directed to a bilateral relationship with the Soviet Union. The Soviet Union would naturally encourage this to retard or prevent European integration. In such circumstances, the differences in security perceptions of the West European nations would prevent them from merging policies not only in security but also in economics, since they could not commit themselves to neighbours without constraining their freedom of manoeuvre towards the Soviet Union. This has already been evident during de Gaulle's period in power, and even now, in the resistance within European Community countries to any common foreign trade policy towards the socialist states. These reservations would be multiplied many times over in a passive or demilitarised Europe of nation states and would probably make the emergence of anything stronger than a customs union quite impossible. This in turn would probably undermine even the measure of cohesion which has already been achieved. Neutrality is a possible policy for individual nations of Western Europe: it is almost certainly not a recipe for a European Community. Like the desire for a super-state, the desire for neutrality, in the form of a search for more civilian and less military forms of East-West relationships, is likely to be a constant of European policies in the years to come, but as a dominant it would disintegrate rather than unite Western Europe.

Europe as a process

The alternative to nationalism or neutralism is the policy of collective action which led to the creation of the European Community itself and which has been pursued in various ways since the war by the West European nations with the sole exception of France under de Gaulle. Western Europe is not self-sufficient in defence and looks unlikely to be so for many years to come. It is positively interdependent with the world economy: the more international production reshapes the world economy, the greater the need for common management of the consequences by the leading powers. In the circumstances, joint action with others, notably the United States, in security and economics, is profitable for Western Europe and any divergence from it can involve heavy losses in wealth, safety and, paradoxically, freedom to choose one's own priorities. Greater cohesion inside a European Community guards against the dangers of a continuing division of Western Europe. If the United States begins to lose interest in Western Europe, or to rate relations with the Soviet Union more highly, or both, the latter could be the residuary legatee and increasingly exercise a hegemonial military-political pressure on the continent. Without cohesion, too,

Western Europe might well find American negotiators of the future, like Mr Connally in 1971, more inclined than their predecessors to exact a high economic price for the maintenance of America's protection of Europe. In such circumstances, a passive Western Europe might find itself faced with the uncomfortable choice of some politico-military subordination to the Soviet Union, some politico-economic subordination to the United States or even subordination to the Dual Hegemony of de Gaulle's nightmare. An effective European Community would, on the contrary, make the most of Europe's chances. It would help to create a significant potential counterweight to the Soviet Union in security terms, able not to replace but to buttress the United States guarantee and discourage the temptation for Moscow to exploit military superiority for political ends. It would strengthen Western Europe's capacity to negotiate on an equal footing with the United States on economic issues. Imaginatively led, it could also create one of the building blocks of an effectively managed world economy. In a period when there are signs of greater East-West co-operation without the total disappearance of recent rivalries, signs too that the old western economic co-operation is becoming more conflictual, a European Community offers the West Europeans their most solid footing to face uncertainty with self-reliance.

The European Community could of course become a very conservative body indeed, protectionist and narrow-minded behind the high walls of a regional self-regard. In pluralist societies, because of the multiplicity of domestic pressure groups, there is a perennial danger of excessively inner-directed politics even in foreign policy: the United States and Japan both offer recent examples. The risk is still greater in imperfectly integrated polities such as the European Community. European integration was originally designed to circumvent the *de facto* veto exercised by all states, even the smallest, in intergovernmental organisations of the type of the Organisation for European Economic Co-operation or the United Nations. But General de Gaulle demonstrated that the process could be stood on its head – that one member country of a Community could hold up the progress of the whole. This has raised a great deal of apprehension about the future of negotiation with the European Community. It is nevertheless probably exaggerated. First, the era of de Gaulle depended on one man's complete indifference to orthodox negotiating, which was and is eccentric to the normal behaviour of modern states, not excluding France. Certainly one would expect the European Community to have difficulty in reconciling different conceptions of policy, in which France both before and during and after de Gaulle has, does and will probably continue to represent a minority tradition; but that is different from the refusal to negotiate. Second, even under de Gaulle the appearances of immobility were sometimes more apparent than real. France may have forced through a highly protectionist agricultural policy with the connivance of farmers throughout the Community, including Germany, but it also accepted the Kennedy Round of steep cuts in the tariffs and other obstacles to trade between highly industrialised countries. When major international issues arise which implicitly affect the system as a whole, the pressures to reach agreement are extremely strong. This was proved again in the dollar crisis of 1971. Third, a Community of Nine will be somewhat different from a Community of Six in that, despite the tenderness of all major states for the vetoes of their equals, the balance will shift away from any minority of one: in the last resort the practical pressures the laggard can bring to bear on what the others really wish to do will be considerably less. Fourth, and of vital importance to the progress of the European Community itself, steps forward within the Community will in many of the most important cases be possible only if broad views of major issues are taken.

Take the international monetary situation. If the European Community fails to strengthen the co-ordination of monetary policy, for instance through a European Reserve Fund, solutions will be found, e.g., in the IMF or between America and Japan and Germany, which take no particular account of the Community: it will be by-passed. Another example is defence. If the European Community is unable to play any role in defence co-operation between its member states, the latter will pursue their policies in East-West negotiations in ways that may easily ignore and even cut across the

Community. Agreements on force reductions in Europe, for example, could treat West Germany differently from the other European Community countries, and so institute a structural distinction between them to add to the present one between nuclear and non-nuclear states. To the extent that solutions to major problems are found outside the Community, these will tend at the best to erode and at the worst actively to impede its aspirations to become a union or even an effective co-operative grouping. Once that situation becomes part of the consciousness of governments in crucial areas, the very idea of a special relationship between Community states which differentiates them in decisive ways from other states with whom they have international agreements, will be undermined, so that the real area of integration may become very small or disappear altogether. There may be exceptions to this. Social conflicts could lead to trade protectionism, for instance. But trade is becoming a lesser part of international economic relations as against, say, international investment; and it is certain that in many areas the frontiers of disagreement on world problems do not neatly coincide with those of the Community. They run between its members, so that the only way to reconcile them between themselves is to reconcile them with third parties. In short, to become a deep-rooted union, the Community must espouse policies which take account of the very wide, because diverse and varying, areas of interest of the members including by definition those interests they share with third parties. The European Community's capacity to be a countervailing power to satisfy its members' aspirations for a parity of benefits and esteem with other major powers in the world implies an ability not only to build up the European Community internally but also to contribute a necessary minimum to Western and even East-West co-operation. That is the price of the minimum consensus needed for significant internal progress of any kind. In crucial areas, the European Community must make the best of international co-operation or it will not go very far itself.

A policy for making the best of the complexities of attraction-and-repulsion of interdependence also has the essential advantage of corresponding more than any other to what the eighteenth century might have called the political genius, or inner nature, of Western European society. This society is in many ways in a unique situation today. The two great wars of the first half of the century have ruined Europe's traditional military and political power, which is why the super-powers virtually meet in the heart of the continent. Extravagant exposure to the horrors of war has also produced one of the most resolutely amilitary populations in the world. Such changes would normally mean the subordination of yesterday's masters to those of today. In Eastern Europe, this has indeed been the case. But in the West, because of the internal diversity, development and similarity of the societies of North America and Western Europe, there has been no such empire. Better still, the nuclear and super-power stalemate in Europe has devalued purely military power and given much more scope to the civilian forms of influence and action. One of these, and perhaps the most important, is economic, and it so happens that Western Europe (unlike its eastern sister) remains one of the four major economic centres of the world. This makes it possible for a European Community to make the most of its assets and to suffer surprisingly little for its past excesses and present weaknesses. It can even aim to consolidate the shift in international relations in Europe from a military to a political emphasis and to profit by it. Europe as a whole could well become the first example in history of a major centre of the balance of power becoming in the era of its decline not a colonised victim but the exemplar of a new stage in political civilisation. The European Community in particular would have a chance to demonstrate the influence which can be wielded by a large political co-operative formed to exert essentially civilian forms of power. This may be almost too good to be true. The fact remains that the unpleasant effects of Europe's decline in traditional terms have been singularly softened by a sea-change in the sources of power. History rarely offers such second chances. They should be taken.

The European Community's interest as a civilian group of countries long on economic power and relatively short on armed force is as far as possible to *domesticate* relations between states, including those of its own members and those

with states outside its frontiers. This means trying to bring
to international problems the sense of common responsibility
and structures of contractual politics which have in the past
been associated almost exclusively with 'home' and not
foreign, that is *alien*, affairs. This is much more than the
common prudence which makes the most of assets and casts
a veil over weakness. It involves the psychological roots of
any foreseeable West European political system. One of the
main reasons for the limited military potential of Western
Europe is not material at all. This is the spontaneous
preference of an urbanised body of citizens, with rights,
values and comforts to secure, for the 'democratic' and civil
standards of the suburbs over those of the armed camp and
the balance of power. The European Community was itself
largely the child of such impulses. Its appeal and success,
despite all the undoubted difficulties caused by its character
as a Leap, and as such something foreign to the everyday
norms of politics, are at least partly due to them. This implies
that the European Community will only make the most of
its opportunities if it remains true to its inner characteristics.
These are primarily: civilian ends and means, and a built-in
sense of collective action, which in turn express, however
imperfectly, social values of equality, justice and tolerance.
To make the most of itself, and mobilise the latent idealism
of affluent societies, it must lay foundations for the political
system of the 1970s and 1980s much as the New Deal and
Welfare Socialism laid the foundations of the West as we
know today. This implies a concern for social justice at home
spilling over in a revival of interest for the poor abroad. It
implies a nose for the policies which can establish a political
peace, that is civilian values, out of the technical peace (to use
Marion Dönhoff's phrase) provided by the nuclear stalemate.
That in turn implies a practical understanding that civilian
standards cannot be maintained unless economic and social
policies sustain the international open society, which we now
take for granted, in conditions which are changing, to the point
where its future may once more be at stake. The European
Community must be a force for the international diffusion of
civilian and democratic standards or it will itself be more or
less the victim of power politics run by powers stronger and

more cohesive than itself. In the long run, as Jean Monnet has said, there is no statemanship without generosity. This applies particularly to a grouping whose influence will depend as much on its functional effectiveness as on material force.

2 The Community and the Changing World Economic Order

Theo Peeters and
Wolfgang Hager

The beginning of this decade has brought uncertain but steady progress towards a negotiated order in East–West relations. Among the industrial countries of the West (which in this context includes Japan), however, relations have been marked by crisis, strife and uncertainty. That part of the international order which is most relevant to our welfare seems to be stretched to breaking point by new demands made upon it. The only reassuring element is the evident determination of all participants to keep some sort of agreed system in operation, even if this means relying on ever more short-lived expedients, tackling symptoms rather than fundamentals. The European Community has a great stake in, and responsibility for, a viable international economic order. Yet this concept has little currency in the Community, and its responsibility is still too often conceived in regional terms.

Largely in reaction to the experiences of the thirties, the founders of the post-war system pursued two objectives. One was economic: to achieve maximum welfare through the international division of labour. The other was political: to avoid a fragmented world, where everybody worked against everybody else's interest, a world without order, a world of war. Neither of these necessities seems to be clearly or strongly enough felt today to be a decisive and compelling impetus to action. Our attitude towards the welfare provided by the international division of labour has changed, partially because we are taking its benefits for granted, and cannot imagine a substantial departure from it. A new emphasis on, and questioning of, the how and why of production, make its material benefits seem less of an end in itself, while stressing the social costs of increased efficiency. And as East–West tensions recede, the threat of international disorder and the danger of fragmentation in the West is faced more calmly.

Yet today, as before, there are economic and political reasons which make international economic order – not necessarily the one we have had, but some kind of viable order – an urgent necessity for the Community and the other developed nations of the West. The economic reasons will be discussed, below, in the analysis of the extent of economic interpenetration which characterises the modern world economy. The political reasons are discussed in François Duchêne's introductory chapter: Europe, weak in terms of political power, must work towards a world governed by rules. As the members of the Community have discovered in their dealings with each other, the acceptance of common rules is the only guarantee of equality. It is also the precondition for moving from a world governed by force, including economic force, to a world governed by contractual relations. In this sense, Europe's long-term security depends on its success in helping to build a world where Europe can assert and maintain its character as a civilian society. The way the Community shapes its international economic relations is thus a highly political issue.

The rise and fall of a system

The international economic system established after World War II has recently come close to breakdown. There are two main reasons for this. One is that it never worked in quite the way it was meant to work, and only survived because one of the participants – the United States – saw to it that it did. Today the US no longer fulfils that role. Secondly the system has fallen victim to its own success. It has helped to create a world economy which has made large parts of the old order no longer adequate.

The two main instruments for liberalising payments and world trade which emerged from the conferences of Bretton Woods and Havana were the IMF and the GATT. The one established the conditions for what was thought to be minimal stability in the monetary field to allow an orderly expansion

of trade. The other established rules – and only later the
machinery – to encourage multilateral dismantling of tariffs
and quantitative restrictions. In both the monetary and trade
fields the founders tried, successfully, to avoid the twin
scourges of the thirties, autarky and bilateralism. The IMF
rules made parity changes cumbersome – to avoid the competitive devaluations which had contributed so much to the
economic anarchy of the thirties – and subject to agreement.
GATT laid down that tariff-cuts, once made, must be irreversible, and more important, concessions made to one country
must be extended to all others: the most-favoured-nation
clause became the corner-stone for the new non-discriminatory, non-fragmented 'one world'.

The system has served us well. For many years world trade
has increased at an annual rate of 8 per cent, compared with 5
per cent for world production. This meant that the trade/GNP
ratio of the great trading nations has, on average, roughly
doubled since the war – evidence that the division of labour
was working and barriers between nations had come down.

We are certainly richer, and live in greater harmony with
our partners, than we would have done without the great
movement towards liberalisation which has marked the past
quarter of a century. But a sign of the weakening of this movement is that trade increases no longer outstripped those of
production in recent years.

But from the very beginning in fact, this system suffered
from a serious internal contradiction, which did not appear as
long as the system was not properly applied, and as long as the
United States added an element – management – which, at
the insistence of the United States, had been left out of the
equation.

The post-war revolution in domestic politics did not carry
over into international life. The thirties had shown the necessity,
and the forties the feasibility, of going beyond blind submission
to the vagaries of domestic economics, and of applying,
with increasing success, the sort of management which we
associate with the name of Keynes. In international economic
affairs, the system that finally came into being was deeply
coloured by the liberalism which had made the period before
the first world war the golden age of international exchange. It

was assumed that if conditions for an adequate operation of the market were created, the international economy would largely be guided by that same invisible hand which had been discredited in domestic affairs. Since, however, countries refused to let external considerations dominate their internal policy-making as they had been forced to do under the iron discipline of the gold standard – something had to give. In the long run it was impossible for interventionist domestic policies and *laissez-faire* international policies not to conflict.

In fact, of course the system was very much managed indeed – by the United States. The chief trade policy instrument of this management was a very selective and gradual application of the liberal precepts subscribed to. In the monetary field, the foreign exchange needed for expansion of trade was made available by direct transfers and loans, while at the same time permitting discriminatory foreign exchange controls. In other words, the system worked because of its exceptions.

Moreover, liberalism was applied only among equals – the Europeans – but not between Europe and America, except in one direction: tariff-cuts negotiated in the first post-war 'Rounds' only benefited Europe, as long as its nations continued to apply quotas and exchange controls against 'third' countries. Among themselves, however, the Europeans were encouraged to liberalise both quotas and payments. Finally came the logical step which established equality: the creation of a European Economic Community. Only then was liberalism fully applied to the rest of the world.

To say that the system worked because of its exceptions, however, leaves out half of the story. For the logic of the system was not so much questioned as suspended: the direction in which progress was to be made – greater liberalisation – was never lost to sight. In fact, with a delay greater than that envisaged by the founders, we now live, and have lived for a decade in the sort of liberal system which they hoped to create.

But the very visible hand which by a self-denying ordinance had given the system the flexibility it needed, at length got tired of the task. One of the reasons for this, undoubtedly, was the more relaxed state of big-power relations alluded to in the beginning. It no longer seems so urgent to ensure the stability and prosperity of Europe and Japan as neighbours to the Soviet Union and China. Concurrently, long-neglected internal demands in the United States have considerably reduced the margin of discretion in economic affairs which was a precondition for the sort of leadership which has characterised the past. For 'self-denial', in the past, had not meant that US economic interests were disregarded but that a long-term view of these interests prevailed over short-term interests and short-term political pressures.

This revealed the grave political danger of relying on leadership by a single power. As soon as the 'self denying ordinance' was suspended, and the US began to behave like the other members by making demands on the system, the disadvantages of its basic inequality became clear. Although unable to avoid major frustrations, the United States had a much greater capacity to impose its own point of view, now increasingly determined by short-term considerations. The interpretation of the rules by one power – once a necessary precondition for the flexibility and management of the system, was now no longer accepted. The reaction, so far, has not been the logical one of establishing a joint responsibility by the major economic powers. Rather it has been a free-for-all, where rules are accepted selectively and interpreted to suit particular interests.

If this disappearance of leadership were the only change in the international economic system, this in itself would make very urgent indeed a profound reflection by the enlarged Community on the implications of that joint responsibility – with Japan, and with the participation of the less developed countries – which must now take the place of the much simpler single responsibility exercised by the United States. Sharing this responsibility will require, from the Community as much as from the other participants, discipline and moderation. More important, it will require that for every single act of policy the Community must ask itself, how such action would fit in with a global concept of economic and ultimately political, order among states. The Community, as a sign of its coming of age, would have to take seriously the principle of 'do as you would be done by others' in all matters of economic policy.

But the precondition for such conduct: a concept of world

economic order, is far from being fulfilled. All participants in international economic exchange are at the scavenger stage in their attitude towards the old system: picking out the parts that suit them (free entry for my goods, but not for yours) but no longer subscribing to the whole.

A new phenomenon: International production

The reasons for this loss of faith in the old system is not only the emergence of a multicentred, hence more complicated world. It is also the changed nature of the international economy. This has made the machinery for regulating economic relations among states increasingly obsolete; and this in turn has increasingly weakened their capacity to pursue internal economic and social goals.

Both internal and foreign policy-making rest on the myth that national economies are largely insulated from each other. Exchanges are thought to be largely of one type: movement of goods, which can be controlled by tariffs and quantitative controls and an appropriate exchange rate. In fact, the sheer volume of transactions made possible by liberalisation of trade and capital movements, and the inclusion of all factors of production in the exchanges now taking place, have left all national economies exposed to influences from outside.

A symptom and agent of this change is the multinational company; its result, international production. The importance of this phenomenon goes far beyond the visible concentration of economic power in the hands of a few giant corporations, although this, too, has helped to weaken the traditional means of economic regulation. The primary effect is much subtler and is brought about as much by the thousands of medium-sized companies now operating internationally. Two characteristics of such companies are especially relevant here.

The first is what might be called their global scanning capacity: the ability to identify much more quickly than national firms variations in market prices, economic opportunity, and costs including labour, capital, taxation, transport etc. The second is their equally world wide capacity to act on this knowledge: to shift production, export markets, suppliers, and resources in general wherever the international market suggests. With only slight exaggeration, one can say that the MNC is on the way to creating what hitherto has only been a theoretical possibility: an international market – and, since this is a market for all factors of production, an international economy.

Our attitude towards the free play of market forces has long been ambivalent. On the one hand we appreciate the efficiency achieved by an optimum allocation of resources. On the other hand, market forces have disadvantages: they favour the strong, impose often harsh adjustments on the weak and may lead to unacceptable fluctuations in economic life. So long as impulses from the external economic environment were only transmitted indirectly, through the movement of goods (and these movements were only imperfectly liberalised), the time available for adjustment, as well as the instruments for it, were sufficient. Until recently, in fact, we were protected by beneficial inertia from the implications of living in an international market.

In this new world, of greatly increased international production, governments found themselves caught between full political responsibilities for the economic welfare of their citizens, and the inadequacy of the instruments (and knowledge) available for dealing with external disturbances. They therefore began to act with increasing bad temper in international affairs. Protectionism, and monetary 'aggressiveness' are symptoms of this frustration.

The new mobility of two factors of production – one of them hardly recognised as such in classical theory – have particularly contributed to making the international economy more volatile: knowledge and money. For many analysts, the multinational company is essentially a device for marketing technological and managerial know-how. It produces abroad in order to draw a maximum benefit from a technology it has developed, whether this is a method of production or a new product. Foreign investment, for such a company, fulfils a different (or additional) function from the classical one of earning interest on capital. It serves essentially to establish a legal claim to the fruits of that other investment, the development of know-how. Foreign direct investment is thus a way of selling a service (knowledge), or rather of extracting a maximum economic rent from the possession of knowledge (including organisational know-how). This means, incidentally, that a restrictive policy on capital movements would not stop the spread of MNCs: they would simply raise all the money locally, instead of three-quarters of it as at present. It also means that we must look at the balance of payments with different eyes. Through the income from the sort of 'service' which direct investment brings, shows up on current account, direct investment itself is part of capital account. Hence, in judging whether there is a balance in the exchanges of a nation, one has to look at the basic balance.

Technology not only means higher efficiency, and hence a considerable welfare gain. It also means that certain ways of production, and certain products are replaced by new ones. This poses an adjustment problem. Productive resources must be re-allocated, a process especially painful for employees. It is this sort of adjustment which modern nations increasingly want to avoid or slow down (through quotas and voluntary restrictions, other NTBs and, more rarely, tariffs) when it is forced on them by imports of goods. These attempts to insulate the economy against impulses from abroad are becoming ineffective, because such impulses are now transmitted invisibly and much more rapidly through the knowledge channels of the multinational companies.

But MNCs have also had a specific impact on trade as such which has contributed to the present restlessness among developed nations, and to protectionist impulses especially in America. Offshore production, i.e. the establishment of production facilities in low-wage countries, is an increasingly typical form of MNC operation. By transferring part of its highly mobile manager class, linked to a global information and decision-making network, a company can overcome the bottlenecks which often prevent technology-based industrial production in less developed countries. For the industrialised countries – and Europe is only beginning to experience this phenomenon – this capacity has led to very dramatic changes in the kind of industrial production in which they thought they had a permanent competitive advantage. Few television sets are now made in the US and German camera production takes place in Asia. Japan is following the same course.

If, in this example, the MNCs create new patterns of comparative advantages, on a more global level, they sometimes ignore the old ones. A growing proportion of international trade is in fact trade between subsidiaries of the same company. The large multinational company increasingly plans the production of its entire range of products world-wide. Parts for a single product may be made in five countries and assembled in yet a sixth. Finished products are imported from various parts of the world to enable the company to present a full 'line' in any given market, etc. While this trade, which is relegated to being merely a by-product of international production, will not stray too far from the logic of comparative advantage, it is at the same time subject to a different logic from classical trade. Internal company objectives like the amortisation of a given plant, and security of supply and market may well take priority over mere cost considerations. While this pursuit of stability may ease internal adjustment problems, measures taken by public authorities to influence trade (devaluations, export credits) which are designed for one sort of world, may not have the same effect in this new one.

Put differently, the MNC, unlike the national firm, is no longer merely the object of economic policy. It makes international economic policy itself, i.e. it pursues long-term strategies which affect sizeable portions of economic activity. International production, i.e. the production of US, Japanese and European foreign affiliates, may amount to 450 billion dollars. If we add to this the value of the home production of these firms, and assume that approximately half this amount represents added value we are approaching an order of magnitude somewhere between the GNP of the Community and Japan. If such a huge chunk of world economic activity no longer plays the game by the familiar rules, it may be time to devise new rules.

Its global flexibility not only allows the MNC to shrug off international economic measures imposed by public authorities, but also frustrates domestic policy goals. A well-known example of this kind is tax evasion. By a number of devices, a company can concentrate profits in a country where they are most lightly taxed. One such device is 'transfer pricing' for intra-subsidiary transactions. The subsidiary of a high tax country can be made to run at a loss by overpaying for goods, licences and loans received from other subsidiaries of the same company: conversely, it can deliver goods and services at artificially low prices. Needless to say, this may have important consequences for a country's budgetary and social policy, as the fiscal burden is shifted from the corporation to the individual, and revenue is lost altogether. More subtly, and perhaps more importantly, countries are discouraged from imposing a 'fair' share of the tax burden on the corporate sector in order to prevent tax evasion – or, given the great mobility of MNCs, not to lose the industry altogether. The United States, and more successfully Germany, have recently tried to plug at least one hole with bilateral double-taxation agreements with Switzerland. In the long run, an adequate solution, can only be found on a global level, such as the proposal by Raymond Vernon[1] for a tax on the overall profits of a company, distributed according to a key system to all host countries where the company operates. Pressures for such a solution may well come from the companies themselves, caught between the contradictory demands of competing national authorities.

A more fundamental challenge to domestic policy-making is the practice known as 'cash management'. Here too, global flexibility of MNCs and of national firms with access to international banking facilities introduces a new element into international economic relations. By being able to rely on a network of production units in different countries, co-operating with each other and with companies especially established for the administration of patents, know-how, and financial transactions, such firms have gained an extraordinary freedom to place their liquid assets in the country of their choice. Subsidiaries can be asked to retard or advance payments for goods and services received in order to concentrate cash in a certain country; a company may ask its business partners to settle their accounts with a specially established financial subsidiary, etc.

This formidable *masse de manoeuvre* is in constant search

[1] *Sovereignty at Bay: The Multinational Spread of US Enterprises* (London, 1971) chap. 8.

of the highest interest rates, or the currency with the prospects of a favourable parity change. In both cases the effects may be negative for the country concerned. High interest rates are meant to reduce total money supply, not to increase it, while a massive influx of foreign exchange in the anticipation of a revaluation may precipitate such an event, or force the country which is the source of the displaced liquidity to devalue. While this activity, like the Euro-dollar market, where much of it takes place, also provides the advantages of an efficient international capital market, the negative aspects will increasingly be thought to outweigh the advantages, unless the former are brought under control (see also Chapter 3). The Central Banks of the industrialised countries, have practised a joint restraint borne out of a common responsibility for the system. The MNCs, though representing a force which is equivalent to that of nations, are not of course parties to the written and unwritten agreements among nations. As a result of huge international flows of private capital these agreements themselves are ever harder to keep, and to operate, as countries, faced with a new inability to pursue domestic policy goals, adopt a *sauve qui peut* attitude.

Other examples of the MNC's ability to frustrate public policy could be added to this list: global price fixing and market sharing by oligopolies – the major oil companies and the pre-war chemical cartels are the most obvious examples; the ability to bargain for special terms (fiscal incentives, relaxed pollution standards) with governments anxious to attract industry to certain regions. But these 'micro-economic' instances of loss of control by public authorities are only minor irritants compared with the stress put on policy-making by the more general openness of nations to external economic events, of which the MNCs are only one aspect. At issue is our ability to enjoy the fruits of international economic interdependence, while regaining control over our economic fate. But, as the foregoing analysis has shown, this can no longer be done by any one country separately. Such control has, in this decade, become more precious, and more essential to governments, than ever before.

The primacy of social policy

The consensus which made possible the American-led drive towards liberalism depended to a large extent on a shared concept of welfare among the developed nations, or at least on its precondition – economic growth. This in turn meant maximising efficiency of production for which the international division of labour was an important prerequisite. True, it was recognised that this was only beneficial in conditions of full employment, and if it took place within an adequate monetary adjustment mechanism. The latter was thought to have been achieved with the Bretton Woods system, leaving to our days the question of who was to decide the amount of total liquidity in the international system, and hence the rate of expansion of the international economy. As to employment, Keynes managed to secure agreement that it was legitimate to impose quotas to protect employment, a step described at the time as 'an economic Munich' by one American purist.

The problem of internal adjustment assumed increasing importance as technological change accelerated. Having what is perhaps the most mobile work force in the world, the US could long afford to ignore the difficulties facing the worker who has to change occupation several times in his lifetime. Total US unemployment had been falling since 1961. But starting in 1969 rising unemployment, coinciding with steeply increasing imports from Japan, from offshore production, and to a lesser extent, Europe, triggered off a protectionist response, whose international effects were felt, dramatically on August 15, 1971.

Although the Nixon measures announced on that date tried to cope with more general problems plaguing the American economy – an overvalued dollar and 'stagflation' – these problems had had a particular impact in declining sectors of industry. The spectacular rise of imports in these sectors, though this was only the visible tip of the iceberg of technological change, led organised labour to turn away from a free trade orientation. In the belief, that their jobs and high wages were in danger because the technology which made these possible was being exported, they also became restrictionist as regards US direct investment. This new and more complex protectionism was more intractable politically, and hence more serious, than the earlier attempts by industrialists to reserve for themselves safe markets and high profits.

But, as pointed out above, unemployment in the United States was not only the result of the difficulties of certain industries. The economy as a whole was running well below capacity. In such a situation, the policy maker has the choice of a number of instruments. Some of these put a burden on other countries. The President, in what may become a dangerous precedent, chose several which hurt the partners of the United States (who had long engaged in the same practices). The United States lowered interest rates at a time when Europe was already choking on unwanted dollars, thus further complicating the task of bringing inflation under control. It imposed an import surcharge and export subsidies in a straightforward attempt to export its unemployment to others. Soon, however, reverting to the logic of the earlier system, it traded some of these measures for a monetary adjustment – against the opposition of several of its partners who wanted to encourage their own exports by means of an undervalued exchange rate. The lesson of August 15, however, remains valid. In a world where full employment becomes an increasingly absolute demand – this now also applies to Japan – a new kind of mercantilism, the export of economic problems, could become the rule.

Implicit in the new protectionism is also a downgrading of efficiency, relative to other concerns. It goes beyond safeguarding employment (still the most important instance) and extends towards safeguarding that broader goal, the quality of life. Symptomatic of this trend – and of its possible implications for the international economic system – was a recent proposal by a progressive personality of the Community, who advocated a 100 per cent tariff on goods produced in ways which pollute and waste resources. More immediately relevant – as yet mainly in Europe, but in the future in the US as well – is the concern for regional balance, which also implies foregoing efficiency, at least in the short term. Again, part of the burden of state intervention for this purpose may be borne by outsiders, both if regional policy is made through the protection of certain sectors of industry, of through subsidised production. The oldest and most important example of such practices is of course the agricultural policy of the developed nations, discussed in Chapter 4.

A host of new and not so new social concerns find their expression in non-tariff barriers (NTBs), or rather in standards of products and production which have the effect of inhibiting trade between nations: safety and health standards, nuisance and pollution control. Non-tariff barriers have, as a result of the drastic lowering of tariffs in the sixties, become much more visible. Their progressive elimination is high on the agenda of the trade negotiations due to start in 1973. In no other field will the confusion between legitimately divergent social goals (you like heavy, safe cars, I like small ones which consume less fuel), bureaucratic obstinacy, and plain old protectionism be greater. **1785251**

If our analysis of a growing concern of governments for 'quality of life' goals is correct, we can expect much more intervention, more standards, and hence, unless care is taken, the creation of more of these technical NTBs. The temptation to use these for straightforward protectionist purposes will be great, unless ways can be found to discuss, in an international framework, those 'purely internal' measures, before they have become the law of the land. Thus, the elimination of existing NTBs, must go hand in hand with the control of new ones. The latter process may even help to shift the former from pure bargaining to a more constructive joint problem solving approach.

The need to by-pass the rules of the liberal system, and to protect certain sectors of industry, has found its strongest expression in the rapid spread since the Kennedy Round, of that quota-like NTB called 'voluntary restrictions' in such fields as steel and textiles. Unlike such equally doubtful and widespread practices as export credits and border taxes, voluntary restrictions reintroduce an element of bilateralism in the system which is in sharp contrast with the universalism of the MFN principle. Also, since these are merely administrative agreements, and worse, increasingly intra-industry arrangements with official blessing, trade policy is removed from the control of democratic processes.

But these ever more ingenious ways of bending or evading the rules of the old system reflect the growing difficulty governments face in pursuing domestic social and economic goals within an international economy guided by the free play of market forces. If we want to domesticate the nascent anarchic urges of the makers of foreign economic policy, we must domesticate the international economy itself.

The problems of interdependence

We are condemned to live in a world of economic interdependence. Too much of Europe's welfare depends on it for any alternative to a world of open economic exchanges to be seriously considered. But, as we have seen, the lowering of economic barriers has increasingly exposed domestic economies to economic events and policies made abroad. Decisions to inflate or deflate one economic area have immediate repercussions elsewhere. Worse, under the present monetary system some important elements of economic policy, like money supply, increasingly escape the control of most national authorities. In this situation of impotence and conflicting national policies, the danger of relying on pure power-bargaining or worse, the anarchy of simple unilateralism is considerable. There is ample evidence of such a trend.

The US pursuit of global political order is increasingly marked by a classical balance-of-power concept. Signs of this way of thinking can be seen in its style of economic bargaining. Japan, which is needed as a constructive participant in world economic order, adjusted its undervalued exchange rate, not from a commitment to the rules of the game, but as the result of massive political pressure. The exercise of such pressures thus becomes vindicated as a normal instrument of economic relations. In the Community, the euphoria of enlargement, combined with the bitter state of international economic relations, has led to attitudes reminiscent of the economic nationalism of an earlier age. The old continent seems not above displaying the immaturity of a post-colonial backlash.

In order to set the implications of the emergence of a world market into perspective, it may be useful to recall some of the arguments which have shaped the creation of the European Community in the late fifties. It was said at that time that the creation of a market free from restrictions on the movement of goods, capital and labour, required important flanking measures to avoid distortions and adaptation problems. Mere free trade, such as the UK proposed at the time, was not thought to be possible or desirable.

In spite of the remaining level of tariffs in the world – 9 per cent on the average for the industrial countries but with an agreement in principle to reduce these further – and in spite of the relative lack of mobility of labour (though, as we saw, managerial mobility can be a substitute for labour mobility) we can say that as regards the freedom of economic exchanges the world economy is beginning to approximate the conditions which were to be made possible in the European Community.

Although the amount of trade among the principal industrial nations is less than that linking the countries of the Community, interdependence is a function of the sensitivity between different economies. As Richard Cooper has pointed out[1] the narrowing of costs differentials for goods and capital, combined with increased mobility, has led the international market to respond to even slight variations of price, interest rates, output or demand. Between Europe and America, where trade cycles are usually out of phase, this responsiveness has had the effect of disturbing not only the economies involved, but also the capacity of policy makers to deal with them.

In the founding days of the European Community, the problems of interdependence were thought to come largely from trade, and less from the movement of capital. Even so, it was recognised that the linking of economic fate which greater mutual exposure implied, meant that in certain fields national autonomy had to be abandoned. For some areas this meant harmonisation, e.g. in the regulation of business activity. In other areas joint responsibility, including financial solidarity, for the victims of the larger market was thought to be necessary. As the crucial importance of monetary influences, and the harmful effects and futility of dealing with

[1] 'Economic Interdependence and Foreign Policy in the Seventies', *World Politics*, XXIV (January 1972).

these separately became apparent, the Community began to consider the much more ambitious project of economic and monetary union.

It may seem utopian to suggest, at a time when progress within the European Community is manifestly difficult and slow, that it is time we took our own theories seriously enough to apply them to the new reality and examine in which fields harmonisation, financial solidarity and joint management are already feasible and necessary on a global scale. But there is little hope that the world will stand still until the Community has completed its slow progress towards full economic union.

Joint economic management

The idea that the lowering of economic barriers among nations does not make sense unless it is accompanied by a minimum of joint management and joint social responsibility, was already seen in the founding days of the present system. The Havana Charter, one of whose chapters is the basis for the present GATT, sought to establish the much more ambitious International Trade Organisation (ITO). This body was meant to deal with the consequences of trade for employment, economic development, and such things as business practices. It was expressly recognised that full employment was a matter of joint concern; and the possible effect of domestic economic policy, like deflation, on the trade and hence the economies of others was clearly seen and guarded against. Decisions were to be taken by majority voting; among them, the decision temporarily to exempt a member from the obligations of the treaty. Also of interest, in view of our present difficulty in integrating the Socialist economies and the LDCs in a global economic system, the Executive Board was to include, apart from the representatives of the principal trading nations, representatives of 'the different types of economies or degrees of economic development'.

The ITO was never implemented, as the US and to an extent Great Britain, would finally not take the plunge which would have robbed them of too much of their sovereignty. Only a decade earlier, after all, the notion that the setting of tariffs was a purely internal matter had still widely been held. To go from there to a joint responsibility for the welfare of others was a large step indeed. Nevertheless, this step was soon thereafter taken, and to an extent far surpassing the relatively harmless provisions of the ITO: with the Marshall Plan and the one way liberalisation described above. But these were unilateral moves, not the result of treaty obligation. Hence they could be abandoned at any moment.

Since the days of the Havana Charter, our understanding of the implications of economic integration has advanced, not least as a result of the Community experiment itself. We are beginning to understand that togetherness does not mean harmony, but conflict; but that we must accept this conflict, not as a sign of failure, but as evidence that, as the border line between international and domestic policy-making becomes blurred, international economic diplomacy takes on the character of domestic politics. But, just as the rough fighting which characterises domestic politics in pluralist societies is only possible as long as a social contract imposes its limits, so the emerging pluralist international economic community needs a minimum agreement on the rules of the game. To achieve this will be a delicate and difficult task. Before looking at some concrete instances of Community policy, it may be useful to restate what we see as the basic predicament of the international economic system, and define more sharply the role of the Community in it.

We have said that further progress towards more freedom in international exchanges increases the efficiency and productivity of the industrialised countries, and is thus the precondition for any policy in pursuit of welfare which wants not only to distribute wealth more equally, but also to increase it. Efficiency is thus not an end in itself, but meant to serve the social objectives of society. Within nations, its implications, and hence the free play of the market are thus increasingly moderated by domestic social policies. This discretion at home contrasts sharply with the lack of discretion in the international economy. There is thus a potential conflict between the general welfare provided by international exchange, and the particular, and often divergent objectives pursued by national policy makers.

To put it differently, this conflict represents a 'load' on the international economic system, which must not exceed the 'capability' of the system to deal with it. The troubled state of present international economic relations shows that the load is growing more rapidly than the capability of the system we have.

There are two ways of dealing with this problem. One is to reduce the load: by retreating from interdependence, insulating oneself from the international economy. To some extent, such a retreat may be necessary, as for example in the monetary field, where, as pointed out in the next chapter, dependence is a better description of the present state of affairs than interdependence. But we have noted the signs of a more general retreat from interdependence: the growth of protectionist practices and attitudes which find their expression in 'voluntary restrictions', demands for the imposition of capital controls, and unilateral economic and social policies whose costs are partly borne by others. A disorderly retreat from interdependence could, as we saw in the thirties, only have destructive economic and political consequences. The Community, as pointed out above, has important economic and political reasons for avoiding such an outcome.

It is here that the second means of restoring the balance between load and capability becomes crucial: increasing the capability of the system to deal with the tensions and conflicts of interdependence. This means acquiring, at a level higher than the national or Community level, the capacity to harmonise and co-ordinate policy and, even more difficult, to undertake joint action.

Such a step forward will not be possible unless there is a Community capable of dealing with the whole range of issues posed by the complex world of interdependence. Why is this so essential?

First, because power and responsibility must be more equally distributed. In any historical perspective, what is astonishing in the post-war period is the restraint with which the US has used its overriding economic strength, not the fact that it has now the tendency to use it without such restraint.

Today it is unlikely that the US and Japan will proceed

very far on the demanding road towards harmonisation, co-ordination, and joint action, unless they are faced by comparable economic power.

The need for a 'counterweight', however, should be understood in larger than balance-of-power terms. Self-restraint becomes difficult unless it is reciprocated. Only a large unit like the Community can, by sharing it, make such restraint worth while.

Furthermore, a Community united in the pursuit of foreign economic policy is a precondition if its member states are to regain the minimum internal autonomy necessary to achieve their social objectives. Separate attempts by the member states to defend themselves against external impulses, through capital controls, exchange rate policy, etc., are bound to fail, if only for technical reasons (e.g. the size of reserves relative to speculative money flows). The attempt would surely put an intolerable strain on the internal workings of the Community itself. Members are not subject to the same degree – for economic as well as political reasons – to the 'load' of global interdependence, nor are they equally committed to keeping it a reality. To seek to cope with interdependence in dispersed order could only have one result: the preponderance of the social and economic objectives of the strongest in the system, the United States.

The achievement of world economic order requires a strong Community participant; this must also be a constructive participant. This means, the Community must learn to see even apparently minor decisions in the context of the world economic order for which it must now become a co-sponsor.

There is, but only superficially, a paradox here: member states give up part of their sovereignty to the European Community, which in turn, and simultaneously, must put this collective sovereignty under the discipline of broader collective action and responsibility.

It is in this framework that we will briefly review the major areas of Community external economic policy, some of which are discussed in greater detail in the chapters that follow.

The monetary aspects

An essential precondition for the maintenance and deepening of international economic interdependence is an adequately functioning monetary system. Without realistic exchange rates, the economic case for the international division of labour is put in doubt: the welfare effects of trade become uncertain. Furthermore, exporting with an undervalued exchange rate is a form of dumping. 'Victims' feel justified to defend themselves with measures which undermine the trading system itself. Though traders are apt to resist flexible exchange rates which introduce an element of uncertainty in their transactions, a greater degree of flexibility, with some international supervision to prevent major distortions, would help to avoid the greater evil, protectionism.

A shift to SDRs as the main reserve asset is crucial for achieving not only the flexibility of currencies, including the dollar, and the deliberate and assured supply of liquidity, but it also opens possibilities for the transfer of resources to the LDCs. For the member states of the European Community, with their joint veto over the creation of SDRs, this represents a much greater control over the total world liquidity than the elaboration of a competing reserve asset of their own. While this might give psychological satisfaction to some, it would leave us with the worst of all possible worlds. Europeans would have no control over the other remaining reserve asset, the dollar; and the possibility of switching between different assets (between gold, dollars and some euro-currencies as at present) would leave us with a very unstable monetary system. A common solution on the global level would therefore give much more real control to Europe than a go-it-alone policy.

The truism that trade and monetary matters are related has led to some confusion, including the proposition that the GATT and the IMF should work more closely together. Trade negotiations are in essence based on strict reciprocity and are concerned with the level of interchanges. Monetary negotiations deal with the balance and adjustment between economies. The confusion has been compounded by recent American attempts to affect their balance of payments by specific trade concessions: the purchasing commitments extracted from the Japanese as an alternative to the revaluation of the yen are a case in point. This bilateral tinkering with the balance of payments through trade is economic nonsense and politically undesirable. It depends on a particular power configuration at a given time. Since some of the heat should be taken out of international economic relations through a return to rules and a reduction of the role of politics, the European Community has every interest to press for an efficient monetary adjustment process, on the basis of which it could pursue its liberal trading interests. In the Japanese example, revaluation of the yen would have reduced pressure, not only on the US, but on Europe as well, thus making less necessary the emerging patchwork agreements on voluntary export restrictions between Europe and Japan.

The present reluctance of the Community to link negotiations on monetary and trade issues is therefore sound in principle. More specifically, the Community may want to avoid making concessions in the agricultural field in return for an arrangement which would meet some of its monetary wishes. If we want to build a sound system for the future, each subject should be discussed on its merits.

There is one area where policy decisions in the trade field directly touch monetary affairs. The imposition of an export or import surcharge may be a substitute for re- or devaluation. As such, the discussion of such measures should take place in the IMF (especially if it becomes a strong, central-bank-like institution, as is implicit in the shift to SDRs), or in Working Party 3 of OECD, if this becomes a more important forum for discussing alternative adjustment strategies.

Trade

As far as major international negotiations are concerned the logical sequence is to have monetary reform before major new initiatives on trade liberalisation. This does not mean that trade issues should be treated with benign neglect for a few years. On the contrary, some sort of major 'Round' should be initiated without delay. But in the present political configuration it cannot make substantial progress towards for instance zero-tariffs among industrialised nations. The immediate political task is to keep a finger in the dam against the rising tide of protectionism. While a trade negotiation is taking place, political leaders can more easily resist particularist pleas for protection. A lengthy negotiation on non-tariff barriers, and the technical preparation of agricultural negotiations, may fit these short-term requirements. Our underlying assumption is that an improved monetary adjustment system, better internal adjustment mechanism for labour, and the gradual realisation by the trade unions that technological change itself, rather than trade, is responsible for much of their difficulties, may create the political conditions for significant advances towards further trade liberalisation. It follows that these external and internal reforms should be initiated with all deliberate speed.

But we must realise that the purely economic case for free trade is getting weaker. The transfer of knowledge, increasingly a substitute for the transfer of goods, has narrowed comparative advantages. The adjustment costs of reallocating factors of production, labour and capital are not only social but also economic costs. Capital sunk in a plant built for fifteen years' production of cameras is lost if home production suddenly becomes uncompetitive. Unemployment increasingly measures, not the relation of jobs to workers, but the time needed to find new jobs (which in turn, depends on the skill differential between the old and new jobs) for the growing number of workers placed in such a predicament.

The real case for a continued commitment to free trade (and the freest possible movement of capital) is political as much as economic. The alternative is likely to be a cumulative retreat from economic interdependence which would not stop before it had seriously damaged prosperity. And this point could not but coincide with an equally low level of political cohesion among the industrialised trading nations.

Nor would the rest of the world remain unaffected by a growing trend towards autarky among these nations. Many less developed countries depend for their welfare on access to developed markets. They cannot hope to keep this access unless the developed countries stay 'open' and hold each other to their commitments. In a longer perspective, moreover, the slow integration of the Eastern European economies in the world economic system would take place, if at all, under very different conditions in an autarchic or semi-autarchic world. Instead of taking their place in a world of economic relations based on rules, they would simply add one more element to a world of political deals based on power.

How can a commitment to free trade be reconciled with a concern for its social and economic costs? As in the past, by making exceptions. The crucial point is how these exceptions are made: unilaterally and/or bilaterally on the basis of political power, or by common consent; permanently or temporarily. In the latter case, every retreat from free trade would have to be justified in social and economic terms, giving the affected partners the opportunity to suggest alternative strategies for achieving the same ends. There would thus have to be much greater transparency – which incidentally would benefit rational discussion of domestic socio-economic policies. There would also have to be greatly increased *droit de regard* by others on the internal affairs of nations. This *droit de regard* would have to extend to the supervision of the – temporary – exceptions made. If textile quotas are allowed in order to give the industry time to adjust, how is this time used? Can the timetable for their abolition be kept? Are subsidies to a declining industry contributing towards making it competitive? If not, why should others allow this subsidised production to destroy their markets?

Even this brief sketch shows the size of the leap in political imagination required to cope with this new world, increasingly one of interpenetrating domestic politics. For the Community, of course, the problem is compounded by the need to cope with similar problems internally as well. Since the Community institutions have great difficulty in getting such issues as regional policies, labour market policies, etc., discussed on a level higher than that of the nation state, these institutions may be tempted to cling to such sovereignty in these areas as they manage to acquire: in the past, for example, any external questioning of the agricultural policy by the many affected parties outside the Community was resented as unwarranted interference.

A more constructive approach for the Community institutions would be to point to the enormously increased scope of foreign economic policy, to suggest that a literal interpretation of article 113 of the Rome Treaty (essentially tariff policy), has therefore become technically obsolete, and that on the contrary the whole range of economic, industrial, and social adjustment policies which have to accompany modern foreign economic policy should fall within its mandate. From being the mechanistic executor of internal economic arrangements in the outside world, the Community institutions would become able, like any responsible government, to arbitrate between, and to harmonise, internal and external policy requirements.

Less developed countries

The capacity for internal and external arbitrage will undergo a difficult test as the Community develops a comprehensive policy towards the LDCs. Not only must the traditional fields, trade and aid, become more closely co-ordinated, and monetary policy added to the external policy instruments, but a whole range of internal policies, starting with agricultural policy, industrial policy, and labour market policy form part of an integrated development policy.

In the trade field, the aim must be a maximum possible opening of our borders for the products of the third world. But there is, as was pointed out above, a real limit to the speed of adjustment which can be imposed on the affected branches of industry. Three conclusions follow from this.

First, the limits of adjustment can be enlarged if labour is sufficiently flexible. Labour market policy (retraining, transition payments, etc.) is thus an element of development policy, as it is an element of trade policy in general.

Secondly, the Community cannot in good conscience commit itself to a liberal import policy, which affects certain member states and regions in different degrees, without financial solidarity in coping with the adjustment costs. Vastly increased resources for the European Social Fund are needed if we want to make our commitment to the LDCs economically and politically feasible.

Thirdly, given the fact that imports of manufactured goods

from LDCs tend to compete with our labour-intensive industries where adjustment is slow, and that in certain sectors
these imports may grow much faster than is usual in trade
among industrialised countries, the basic liberal approach
must be tempered by external management as well. The
present system of generalised preferences, with its built-in
quotas, is an effort in this direction. But it errs on the side of
caution, is very complicated, and introduces an unnecessarily
large element of uncertainty into the calculations of would-be
exporters.

Of even more fundamental importance to the future relations of the Community with a part of the less developed
world are the preferential agreements with most of the
Mediterranean and African states. Unlike the generalised
preferences, these are reverse (two-way) preferences, linking
the Community with these countries in nascent free trade
areas. Where generalised preferences acknowledge inequality,
reverse preferences maintain the fiction of equality. Where the
former are universal, the latter create special relationships of
dependence. These dependencies are aggravated, whatever the
short-term economic benefits, by special aid links and agricultural import arrangements.

The Community is in a position *vis-à-vis* its southern neighbours similar to that of the United States *vis-à-vis* early post-
war Europe. Like the US, Europe should aim at creating
viable partners rather than dependencies. This means allowing
discrimination against the stronger partner, encouraging
regional groupings among the LDCs and transferring real
resources as a function of development needs rather than as a
form of export promotion.

The Community must also recognise that increased economic interdependence, which is the aim of its Mediterranean
and African policies, puts a much heavier strain on the LDCs
than on us. The treaties linking us with these countries introduce an element of rigidity, not to say a lack of freedom of
action, which is politically undesirable among non equals,
and may be economically harmful. This point is further
developed in Chapters 9 and 10, on the Mediterranean and
the developing countries.

In a few instances, notably for a number of commodities

for which it is the main market, the Community can by itself contribute towards development. In most areas, particularly aid policy, only a joint approach by the rich countries can make a dent in the problem. The untying of aid, for example, could increase by a third the real value of aid received by the LDCs. How can Japan and the US agree to such a policy if their export possibilities are distorted through reverse preferences granted to Europe?

Preferential agreements are of course also a symptom of that more general phenomenon, the disregard of spirit of GATT by all contracting parties. If we want our developed partners to play by at least some of the rules which have served us well in the past (universalism is one of these), we should be prepared to reconsider the most notable transgression by the Community in this field. The fact that this happens to be an important item in the American negotiating position should not prevent responsible Europeans from overcoming bureaucratic inertia and dismantling a set of arrangements which is not really in harmony with the economic and political views of the Community of Nine.

The alternative to a sphere-of-influence approach is a multilateral approach to the problems of development. Multilateral aid-giving, for example, through the World Bank, lessens the direct political link between donor and receiver countries. If such aid is subject to conditions, these have to be explicit and formulated with regard to development objectives. The multilateral approach would also help to persuade our rich partners to subscribe to long-term contractual engagements *vis-à-vis* the third world, to co-ordinate our efforts, and to give a participatory voice to the third world. It is of course necessary that the Community be represented as an entity in world bodies dealing with economic questions. The organisational and intellectual resources of the European Development Fund could thus be partially used to formulate Community policy positions in the World Bank.

East–West economic relations

As in the case of the less developed countries, the introduction of the centrally planned economies into the world economy presents special problems. Here the problem is not to change and adapt a long established relationship, from dependence to interdependence, but to create new links of interdependence. While the difficulties in dealing with the LDCs are diffuse, those with the socialist economies are very visible: a highly elaborate economic system operating on very different principles.

The conciliation of the two systems presents real technical and political difficulties. It is in Europe's interest to depoliticise economic relations as much as possible. This means the elaboration of multilateral contracts (in GATT, IMF, etc.) rather than a series of political bargains subject to the vagaries of political relations. A number of individual agreements between, say, the Soviet Union and the three major industrialised powers would, while favouring one or the other, in the end weaken all. This is also true, of course, for specific issues, such as interest rates on long-term loans, where competition for exports may lead us to engage in an involuntary aid policy.

In one respect the socialist countries resemble the LDCs. The development of an industry able to compete on equal footing with those of the West is a long-term task which necessitates at least some imports of capital goods from the West. The scarcity of convertible currency may force these countries to a restrictive bilateral balancing of trading accounts. For these reasons, the West should be willing to provide sufficient liquidity to finance balance-of-payments swings, thus priming the pump of international trade, and to finance sustained deficits, for example by a joint low interest loan, making possible a greatly increased productivity in the future. Unless the gap in economic development between Western and Eastern Europe is narrowed, there can be little hope of an eventual growing together of the two parts of the continent.

Conclusion

World economic management, in the future means coming to grips with the formidable problems of industrial, regional, and conjunctural policy on a world scale.

All governments now accept ever greater responsibility for domestic economic welfare, but the international economy which contributes to that welfare, increasingly limits the effectiveness of national control. The rules which now regulate international economic exchanges cannot, by themselves, contain the political pressures. Furthermore, these rules have in part become technically obsolete. The character of international economics has changed through international production, and the entrance of new participants: the LDCs and the centrally planned economies.

The increased strain on the post-war economic system has coincided with the loss of such management as it had in the past. During this period of nascent anarchy all rules are being broken, the good with the bad. What is now needed is a recommitment to some of these rules by the major participants, agreed procedures to temper the application of the rules, and, new rules, especially in the monetary field.

For the Community, this task is as difficult as it is vital. Difficult, because member states will find it hard to agree on basic lines of economic policy; because delicate internal bargains could be called in question; and because participation in world economic management would require a greatly increased capacity, at the centre, to harmonise internal and external requirements. Vital, because without such a capacity, member states will break the constraints imposed on them by an ineffective Community, and each will seek to face the new economic challenges by itself. Not only would they fail, but the absence of a constructive Community would have profound consequences for global economic order itself.

3 Europe and the International Monetary System

Albert Kervyn

In discussions of the international monetary system, the only unanimity is on the need for fundamental reform. Clearly, the agreement reached at the Smithsonian Institute in Washington in December 1971 only solved part of the problem: it was a temporary papering-over of the cracks, an interim solution pending the negotiation of a new overall settlement. Even before this new negotiation had begun, the Smithsonian agreement has already been called in question. Since June 1972 the pound sterling has been floating; and it was only after hard bargaining that European Ministers were able to announce their intention to abide by the Washington agreement.

There is no disguising the fact, therefore, that the present system will only survive until the next crisis or until it is replaced by a new settlement. The pages that follow will seek to examine what Europe's interests are in the necessary reform, and how European countries could effectively act to prevent a worsening of the international payments situation. The choices open to Europe in this field will be discussed in relation to the steps undertaken towards economic and monetary union, since although the internal details of such a union are outside the scope of the present chapter it is nevertheless necessary to analyse their relationship with any international system. In this international field, the central problem today is that of the dollar, and the three main actors on the scene are the United States, Europe, and Japan. What will be expounded here is a European viewpoint; and without neglecting the broader international context of any negotiations, it is from this angle that the technical aspects of the problem will chiefly be considered.

Bretton Woods and after

The contents of the Bretton Woods agreements, and their subsequent history, are too well known to make necessary more than a reminder of a few salient points that are significant for the present discussion.

The year 1958, which saw the beginning of the Common Market, also marked the great return to 'normalcy' in the monetary field: the world's leading currencies once more became convertible, and the movement of capital was partially liberalised. When the exchange markets were re-opened, the dollar was officially enthroned as an international reserve unit alongside gold. All Central Banks agreed to maintain the dollar parities of their national currencies on their national markets, while the Federal Reserve Board agreed to buy or sell gold at a fixed dollar rate. The gold exchange standard was established, the International Monetary Fund was reduced to a subordinate role, the European Payments Union was abolished, and the recurrent weakness of sterling became an embarrassment rather than a serious threat. The Federal Reserve, with its large gold stock, was the ultimate guarantor of world liquidity.

This, however, had only become possible as a result of the United States' balance-of-payments deficit, which had enabled European Central Banks to build up their own gold stocks at the expense of Fort Knox, and to accumulate the dollars that were necessary for their current interventions on the markets. The equilibrium thus achieved was not to last. As the American deficit continued, a 'dollar glut' soon followed the 'dollar gap'. From 1963 onwards, the continuing fall in their gold reserves led the Americans to put pressure on the Central Banks to retain their dollars without seeking to convert them into gold. At the same time, the United States tried to limit the private export of capital, which had become a more important element in the deficit than official transfers. Thus began an almost imperceptible shift from the gold exchange standard towards a dollar standard pure and simple.

Then came the gold crisis. From 1966 onwards, private purchases of gold on the London market began to exceed current production (and Russian sales). At the beginning of

1968, speculation on the revaluation of gold turned into a torrent, and the Central Banks decided to cease maintaining the price at $35 an ounce. From then on, they would no longer either buy gold or sell it. The existing stock continued to circulate among them in order to settle deficits, but without reference to the price on the free market.

This clearly threatened to lead to a shortage of liquidity in the international payments system. World trade was expanding at an unprecedented pace, and capital movements were growing ever larger. There was a parallel increase in the need for international reserves to cover temporary payments disequilibria. But there was now only a fixed stock of gold, and many Central Banks were now no longer keen to accumulate more dollars. Of the two pillars which had been intended to uphold the growth of the system, one had become unavailable, the other unpopular.

Certain economists (chief among them Robert Triffin) had long pointed to this danger, and proposed the establishment of international reserves with machinery for ensuring their controlled growth. This time, after years of discussion, governments were obliged to take action; and in 1969 they decided to create Special Drawing Rights in the International Monetary Fund. This agreement, although its immediate effects were limited, was hailed as the start of a new era in monetary co-operation.

Meanwhile, the expansion of the private international dollar market created new problems. From modest beginnings, the Euro-dollar soon proved to be a flexible and efficient means of financing international transactions. 1968 and 1969 were the years of its greatest growth. By the end of 1969, as a result of the restrictive monetary policy practised by the Federal Reserve, American banks had borrowed more than 15,000 million dollars on the market to meet the credit needs of their clients, using as intermediaries their overseas branches. The result was an exceptional rise in interest rates, which attracted to the dollar all available liquidity. The reflux which followed the slowdown of expansion in the United States and the change in the Federal Reserve's policy, while it led directly to the monetary crisis of 1971, checked but did not halt the expansion of the Euro-dollar market. First the multinational companies, then other firms with excess liquidity, saw the advantage of placing their funds where they would earn the highest rate of interest; later, they took to shifting them in order to avoid losses or to make profits whenever a change of parity seemed likely.

If the 1971 crisis began with the reflux of some 10,000 million Euro-dollars, it was increased by short-term movements of capital out of the United States. During the first three quarters of 1971, in fact, nearly 12,000 million dollars were exported, almost 10,000 of which appeared in the balance-of-payments statistics under the heading 'Errors and Omissions', probably the largest error in monetary history.

The Central Banks of those countries whose currencies were regarded as strong by 'speculators' (in the sense defined above: companies operating in several countries and able to shift funds rapidly) were forced one after another to let their parities float when they were no longer willing to buy up all the dollars that appeared on their markets. This period of floating exchange-rates ended with the Washington agreements of December 1971, which established a series of fixed parities, although with wider bands. The dollar, which had been virtually inconvertible whenever large sums were in question, and which had become officially inconvertible in August 1971, remained so.

This brief summary of the difficulties experienced in recent years has a number of lessons to teach us if we seek to achieve effective reform. To quote a *locus classicus*, 'Those who are ignorant of history condemn themselves to repeating it.'

First an exchange standard system based on more than one reserve medium is not in the long term viable: one of the assets grows too scarce, and the other over-abundant. This was already the fate of bimetallism in the nineteenth century. The same was true of the gold-exchange standard in the inter-war period, when sterling was the reserve currency and in the 1960s, when the dollar had largely taken its place.

Some American economists deplore the Central Banks' irrational preference for gold. In one sense they are right, since gold is virtually useless unless converted into dollars, which alone can buy goods throughout the world, whereas dollars have no need to be convertible into gold in order to be used or to earn interest. This practical advantage, however, is more than offset by the dollar's weakness as an asset. The over-abundant unit will always risk depreciating in terms of the scarcer unit, and hence will emerge as a less desirable asset.

This is the fundamental problem for any reserve currency. As the League of Nations already realised in the 1920s, gold is scarce and cannot be used to finance a growing volume of trade: hence the need for a reserve currency. But such a currency cannot play its reserve role unless the country that issues it is willing and able to make growing quantities available to the rest of the world: in other words, unless it has a quasi-permanent deficit in its balance of payments. And the existence of this deficit, necessary though it is, ends by destroying confidence in the reserve currency itself.

To speak today of the 'bankruptcy' of the dollar, and to imagine replacing it by a European reserve currency, would be to enter the same ultimate impasse.

Secondly, a country with a reserve currency faces major adjustment problems when it has to correct a persistent deficit. The United Kingdom paid a high price to learn this lesson, in terms of employment and growth. Except in a crisis like that of 1971, the reserve currency cannot be devalued without dragging with it most of the others: it cannot enforce a change in relative parities, which for the external balance is the only change that matters.

It is necessary also to bear in mind the asymmetry that is a characteristic feature of such adjustment problems. Countries in deficit, that is, are from time to time obliged to devalue their currencies *vis-à-vis* the standard, whereas there is no comparable pressure on countries in surplus to revalue, so revaluations remain the exception. The result is that the reserve currency therefore tends to become over-valued, and this 'hidden revaluation' is only acceptable if the country in question is less inflationary than its partners. If not, it must sacrifice either its international commitments or its level of employment and its growth rate. This dilemma underlies all the monetary debates between Americans and Europeans during the last ten years.

Thirdly, the period of floating exchange rates, although

short, was long enough to dash the hopes of an influential group of academic economists who had advocated this as a solution, believing that parities should be determined by the interplay of supply and demand. This, it was thought, would automatically ensure balance-of-payments equilibrium and eliminate the reserve currency problem.

However, industry and commerce expect of Governments, more than anything else, some limitation of the many uncertainties that surround their operations and decisions. Pressure from the business world, therefore, is always in the direction of fixed parities, with the narrowest possible dealers' margins. No doubt the experts employed by the larger corporations can put up with floating exchange rates, and even make a profit from them. But for the mass of medium-sized exporters they are a real hindrance to trade. Such firms will always seek their abolition.

Fourthly, modern economies all operate with surplus liquidity: this was the basis of the Euro-dollar market. The supply of Euro-dollars comes both from Europeans who hold funds for which they have no immediate use in their national currencies, and from Americans who leave their surplus dollars offshore. As soon as market institutions arise which make it possible to pool these funds and distribute them according to demand, the advantages become obvious. The size of the market itself ensures that it is fully competitive, and unlike national markets, which are often small, it has sufficient liquidity to make loans of almost unlimited amounts. The world's largest firms, and some governments, can use it as a source of finance, and Central Banks can operate on it for monetary or other purposes without danger of disruption.

So it has to be reckoned that an international market capable of assembling and deploying very considerable sums will be a permanent feature of the monetary scene. It is difficult to follow the reasoning of those French economists who consider it a temporary or peripheral phenomenon, a mere by-product of United States Regulation Q. Indeed, it is noteworthy that operations on the Euro-dollar market have hardly been checked at all by either the abolition of that Regulation or the crisis of confidence in the dollar. All that happened was that in 1971 its expansion was less rapid than that of transactions in other Euro-currencies. During the two years when American banks' borrowings from their overseas subsidiaries fell by 10,000 million dollars, borrowings (in dollars) by foreigners increased by 20,000 million, and their deposits by 10,000 million. At the end of 1971 the monetary basis of the Euro-dollar market consisted of 15,000 million dollars' worth of debts owed by American banks to foreign firms (leaving out of account official institutions); and to estimate the volume of transactions involved, this figure must be multiplied by three or even four. By way of comparison, it may be noted that the total exchange reserves of the six Common Market countries at the end of 1969 amounted to less than 21,000 million dollars.

Alongside its undeniable advantages, from a European point of view the Euro-dollar market has some serious draw-backs. First of all, it is still dominated by the American mone-tary market, and in particular by the policies of the Federal Reserve. This is a simple matter of size. Ten or fifteen thou-sand million dollars are not much by comparison with the credit volume of American banks, but their weight on the European markets is huge. The result is that the European Central Banks have largely lost their autonomy in monetary policy: their discount rates are obliged to follow the evolution of the Euro-dollar market, which itself is determined by the restrictiveness or otherwise of the policies pursued by the Federal Reserve. Credit restriction in Europe is either ineffec-tive or highly discriminatory if the larger firms can evade it by turning to the Euro-dollar market.

Furthermore, the movement of funds across that market is a constant threat to the system of fixed parities. Experience shows that Central Banks find it hard to resist capital move-ments resulting from the expectation that one currency or another is to be devalued or revalued. When the authorities are no longer able or willing to defend their parity, 'specula-tors' trigger off the change that they have been expecting, and their judgement thus becomes a self-fulfilling prophecy. This happened in 1967 with the devaluation of sterling, and in 1969 with the revaluation of the D-Mark. In 1971, one currency after another had to break away from the dollar. In 1972, an attack on the pound was once again justified in retrospect by its downward float. It is hardly surprising that in these circumstances the credibility of fixed exchange rates is gradually eroded; and this loss of confidence is reflected also in the rise in the free market price of gold.

A psychological climate in which any disequilibrium in balances of payments, however temporary, is likely to be interpreted as heralding a parity change, makes very clear the need for a robust system in which the monetary authorities are in a position to defend themselves against sudden shifts in liquidity.

Finally, there is an obvious dilemma. A nation may seek to insulate its economy from the Euro-dollar market, or it may look for ways in which to live with it. The former solution is never entirely practicable, since capital movements can too easily be disguised as commercial transactions.

With monetary union in prospect, there is surely no option but Community action. Any solution but the most restrictive must take account of the fact that the national monetary entities to which we are accustomed are now too small to be effective. The concept of an optimum currency area, proposed by Robert A. Mundell, has never been quantified in practice. In theory, it would be an economic area large enough for an independent monetary and exchange-rate policy to be able to ensure economic growth; but economic interpenetration, the response of wage rates to the rising cost of living, and now the development of a private capital market, alter the very terms of any such definition. Any area that is too small has lost all possibility of pursuing an independent policy. Now that economies of scale have become important in the financial field, a small country that fancied it could defend its own autonomy would very soon see the dollar become its second national currency and, for all important financial transactions, its first.

Europe and the situation in 1972

The exceptionally rapid growth of European economies during the last twenty years, and the rising living standards which this has made possible, have been associated with an even more rapid expansion of international trade.

Europe, like Japan, is much more dependent on this than either the United States or the USSR. Pre-war experience has amply shown that world trade cannot expand without a viable payments system. This is a fact that Europe cannot afford to ignore.

But Europe also needs a degree of independence. The political and other objectives discussed in the present book all point to the need for European unity. But from the specialised viewpoint of the present chapter, monetary union is Europe's only hope of establishing a currency area large enough to cease being an involuntary appendage of the dollar zone, which it at present is.

The details and disadvantages of this situation will be examined later. But it must be pointed out at this stage that neither of the two imperatives mentioned above has any chance of being met unless there is a consensus of opinion in Europe adequate both for international negotiations, i.e. a joint approach to the United States, and for each stage of the move towards monetary union. This is not the place to discuss the internal details of such a union and the degree of co-ordination of national policies, or the delegation of sovereignty to Community institutions that it will involve. But it must be clear that a change in political attitudes on the highest level is necessary if a Community point of view is to replace the spread of national viewpoints as they at present exist. The unhappy experience of 1971 must not be repeated. Then, the Council of Ministers' decision on mutual consultation and the commitment to monetary co-operation were forgotten as soon as difficulties arose. Agreement to start on the process leading to economic union was followed, after only a few months, by the most lamentable inability to agree on what attitude to take in the face of the dollar crisis. From May to December 1971, all the Commission's recommendations were without effect, and all the meetings of the Council of Ministers were failures.

It is be hoped that the bitter experience of 1971 may have been useful and have led to a resurgence of the political will to achieve effective co-operation. The decisions taken in the spring of 1972 were a first step in this direction: they were a first attempt to give some reality to monetary union in Europe.

The sterling crisis that occurred later in that year gave a new sense of urgency to the need to act together. The French agreed to the potential sacrifice of a certain amount of gold to persuade the Italians to accept their policy and the Germans followed them, even going so far as to sacrifice one of their key Ministers, less in the conviction that the policy adopted was a good one than in a spirit of European solidarity.

These recent signs are hopeful. But there still is a long way to go. The sections that follow will suggest that a real reform, safeguarding Europe's long-term interests, will require fundamental decisions that impinge on certain cherished elements of national sovereignty. The responsibility for these decisions can only be taken at the highest political level: no negotiation among experts could achieve the necessary changes without precise political instructions on the principles to follow.

Before discussing the options that are open to Europe, it may be well to describe more precisely the results of the Washington agreement of 1971.

This re-established a system of fixed exchange rates. The widening of the bands around central rate may indeed limit the very short-term interventions of Central Banks on the exchange markets, since private buyers and sellers will time their operations according to market fluctuations. If the currency they need is temporarily dearer, they may take the risk of borrowing for a few days or weeks in the hope of obtaining a better rate later on. With such flexibility speculation may have a stabilising effect at least so long as dealers believe that the central rate will be maintained. Flexibility also increases the risk of losses on speculative movement of capital, and may discourage it if the prospects of a parity change are not very great.

These, however, are only short-term effects. Over a longer period, the supply and demand of any given currency are determined above all by the economic operations that give rise to the transactions on the exchange market – buying or selling, investing, etc. And it is very unlikely that these will be greatly affected by the widening of the band. The extra element of uncertainty that this introduces may well make some transactions a little more difficult or costly, but even the most enthusiastic of advocates of widening the bands have never claimed that this in itself could ensure balance-of-payments equilibrium.

As in the past, therefore, fixed exchange rates impose on the Central Banks an unlimited obligation to buy or sell dollars against their national currencies. True, this no longer applies to transactions inside the European Community, but it remains true for the European Communities' net settlements with the rest of the world.

In a system of fixed exchange rates, the problem of exchange reserves remains central. Here, the present situation is full of paradoxes. International reserves have never increased so rapidly as in the last few years; they have now reached a level at which there seems to be a glut rather than a shortage as was long the case in the past. Between 1964 and 1969, they went up by 13 per cent, 2·5 per cent per year. In 1970 and 1971, they rose at the rate of 30 per cent per year.

And yet there is less real liquidity now than for a very long time. The dollar, its credibility weakened, has become an inferior asset, and any Central Bank which is a creditor is anxious to receive gold or SDRs, or to force its debtor to pay in its own currency, acquired from the IMF. The IMF itself refuses to buy dollars or to accept repayment in them. All international settlements now have to be negotiated, and in this respect the world has returned to the worst days of inconvertibility, when everyone was trying to accumulate claims in hard currency and to get rid of weaker currencies. This is the result both of the inconvertibility of the dollar and of doubts about the possibility of long maintaining its present parity, as well as of the rise in the gold price on the London market. Even if the Central Banks continue to evaluate their stock at $38 an ounce, they can hardly avoid casting a sidelong glance at the profits they would make by selling it at $60.

The conjunction of a shortage of real liquidity with a plethora of reserves, which dominates the discussions among the European Central Banks, does not, however, apply to the private international market, or to the less developed countries: the 4,000 million dollars which they acquired in 1970–2 is for them a real increase in liquidity.

Certainly, a large and prolonged surplus in the American balance of official settlements would restore the full usefulness of the dollar for effecting official settlements. If such a surplus could be expected as a result of the realignment of parities in 1971, there would be less urgent need for reform.

But as things stand, the European countries are in a most unenviable position. So long as the international system is based on fixed exchange rates, the Europeans' overriding interest in maintaining these parities obliges them to buy all the surplus dollars that are offered on their markets. In the short term, to limit capital movements, they are forced to go on aligning their policy on the American money market, rather than acting, according to the state of their own economies. In particular, if inflationary pressure becomes stronger in Europe than in the United States, the Central Banks are robbed of their traditional weapon against inflation, an increase in interest rates.

The freedom lost on the European side is acquired by the Americans. Under the present system, there is no balance-of-payments constraint on the economic policy of the United States. Even the dilemma of an internal recession which calls for expansionary policy, coinciding with an external deficit, which would normally call for a squeeze, presents no problem. There is no need to worry about the external consequences of policies dictated purely by the internal situation. In so far as they cause or worsen a balance-of-payments deficit, the latter is automatically financed by the European Central Banks, which buy dollars on an unlimited scale to maintain their own parities.

What appears as freedom from an American point of view, is resented as domination by the Europeans. It is true that, while nothing in the system obliges the Americans to take account of their partners' interest, they may nevertheless decide to do so for long-term policy reasons. This would be what Richard Cooper, in a recent article in *World Politics*, has called a constructive reaction; but such a reaction cannot be counted on, at least if the decisions of August 1971 are any guide. These, in Cooper's classification, would be characterised as aggressive.

What is advocated here is a constructive solution on both

the international and the European level. As will be seen, moreover, European co-operation has two aspects: first, a joint approach to the Americans, and secondly, internal arrangements among Europeans themselves. The optimum solution would be a combination of these two. If, however, that proved impracticable, Europeans would have, to fall back on a defensive solution *vis-à-vis* America which would, however, itself presuppose a constructive solution among themselves. The discussion that follows will indicate both the advantages, even on a purely international plane, of achieving monetary union and the difficulties involved. For this purpose, it will be necessary to sketch the broad lines on which monetary union could be gradually established. Full treatment of this theme would, however, be out of place here: the reader who seeks it may be recommended to examine one of the most complete and clear-sighted analyses of the subject, the study published by Magnifico, Villiers, and Williamson in their report for the Federal Trust.[1]

A co-operative solution

Before proceeding further, one pseudo-solution must be ruled out: that is, the proposal for a massive rise in the gold price. This would be unacceptable to most countries, not only for political reasons (the power it would confer on South Africa and the USSR and the unfair distribution of the resulting profits), but also because it would only solve the problem if the official price were tripled or quadrupled in order to ensure that the excess of production over industrial needs would be large enough to supply the necessary additional liquidity each year. And even if there were such a price rise, the result would be unpredictable: how would private holders of gold react?

The only viable solution, therefore, would be to apply the long-standing proposal made by Robert Triffin, that is, to internationalise exchange reserves by the creation of a new asset the supply of which would not depend on the external deficits of reserve-currency countries. One step has already

[1] *European Monetary Integration* a Federal Trust Report (London, 1972).

been taken in this direction with the establishment of SDRs, but so far this is only a minor addition to the existing reserves system. What is needed is to go much further and make this new asset the central instrument of world liquidity supply, alongside both a stock of gold which could remain more or less frozen as it is today (but then without causing any major inconvenience) and lines of credit with the IMF or opened by the Central Banks.

In 1960, this proposal would have been relatively easy to apply. Today, the consolidation of the dollar (and sterling) balances, which is the precondition for such a SDR based system, would lead to serious conflicts of interest. However, a great deal has been learned during the past twelve years; and even if it is more difficult, such a reform may today be more practicable, now that the disadvantages of any alternative have become clearer.

Since what is in question is essentially the move from a dollar standard to an international standard, a crucial question is the attitude of the United States. Fred Bergsten has provided an admirable analysis of the fundamental interests which the American delegation should defend in such negotiation.[1] He sets forth three requirements for any acceptable reform:

> an effective adjustment mechanism which gives the United States the same possibilities as other countries;
> the elimination of surplus dollar balances;
> machinery for the creation of new reserves in line with world needs.

Let us take these three points in turn and examine the problems that they raise.

Given the unwillingness of surplus countries to revalue their currencies, it is understandable that the United States should wish to enjoy the same possibility as other deficit countries, that of restoring equilibrium by means of devaluation. The difficulty lies not only in the monetary situation of the dollar, but also in the industrial power of the United States. Some

---

[1] See ' International Monetary Reform: A Viewpoint from the United States' in *Europe and the Evolution of the International Monetary System* (1972).

Europeans demand that the United States eliminate its external deficit because it causes inflation in Europe, and almost in the same breath express the fear that they may not be able to meet American competition. Is the dollar too strong or too weak? The usual French reply is that the commercial dollar is strong, but that its weakness arises from the fact that Americans are buying up European firms. In fact, for the three last years that can be called 'normal' (1968–70) the balance of payments of the United States shows that the net flow of direct investments into the Common Market and the United Kingdom was slightly less than 2000 million dollars, while Europeans bought more than 4300 million dollars' worth of American securities. From the balance-of-payments point of view, it is not the Americans who are buying up European industry, but the Europeans who are buying into American industry.[1]

Since the Europeans would no doubt be unwilling to allow the dollar to be devalued against their currencies by a unilateral decision of the US Government, procedures for discrete consultation and implicit negotiation need to be worked out in order to make effective the abandonment of the dollar standard and to give back to the Americans that margin for manoeuvre which is necessary to maintain dollar convertibility.

The conversion of the dollar balances into SDRs raises other problems. The United States could scarcely accept less than the almost complete conversion of the sums at present held by the Central Banks. Expressed in devalued dollars, the exchange reserve of the United States at the end of 1971 amounted to 13,000 million dollars, of which 10,000 million were gold which must be considered frozen. After an increase of nearly 35,000 million dollars in two years, the dollar balances held by the Central Banks at the same date can be estimated at some 52,000 million.[2]

[1] *Survey of Current Business*, June 1971.
[2] The figures that the Central Banks reported to the IMF are very much higher; the total amount of foreign exchange in their reserves was 80,000 million dollars, 8,000 million of it in sterling. The difference – some 20,000 million – is explained chiefly by the fact that part of it is counted twice, through investments on the Euro-dollar market made by the Central Banks (or by the Bank for International Settlements on their behalf) and through

To this must be added more than 15,000 million dollars in the form of private balances on the Euro-dollar market, to mention only its monetary base, part of which is liable to flow back to the Central Banks.

These figures show clearly enough that once doubts have arisen about the dollar, the United States could only return to convertibility if the quasi-totality of its liquid debts were consolidated, i.e. if those who hold them were no longer able to change them into other assets. The simplest solution would no doubt be to convert them into a long-term American Government loan, accompanied by an exchange guarantee.

Such a solution would only be very partially acceptable to the Europeans and the Japanese, who could hardly agree to so dramatic a drain on their liquidity. About 27,000 million dollars out of the 35,000 million accumulated during the last two years is the result of short-term capital movements.[1] But what has left the United States or the European dollar market can always return. Even if this hypothesis at present seems unlikely, the European and Japanese Central Banks cannot take the risk, and they would certainly want to retain sufficient liquidity to meet it. They could therefore only accept a very partial conversion of the dollar balances into a long-term debt.

The contradictory demands of the United States and Europe could only be reconciled if the dollar balances were converted into assets which remained liquid but were no longer United States debts. This would be the case if they were converted into SDRs which, while remaining liquid from the creditor's point of view, would no longer create a threat to the debtor's liquidity. The IMF would then hold the bulk of the American Government's long-term bonds. Since the IMF would then be in the position of a Central Bank *vis-à-vis* the whole world, it would have no liquidity problem.

the use of swap facilities. These figures also include other currencies, such as Deutschmarks, Swiss francs or, in the franc zone, French francs.

[1] More precisely, the deficit in the official United States balance for 1970 and 1971 was 39,500 million dollars, 4500 million of which were settled by a lowering of exchange reserves. Of these 39,500 million, only 12,000 million were the result of a deficit on current transactions and long-term capital movements (and even this figure is swollen by the inclusion of short-term capital disguised under these headings). The remaining 27,500 million came under the heading of short-term movements.

What is more, the exchange guarantee desired by its creditors would be automatic since the SDRs would be the standard against which other currencies were valued.

The SDRs could thus become 'the' international currency, and the United States and their partners would no doubt desire as complete a dollar conversion as possible, leaving only minimum working balances. The chief problems would then be interest rates and amortisation. On interest rates, Bergsten has made what seems an eminently reasonable proposal: that SDRs, being a liquid asset, could pay a fairly low rate of interest, and the long-term debt a higher rate, the difference being made over to the World Bank for development aid. Since the amounts to be converted would exceed 50,000 million dollars (the figures quoted above referring to the end of 1971, and the balances having reached 60,000 million dollars in September 1972), a difference of two percentage points between the two rates of interest would give an absolute difference of 1000 million dollars per year.

The only genuine amortisation of the long-term debt would be for the American Government to exchange it for SDRs when it fell due. This would mean a loss of international liquidity. Even more important, both the interest payments and amortisation would require a surplus in the American balance of payments. Assuming a figure of 50,000 million dollars, at an interest rate of 4 per cent and repayable in twenty-five years (extremely favourable conditions) the annual surplus needed in the American balance of payments would be 4000 million dollars. In practice, this would mean a comparable balance-of-payments deficit in Europe – and thus probably, in practice a big enough devaluation of the dollar to secure such a United States surplus year in, year out. Europeans ought to consider very seriously the conditions they seek to impose for the conversion of the dollar balances.

The third American requirement is for a reasonable rate of liquidity creation in the future. Clearly, the American economy would scarcely be able to run with its level of effective reserves as low as at present, and the United States could not count on achieving an immediate surplus in order to reconstitute them. Here, it may be more difficult to reach agreement. Four years ago, the member nations of the IMF decided that liquidity needs could be met without danger of inflation by issuing SDRs at a rate of some 10,000 million dollars in three years. During the past two years, however, total exchange reserves reported to the IMF have increased by more than 40,000 million dollars. The Europeans and the Japanese have by no means digested the inflationary effects of this influx on their national currencies: would they be ready to agree that there is still a shortage of international liquidity? Or would they agree – which would be the most reasonable solution – that SDRs should be issued to benefit only the United States and the less developed countries? Might they propose some formula by which, once the total amount of new SDRs had been fixed, they should be distributed to those countries whose reserves were inadequate in view of their balance-of-payments situation?

Any international solution requires that the dollar should once more become convertible. But while the conditions for achieving this are relatively easy to define they are likely to be more difficult to fulfil. Clearly, the internal policy of the United States cannot be determined solely by its balance of payments. To wipe out the present deficit, how many Americans would have to lose their jobs? Foreign transactions form such a small part of the American national economy that balance-of-payments considerations cannot be allowed to rule it. Europeans, therefore, must look for other ways of restoring equilibrium. As has already been seen, long-term capital movements are at present helping to do so, and to restrict them would simply aggravate the problem. Would Europeans, then, be prepared to see an end of United States military commitments in Europe? Would they be prepared to finance them? Or would they prefer a further devaluation of the dollar (if the most recent devaluation was insufficient), making American exports much more competitive and European exports less so? That might be preferable to a new wave of protectionism, which is the other alternative. But whatever the solution, Europeans must realise what it would involve.

It should be added, however, that all this is for the moment premature: there is no immediate prospect of equilibrium being restored. The figures for the last ten years show a fairly constant relationship between the United States' trade balance and its basic balance (current transactions plus long-term capital); the difference between the two is in the region of 5000 or 6000 million dollars and is tending to increase. Given a trade deficit of more than 6000 million dollars in 1972, simple extrapolation would suggest an overall deficit of some 12,000 million dollars for the whole year. If an agreement of the type discussed earlier had been concluded on January 1, 1972, the exchange reserves of the United States would have been unable to resist, and dollar convertibility could only have been maintained for a few months.

This shows how precarious it would be to attempt any such reform before achieving some degree of external equilibrium. A fundamental reform of the system based on co-operation must therefore be envisaged as a medium-term hope rather than an immediate possibility. Europeans themselves, moreover, need time to agree on the kind of price that they would be ready to pay in order to re-establish international order. What is more, the debate so far has centred on relations at Central Bank level; and in the world of today, as has been seen already, these are only one aspect of the problem: another is that of the international money market, which cannot be ignored. The solutions discussed so far would meet Europe's first need – interdependence – but not the second – effective independence. Even if the dollar standard were indeed eliminated from official transactions, it could once more assert itself in private transactions through the Euro-dollar market.

To meet their second objective, Europeans need to go further than deciding on a joint position for international negotiations: they need to make arrangements among themselves to establish a European market which would be in some degree independent of the dollar and hence of American monetary policy.

The pages that follow will suggest that this can only be achieved in practice as part of an approach to monetary union; and that institutional progress of this kind would at the same time enable Europeans to find a second best solution pending an international solution for which the time is not yet ripe. Let us therefore consider such a European solution,

first on the assumption that international agreement has been
reached on the dollar problem, and secondly on the assumption
that no such world solution has yet been achieved and that
the European or 'second-best' solution must apply to both
private and official transactions.

European solutions in the context of a world solution

In the present situation, the dollar is *de facto* 'the' European
currency: in so far as a European credit and capital market
exists, the dollar is the currency in which it operates. The
disadvantages of this situation are well known, and have
been summarised above.

There are two alternative ways out. The worse would undoubtedly be general restrictive measures seeking to limit
international capital movements, with every country setting
up frontier controls for fear of the dollar and the instability
that its unchecked movement may bring about. Such a policy
would effectively prevent the development of a European
market, without offering any alternative to the Euro-dollar
market: the latter would continue to be the only international
market and the Euro-dollar would remain the European
currency, in so far as there continued to be one. The extraordinary success of the Euro-dollar market in the last few
years shows clearly enough that it meets a very important
economic need. Restrictive policies could make it impossible
to establish a truly European market, but they would not
prevent recourse to the Euro-dollar market – or, indeed, a
flight into this market wherever there was a loophole in the
regulations.

The opposite of this nationalist and ineffective course would
be a European solution which sought to give financial institutions and firms a better alternative to the dollar for transactions
in Europe.

The simplest such solution would obviously be to use one
of the European currencies. But this would have very serious
disadvantages. From the point of view of the country whose
currency was thus used, this apparent privilege would be a
heavy burden (as Germany has clearly realised, since it has
been trying to prevent the growth of a Euro-mark); while

from the point of view of the other European countries the burden would look like a privilege carrying with it exceptional power. In other words, one Central Bank cannot be made responsible both for running its own national monetary policy and for supervising the European monetary market. The resultant conflicts of interest would in fact lead to the breakdown of the system.

The only alternative is a European solution; but its implications are very profound. The responsibility which cannot be undertaken by any one of the Central Banks must be entrusted to a body which represents all of them (as the Werner Report proposed). The first responsibility of such a body would be to establish a European unit of account, which could be defined, for example in terms of SDRs, and against which the parities of the European national currencies would be fixed – without, however, necessarily ruling out future parity changes. The next step would be the gradual introduction of monetary instruments denominated in this new unit of account, that is, its gradual assumption of the role of a genuine currency for Europe. This might be begun, for example, by means of Treasury Bonds denominated in units of account, issued by the joint body on behalf of one of the member states, and convertible without charge into any European currency.

Clearly, if the joint body were gradually to develop into a European bank, this would be entirely compatible with existing arrangements at Central Bank level. In particular, it would not imply that the snake in the tunnel became as thin as a wire, or that there was any irrevocable commitment to maintain for ever the present parities among European currencies. But what it would imply is much closer co-operation among Central Banks: the rapidly growing inter-penetration of their markets would make it necessary for them to co-ordinate their policies and gradually to achieve joint management of a European market. Although interest rates would have to become uniform throughout Europe, the Central Banks would on the other hand recover an instrument of national monetary policy through open market operations between the unit of account and their own national currencies.

It is also likely that, once they have become accustomed to

it, banks and firms would come to favour the new asset: its flexibility, and the possibility of converting it into European currencies without charge would give it undeniable advantages which would themselves increase as the market expanded. Based in Europe, it would avoid the uncertainty that hangs over the future of the dollar and for Europeans it would become preferable to the Euro-dollar, although offshore dollars would no doubt continue to be used on the international market outside Europe. At the same time, it would be easy to erect certain barriers between the European unit-of-account market and the Euro-dollar market, if only by charging for conversion or forward cover.

Europe's double interest in interdependence and autonomy, in other words, requires both a reform of the international payments system through the development of a new reserve unit to replace the dollar, and the promotion of a European capital market to replace part of the Euro-dollar market. As has been pointed out already, the former goal can be prepared but not yet achieved, so long as United States balance-of-payments deficit has not yet been more or less eliminated. The second goal too cannot be reached overnight. It will take time to build confidence in the new asset and establish the habit of using it. It will be argued below, however, that the importance of this second goal would be greater rather than less if no co-operative solution on a world level were to be found. The fact that a European capital market cannot be achieved overnight, therefore, makes the first steps towards it even more urgent.

A purely European solution

We have seen what European solution might be possible for private transactions if an international solution were reached at Central Bank level. Let us now consider the less promising alternative. If the dollar problem were to remain unsolved, European Governments would have to seek an intra-European solution which would enable them to leave the dollar zone without seriously disrupting world trade. Once again, the solution would have to be sought through joint machinery set up among the Central Banks, operating not only on the private market but also at official level, managing reserves and exchange-rates.

This would imply the achievement of monetary union, and would effect in particular its external aspects. The discussion that follows will examine the options open to Europe on the supposition that monetary union is in process of being achieved, but will leave aside internal problems, whether monetary, economic, fiscal or regional, since to go further would lead us away from our present subject. Nor is this as unrealistic as it may at first sight appear: unity, like an alliance, is usually a response to an external danger; and it may well be that the dollar problem, whatever difficulties it causes, will also provide the main pressure for rapidly achieving monetary union in Europe.

In this case, the joint body referred to earlier would become a true European Fund, entrusted by the Central Banks with the management on their behalf of a large part of their external affairs. At the same time, the unit of account, which from now on we shall call the 'Europa', as in the Federal Trust study cited earlier, would become the currency of this Fund and would be held by the Central Banks in exchange for dollars transferred to the Fund. In what follows, we shall speak of a European Fund and its intervention currency. But that is simply to facilitate the discussion: as will be seen, the real problem lies in establishing a common policy. This would no doubt be assisted by the institutional developments envisaged here, but these are in no way indispensable, and the problem would remain basically the same if such institutions were only established later.

Let us, however, suppose that they exist. The European Fund would centralise intervention on foreign-exchange markets. The crucial economic-policy problem would then lie in the instructions to be given to the Fund by Central Banks and governments: on what principles should it operate? (Alternatively, what common policy should the Central Banks agree to apply individually?) Assuming, as we do here, that no international solution has been achieved, because the problem of the dollar or the American deficit has not been solved, the Community must to some extent protect itself. If, in these circumstances, the Community is free to decide on its exchange-rate policy, how should it act to safeguard its own interests while taking due account of the international context which it cannot ignore?

We propose to examine two hypotheses, with a variant for the second: a floating exchange rate, and a double exchange-rate system. Each corresponds to a different aim in economic policy. In order to simplify the problem, we shall assume that the less developed countries use all the foreign currency that they receive, so that their balance of payments is in equilibrium and the Community's surplus is equivalent to the American deficit minus the global surplus of Japan.

On the first hypothesis, the Community would seek global equilibrium in its balance of payments and would therefore refuse to accumulate any more dollars. In this case, the European Fund would be instructed to organise an exchange market in which the dollar would float freely against the Europa. That is, the interventions of the Fund would be too limited to cause large net purchases of dollars.

On the second hypothesis the Community would agree to have a surplus in its commercial transactions, or on current account, or in its basic balance, but would wish to protect itself either against an influx of short-term dollars, or against any movement of capital, or against any transfers not arising from a payment for goods and services. In this case, the European Fund would have to organise a double exchange-rate system. On the commercial market (which might possibly handle certain other operations agreed in advance) it would intervene to maintain a fixed parity; the financial market would be left to fluctuate freely.

The first hypothesis, that of a joint float, would offer complete protection against an unwanted accumulation of dollars, and at the same time great freedom of manoeuvre. At the present time, for instance, one might envisage that the Fund would be instructed not to buy dollars, but to sell them freely, although without letting the Europa depreciate should floating capital decide to return to the United States. The price of such an arrangement, however, would be the risk of large exchange-rate fluctuations. Thus, if there were speculation against the dollar, i.e. if a majority of holders of funds were convinced that it was likely to depreciate, they would sell enough to bring about precisely the degree of depreciation that the majority of them was counting on. Such floating would work well enough if one were able to rely on the classical hypothesis which presupposes a large number of decisions being taken independently. But this is not the case: dealers' reactions are cumulative rather than independent. Hopes and fears spread rapidly, often irrespective of the real economic facts. One can hardly use the market's speculative estimate of the value of any currency at a given moment as an indication of the exchange rate which will assure the market's long-term equilibrium. A typical example is that of the Belgian franc, against which there was strong speculative pressure in 1969. The expected devaluation did not occur. The trend was reversed, and in the following year, when the franc was floated, it appreciated and in December 1971 was revalued. Who could claim that these changes in the market's estimate of the position between 1969 and 1971 reflect a fundamental alteration in Belgium's competitive position?

But the danger of speculation should not be exaggerated. The mere existence of floating exchange-rates may discourage certain short-term capital movements. The uncertainty inherent in this system makes forward cover dearer, which in turn has two results – one desirable, the other not.

As far as capital is concerned, uncertainty means that a difference between the interest-rate on dollars and that on Europas would not lead so readily to the shifting of funds: in this respect, the European zone would enjoy greater autonomy in its monetary policy.

But the self-same uncertainty is a disadvantage from the point of view of trade. This explains the unpopularity of floating exchange rates in 1971. The price to be paid for a 'second-best' solution of this type would be the division of of the world into three or four monetary areas, with exchange risks involved in dealings between them. The disadvantages of this should not however be overstressed. The majority of European economic transactions would take place within the European monetary area (it should be recalled that the United States accounts for less than 10 per cent of the trade of the Nine, and that even the dollar area which might in such circumstances emerge would still account for less than 20 per cent). A system of large floating areas, unlike one in which every currency is floating, would supply a big enough volume of trade to make it possible to organise an effective forward market. In this case, the disadvantages of floating exchange rates would be limited.

If the overall equilibrium of the balance of payments were achieved in this way, the question would then be on which items of the balance of payments adjustment would take place. The United States has usually had a surplus on current account and a large deficit on long-term capital movements (*vis-à-vis* the Common Market the basic balance has usually been in surplus, but it is not this bilateral relationship that counts here). If there were no speculative movements, would adjustments occur chiefly in the field of goods and services, of transfers, or of capital? Most Europeans would no doubt prefer this last item to be the most sensitive to exchange-rate variations, so that overall equilibrium could be achieved without large parity changes and therefore without great alterations in the competitive position on export markets. But there is no guarantee that this would be the case. The devaluation of the dollar is too recent for its impact to be judged, especially since its effects are at present more than offset by the recovery of the American economy. Even so, the system of floating exchange rates does carry with it the risk that commercial interests, and therefore employment, may be sacrificed to the free movement of capital.

The third problem is one which might arise within the Community itself. The supply and demand of Europas against dollars would above all be determined by British and German transactions. A surplus on the part of these two countries would lead to the appreciation of the Europa, and would thus make it more difficult for other European countries, which might be in deficit, to sell on the export market. This is not the place to discuss in detail a problem which concerns the internal aspects of monetary union; but, as was argued earlier, a floating Europa might be established without permanently locking exchange rates between it and all Europe's national currencies, whose parities might still need to change at intervals for a long time to come. A joint float with fixed internal parities would require greater solidarity or better harmonisation of policies: the maintenance of fixed parities presupposes an inflation rate comparable to that of the world and which is beyond Europe's control; a joint float presupposes inflation rates adjusted among the member states, and depending therefore, at least partially, on the policies decided within the group. Difficulties are always likely to be greater when the invisible hand is replaced by one's neighbour's visible action.

Finally one further point whose economic importance is relatively small but which might be a political obstacle: who floats against whom? Since only relative prices matter, the question has little point: an appreciation of the Europa or a depreciation of the dollar both have the same effect on the competitive positions of the two areas *vis-à-vis* each other. But the question may still be important in a world which is still pursuing the chimera of some absolute measure of value. For some Europeans at least, a joint float would be more acceptable if it were the dollar which floated against SDRs or against gold (at the official price), while the parity of the Europa remained fixed.

If the first hypothesis – a joint float – is more liberal or 'German', the second – a double exchange rate – is more mercantilist or 'French'. It would admit the accumulation of dollars, arising from a surplus on current transactions (in other words Europeans would agree to finance the American deficit on such transactions); but it would not allow capital inflows to affect the exchange rate and thus make exports more difficult.

If one defines Europe's objectives in these 'mercantilist' terms, this solution is clearly better than the first – at least so long as present parities do not lead to excessive disequilibrium in the current balance. At the same time, a free money market, in which the Fund did not intervene, would lead to a floating exchange rate under which capital movements would be automatically in balance. But this system would raise two kinds of problem – the first, administrative or technical; the second, the choice of economic policy objectives.

Under the European solution, transfers would be freely possible within the area. A double exchange-rate system therefore would require agreement on which operations came under which heading and on how the resultant regulations were interpreted; countries associated with the area would no doubt also have to be party to the agreement. Equally, the exchange controls involved would have to be applied with the same degree of rigour by all national authorities.

This is comparable to the need for a common external tariff in a customs union: without it, trade would seek out the point where the tariff was lowest. In the case of goods, transport costs would discourage such trade diversion. In the monetary field, financial transfers involve virtually no transport costs, so the need for uniform regulations is all the greater. If these conditions are not fulfilled, the double exchange-rate system loses the greater part of its effectiveness, and becomes no more than a small additional widening of the bands.

The economic policy problem will be that of defining those types of transaction to be allowed on the commercial market where a fixed parity is maintained. In general terms, the problem can be defined as follows: what are the operations which are so important that a surplus on them is acceptable, i.e. those which justify the accumulation of dollars? And what implications do these options have for Europe's position *vis-à-vis* the Third World, including those countries which choose to link their currencies to the European area and those which prefer the dollar area?

The two systems sketched here, a floating exchange rate and a dual exchange market, have been singled out as examples because they are the subject of official discussion and even official proposals. Many other systems and combinations of systems are possible; among these an agreement, tacit or institutionalised, to undertake more frequent, and small, parity changes seems most likely at this stage. But all Community solutions raise the basic problems of a common policy *vis-à-vis* the dollar, and the structure of the European Community's balance of payments.

Conclusions

First: among the problems at present facing the Community, that of a joint approach to the United States in view of an international solution is no doubt the easiest to solve. It may not, however, be the most important. It has been pointed out above that a solution that would enable the United States to restore dollar convertibility would presuppose approximate equilibrium in the American balance of payments. This would mean an improvement of some 10,000 million dollars over 1972. Is this really likely?

The international monetary scene is in such a state of flux that Central Banks are pleased when a whole week goes by without the need to buy dollars. But this, of course, means very little. Thus, if a minimum degree of confidence in the dollar were to be re-established today, the private market could easily reconstitute its assets and finance a large United States deficit without the Central Banks having to intervene. This was the situation in 1968 and 1969, and it laid the foundations of the 1971 crisis. But so long as the United States' overall deficit continues, the volatility of increased private dollar holdings remains a threat for the future. And if the private markets were to accumulate, say 20,000 million dollars, the next crisis would certainly be delayed, but even more serious than the last.

Failing a large-scale recovery on the American side, Europeans ought rather to devote their efforts to preparing alternatives to an international solution.

Secondly, agreement among Europeans on these alternatives is very difficult to reach today. It was pointed out earlier that this would in fact imply a decisive move towards monetary union. From the point of view which concerns us here, this means agreeing on a balance-of-payments policy and establishing joint market machinery or controls to put it into practice. The foregoing discussion has been concerned with exchange-rate policy; but the same conclusion would apply whatever the instruments chosen as the means of pursuing a common policy.

Without such a policy, each European country would resort to its own means of control or 'deterrence' against capital movements. The national barriers which they would thus seek to raise against the dollar would in fact be much more effective in isolating them from each other. If a European capital market is not established, the dollar will remain Europe's common currency, the only one in which important private transactions take place and the only one, therefore, from which no European country can effectively insulate itself.

If Europeans wish to escape from continued dependence on the dollar, they must first endeavour to lay the foundations of monetary union among themselves. External pressure is at present their strongest incentive to make rapid progress towards monetary union, even if, in economic integration, this entails certain risks.

Thirdly, it was suggested earlier that the establishment of institutions – a European Fund, and a unit of account which could develop into a true currency – would facilitate the carrying out of a European policy, but that it would not be indispensable to the solution of international problems. To solve the internal problems of the monetary union, however, institutions are essential. Here, it would be necessary to have means of transfer and settlement between member countries which did not involve their Central Banks, and which therefore did not affect their exchange reserves or their lines of credit. A commercial bank whose clients are in deficit *vis-à-vis* those of another elsewhere in the Common Market must be in a position to make settlements directly by transferring assets which are uniformly negotiable or liquid throughout the Community. There must, therefore, be a large supply of assets (Treasury Bonds, bills of exchange, loans) denominated in units of account; and a market in them must be developed.

Only in these circumstances will settlements within the Community acquire the automatic character which such settlements at present have within a country, i.e. a single monetary area. So long as this condition is not fulfilled, the problem of making over exchange reserves or mutual credits will continue to weigh on the future of the union. And we have seen that as long as an international agreement is not achieved, existing exchange reserves, although theoretically abundant, will remain inadequate and difficult to deploy. This fact has been underlined by the agreement on the use of European currencies by the Central Banks: overall settlement is to take place at the end of every month, and the question of which currencies to use for settlement has been the subject of acrimonious debate.

In the external field, we have used the concept of the Europa mainly to facilitate the discussion. But for the Community's internal affairs, the Europa would be an instrument of crucial importance.

The foregoing discussion suggests that the Community has some very weighty decisions to take in the monetary field. In fact, the Community is seeking its own monetary identity at a time when the international system is undergoing a fundamental crisis which endangers its very existence. This means that the Community must take decisions and agree on common policies at a moment when it is perhaps not yet ready to do so.

But the problems are very serious. Robert Triffin recently expressed the fear that the breakdown of the international system could lead us back to a situation similar to that of the 1930s, when the escalation of mutual protectionism brought about and prolonged the great depression. As the world's largest trader, the Community has an immense responsibility and a vital interest in preventing such an outcome. Internationally, its role is already essential as the leading partner in negotiations with the United States. But if Europeans are to have a guarantee of a stable future, it is no less important for them to organise their internal monetary union, which depends on them alone.

4 European Agriculture in the World Economy

Adrien Zeller

Introduction

The common agricultural policy is without doubt the most important achievement of the European Economic Community. It directly affects the income and the future of ten million people and determines the development of the whole agricultural and food sector of the economy. In the short term, it is crucial to the prosperity of the Community's agricultural areas. It has greatly influenced the standard of living of consumers, and especially the poorer sections of society. What is more, it has led to a reshaping of the Community's economic links with the rest of the world in this particular field.

This reshaping occurred when the common marketing organisations were established for various products between 1962 and 1970. These marketing organisations, it will be remembered, determine both the conditions of external trade and the production and marketing policies for the various products.

When these organisations were set up, and the essential decisions were taken, comparably little attention was given to the problem of integrating Community agriculture in the world economy. There were three main reasons for this. First, it was very difficult to integrate six national agricultural policies which were profoundly different, relatively rigid, and for a large part ill-prepared for competition. Secondly, Europeans were concerned not to lose the influential support of farmers and farming organisations in the process of integration European agriculture. Thirdly, their initial priority was to ensure that the common agricultural policy furthered European integration. The fact that world markets for agricultural produce have long been in a state of new anarchy with unstable and artificial prices has obviously not made it any easier to integrate the Community's agriculture in the world economy.

At the same time, it was the way in which the machinery established for the common agricultural policy came to be used in the course of the years determined the volume, the nature and development of the Community's agricultural trade with the rest of the world.

Community efforts to undertake a reform of its agriculture are recent. Until now, the common agricultural policy has chiefly been limited to the establishment and organisation of a common market in agriculture, which, among other things, gives farmers the basic security they need to sell their produce and maintain their incomes. In terms of the interpenetration of markets, and of real Community solidarity, in dealing with the many economic, social, and indeed human problems of a vital sector of economic life, the European achievement is considerable. It is this which makes it so important for the Community to undertake the necessary efforts to consolidate the system: to make it viable in the long run by introducing the necessary changes and eliminating the remaining contradictions.

For it has to be admitted that the operation of the present system, including above all the price and support policies, has not so far brought about a satisfactory solution of the Community's internal problems. For some of them, indeed, it has not even led to the beginning of a solution. The earnings and material conditions of large parts of the farming population of the original Six have lagged behind those of the rest of the population. Within the farming sector itself, sizeable regional differences are emerging. The average productivity of a farmer in the Six remained far behind that of his counterparts in the new member states, Denmark and the United Kingdom, as well as in many countries such as Australia, Canada and the United States. Agricultural markets are constantly exposed to the danger of large and costly imbalances. Most agricultural and food products remain more expensive than those in other countries, despite the Community's broadly favourable agronomic potential. Nor can it be claimed that the Community's agriculture is fulfilling in a satisfactory way the new non-market function that post-industrial societies expect from

agriculture, such as the maintenance of a minimum population
in certain areas with no economic alternatives, or the conservation of nature and the maintenance of natural landscape
in mountainous or other unspoiled regions. In fact, the areas
in which such problems arise are at present neglected, and
the farming population and farming activities are in full
retreat.

Meanwhile, this same policy, although it has not prevented
an overall increase of agricultural trade with the rest of the
world, has involved the Community in a number of trading
conflicts with both developed and less developed countries. In
some cases, the gradual establishment of the common agricultural policy has caused considerable deflection of trade, e.g.
with Denmark, or threatens to do so with other countries now
that the Community is enlarged. At the same time, for reasons
often entirely valid in a short-term perspective, the Community has repeatedly refused to include agriculture in
bilateral or multilateral international negotiations, thus ignoring the often large and highly competitive export possibilities
open to other areas of the world; and it has established expensive systems subsidising the export of its own surpluses on
world markets. On the other hand the very positive proposal
made by the Community in the course of the Kennedy Round,
to conclude an international agreement to consolidate the
levels of support for agricultural products, was not taken
up.

Given the historical, political, and institutional circumstances of the creation of the agricultural policy, the Community may have had little choice but to proceed as it did.
But, in the light of the foregoing analysis, the question whether
this policy as it is applied today truly reflects the economic and social interests of the farming population at large, can
no longer be ignored. There is also the question whether
either its internal or its external aspects meet the real interests
of the Community as a whole.

An answer to the second question must take into account
that most countries of the world intervene substantially in the
agricultural sector of their economies. Research carried out
by the EEC Commission showed that market support schemes
and protection accounted for 50 per cent of agricultural

incomes in the Community, and for 45 per cent in the United States.

The extent and modalities of such intervention depend on internal priorities and, in the final analysis, on the political context, where purely economic and social considerations can be secondary or even neglected altogether. Indeed, it can easily be shown that each particular decision largely depends on the power configuration among social groups and among the farmers themselves.

But measures of intervention decided under such conditions tend to have important short- and long-term consequences for international markets and for the commercial interests of others. There have been repeated calls for international co-ordination, harmonisation, and regulation of domestic intervention in agriculture to deal with this situation. There are good reasons for the absence of such co-ordination at present: the establishment of international order will require a radical change of attitude among public policy makers – not least those of the Community.

A precondition for such a change of attitude, or perhaps the first manifestation of such a change, would be for those who decide on internal measures of intervention to try to forecast the short- and long-term international consequences, whether commercial, economic, or social, of decisions often made with a rather short-time horizon. Internally, a greater stress on the general interest, as opposed to that of specific groups of producers, would complement and facilitate international agreement.

The purpose of this paper is precisely that: to undertake a critical analysis of the common agricultural policy both as regards its international consequences and seen against the requirements of the general interest of the Community itself, in the conviction that the Community cannot, in a world which is growing more and more interdependent in economic and social affairs, effectively safeguard its own true interests without taking into account in its agricultural policy, as in all other fields, the agricultural interests, problems and potentialities of its partners.

The mere fact that the direct and indirect economic and social costs of the present common agricultural policy are not an impossible burden for the Community is no reason for the maintenance of the *status quo*. From the point of view of the Community's internal development and the pursuit of European integration, it is surely vital that the common agricultural policy – which is the only true common policy the Community so far has – should achieve its aims for everyone's benefit and thus be a practical demonstration of the potential, the effectiveness, and hence the advantages of the Community.

From the point of view of the Community's relations with the rest of the world, the need for change in the sense of a more responsible use of the existing price and market instruments is no less evident. Since some of the Community's trading partners have a great deal to gain from liberalising agricultural trade, the Community might be able to secure greater openings on their markets by adopting a new attitude in the agricultural field. What is more, many less developed countries depend very heavily on their exports of agricultural products, and the Community's agricultural policy, often protectionist at home and sometimes, to state it bluntly, aggressive abroad, could have an unfortunate or even disastrous effect on those less developed countries that are most dependent upon exports. Finally, by exporting at quasi-dumping prices the results of its own insufficient ability to limit production and solve its agricultural problems, the Community risks becoming an important source of political and commercial tension. It increases the dangers of an uncontrolled breakdown of the international trading system, and it threatens to unleash chain reaction which would be to everyone's disadvantage.

Protectionist escalation

There can be no doubt about the protectionist nature of the Community's agricultural policy, even if in today's world it is not alone to merit this adjective. Together with special cases like Norway, Switzerland and Finland (and perhaps Japan), the Community is among the countries with the highest guaranteed farm prices in the Western World – although it does not have either the highest wage and other costs nor the highest average earnings in this field. Despite the difficulty of making precise statistical comparisons, there can be no doubt of the gap between the Community's agricultural prices and the internal prices of the most important agricultural producers in the developed or the less developed world: although this gap varies according to the product, prices in countries outside the Community are often thirty or forty per cent below European prices for the key products.

It is generally agreed that these high European prices derive from three main causes.

First, the inadequate and uneven structure of European agriculture and in particular the excess of manpower in relation to land under cultivation. This factor is responsible for the high prices for large-scale crops, and in particular for grains. A long-term encouragement can be drawn from the fact that during the period between 1967 and 1971, when the common agricultural policy was first fully enforced, about five per cent or more of the farm population left the land every year. In other words, the Community's high-price policy has not prevented structural change and the gradual shift of surplus manpower, even if the latter has not been rapid enough to prevent surplus production, market disruption and further investment in marginal farms.

The second reason for Europe's high prices has been the continuation – and in some cases the establishment – of subsidies for climatically marginal production. For example, even with the help of advanced technology and modern organisation, the production of beet sugar would still be dearer than tropical cane sugar production, as is shown by the results obtained in Australia, Brazil, Argentina and the Caribbean. The comparative advantage enjoyed by tropical sugar producers becomes particularly clear if opportunity costs are borne in mind. In the tropics, there are few if any alternative employment possibilities for either the land or the men who work it, and opportunity costs are therefore very low. The alternatives open to sugar beet producers, however, most of whom are located in the richest parts of Europe, are by contrast very varied, and their opportunity costs are correspondingly high.

The third reason is linked to the first: that is, the scarcity of usable land has led European agriculture in many areas to pursue intensive cultivation and production, which uses a comparatively large labour force and results in a high output per acre. Today, these crops (low-grade wine production, fruit crops, tobacco, vegetables, etc.) are scarcely any longer competitive with those of countries, chiefly in the Mediterranean, which have not yet achieved industrialisation, and which have abundant manpower and at least equivalent climatic and natural conditions.

What is more, although abolishing all quotas the Community's level of agricultural support and protection seems significantly higher than that of its member states before the establishment of the common agricultural policy. The common prices were established at levels higher than the weighted average of the previous national prices. The common system of market protection and support is more automatic than in most previous national systems; and the Community, finally, has abolished the quite effective production controls that were in force in some of the member states (France, the Netherlands).

True, the global protectionist effect of the common agricultural policy, as reflected in the trade figures, seems not to have been enormous: the Community's trade balance in products subject to the common agricultural policy went from a deficit of 2500 million dollars in 1963 to a deficit of 2700 million dollars in 1970, compared with Community production valued at 35,000 million dollars. In this sense, the common agricultural policy has so far been a rather incoherent synthesis of previous long-standing protectionist policies. But the global figures are somewhat misleading. The common agricultural policy did not have its full force until 1967, and in some cases, such as wine and tobacco, until 1970. Moreover, there is always a time-lag between economic policy decisions in agriculture and their practical effect. For these reasons, the full effect of the common agricultural policy may not yet be apparent. Furthermore, the slight increase in the Community's agricultural trade deficit in reality marks a large reduction in the part played by imports in Community food consumption, and a notable increase in its degree of agricultural self-sufficiency. It is significant that this increase has taken place at a time of growing disparity between Community price levels and those prevailing in the other agricultural regions of the world – which suggest that the Community's competitive posi-

tion has worsened. This would seem to justify a structural
shift in the European economy and a much greater reliance on
food imports.

There is no reason to believe that this situation is merely
temporary and can therefore be ignored. For most large-scale
crop production, only part of the Community's acreage can
hope to rival the mechanised farming of the American, Canadian, Australian, or Argentinian prairies. Similarly, for intensive production with a high labour input (grapes, olives,
tobacco, horticulture, etc.) the disparity between labour costs
in the developed and less developed countries can only
increase in the medium term, as no doubt will the scarcity of
temporary manpower in the Community. The less developed
countries should therefore enjoy an increasingly more favourable competitive position in these fields. Finally, for those
European products that compete directly with tropical products (oilseeds, rice, sugar, cassava flour), the only acceptable
working hypothesis is the economic development of the tropical producing countries; and this – at least in the first instance
– must mean an increase in their exports of the products concerned, the more so since they enjoy more favourable natural
conditions and lower labour costs.

All these arguments are made more cogent by the constant
reduction in transport costs and the growing improvement of
storage and conservation techniques, which make long-
distance imports very much easier.

Finally, the Community seems to have improved its competitive position in recent years only in a limited number of
sectors, notably in beef and dairy production, and in pigmeat,
poultry and eggs. These are products requiring high-grade
technology, sizeable capital inputs, and a temperate climate –
all three factors in which Europe seems likely to enjoy permanent advantage. And the prospect for a long-term world
shortage in these animal proteins suggests the direction which
future Community production might profitably take.

Expensive contradictions

Nor are the disadvantages of the present shape of the Community's common agricultural policy limited to its generally

high protection. As often pointed out by the Commission, this policy is also characterised by several inconsistencies. So far the Council of Ministers has been unwilling to act.

At one and the same time the EEC has produced costly surpluses of wheat, milk, sugar, and fruit, and has tended to neglect those products which the world is likely to need in growing quantities during the coming years, and in particular, beef. What is more, the fact that the Community accords very different levels of price and protection to competing products which are either partly or wholly interchangeable has introduced considerable and costly distortions in its own production and consumption pattern as well as into world trade. Finally, one can note that the Community has tended to pay the highest prices, and to give the highest level of protection, not to those products that emanate chiefly from its poorest regions and its poorest farmers, but to products which mainly come from regions that are already prosperous and better able to face international competition.

The core of the problem is the relationship between prices fixed for beef on the one hand and crops on the other (mainly grains, but also sugar beet and colza). The high prices fixed for the latter have led to an artificial increase in Community production which could, at least partially, be replaced more cheaply by imports. At the same time, they have penalised cattle-raising at a time of growing world shortage and rising prices. In regional terms, this has meant that a farmer in the Limousin, a poor agricultural region relying chiefly on cattle, has average earnings only a quarter of those of his counterpart in the Paris region, from which he is obliged to buy the feed grains he needs at artificially high prices. This for producing beef for which there is a world shortage and which, meanwhile, the Community has to import at a high price. And when a cattle farmer and a grain producer compete to buy or lease farmland, the grain producer can easily supplant the cattle-breeder because of the high prices guaranteed by the Community.

By the same token, if the quality of his land makes possible a yield of thirty quintals of grain (which in European conditions is very moderate), the cattle farmer has every interest in ploughing up his grassland to grow wheat, which will add to the Community's surplus and be dumped on the world market with a subsidy from the Community's agricultural fund. All this has of course been pointed out by many analysts.

Apart from encouraging overproduction within the Community, the high price of feed grains has the further effect of restricting demand from the animal transformation industry, thus causing a further trading loss for competitive producers of feed grains in and outside the Community.

The negative influence of this policy on world trade and specialisation are as clear as its effects on consumer, on the taxpayer and the many poor farming regions within the Community itself.

But there are also more unexpected effects. The high level of protection accorded to the Community's grain market greatly encourages the sale of substitute feeds, such as oil-cakes, including soya-based feeds from the United States which, unlike grains, enter the Common Market without restriction – a further and major contradiction in the Community system. Partly, at least, United States losses as a result of the Community's grain policy have been balanced by large and rapidly growing exports of soya beans, but Canada and other large grain exporters do not enjoy such possibilities and make a net loss. Meanwhile, the sale of large quantities of low-priced soya cake has flooded world markets with large quantities of its by-product, soya oil, which threatens the vegetable-oil exports of the less developed countries. This is one of the main reasons for the recent serious crisis in the market for groundnut oil, which is the chief export product of a country like Senegal.

Disruption of world agricultural markets

The Community is not by any means the only 'power' which intervenes on the agricultural market and thus on world markets, and which wholly or partly shelters from the laws of free trade. Indeed, it is not isolated or combined agricultural producers who compete on world markets, but national or international agricultural policies. As the result, the international division of labour scarcely applies. In many cases, a country becomes an exporter of a given product not for any

objective reason, but because its producers have been able
to extract from the public authorities a particularly favourable
guarantee and/or a particularly effective or automatic system
of export aids.

Thus, in 1969, Canadian wheat went to waste while Community wheat grown at twice the cost was able to conquer
the markets of the Far East with generous aid from the
Community's agricultural fund, which covered the price
difference and the transport costs.

As regards sugar beet and sugar production, the price
support given by the Community has been such that the Six
have produced fifteen to twenty per cent more than they need
– a surplus of 1 to 1.4 million metric tons – three or four times
the surplus that existed before the Common Market system
was set up. These surpluses have, until the recent relative
shortage, had to be turned into animal fodder or, more
frequently, sold on the world market thanks to substantial
public subsidies.

By using its economic power, rather than self-restraint by
taking part in the International Sugar Agreement, the Europe
of the Six has long contributed to the depression of sugar
prices on the free market and has played a large part in
discouraging sugar investments in the less developed countries.
The poor export prospects for these countries, together with
the partial failure of Cuban sugar crops, and the poor harvest
in the USSR, explain the relative shortage which occurred in
1971. But this cyclical and artificial shortage, which today
makes it easy for the Community to dispose of its surpluses,
is no justification for the policy which has helped to provoke
it. All that has happened is that the Community system has
enabled Community sugar producers to evade the laws of
competition in a period of glut by distorting the world market,
and then to occupy the ground left free by those whom the
glut has helped to ruin.

If it be agreed that the capacity of any country to subsidise
its farm exports is inversely proportional to the part played
by agriculture in that economy, it can be seen that the brunt
is borne by those countries which are mainly agricultural
and/or less developed. Far from being able to subsidise exports, many of these countries are even obliged to tax their

exports in order to increase the revenue of the state (as, for for example, is the case with Senegalese groundnuts, with sugar, and with beef and cereals in many Latin American countries). The inevitable depression of world prices is therefore paid for by those producers and countries which derive the essential part of their revenue from the world market. In this way, the growth of the market support and price guarantees given in order to help inefficient farmers, as in the case of the common agricultural policy, however justified this may be by their low incomes, generally leads to very great difficulty for others including not only the farmers in the developed countries which are large agricultural exporters, such as Denmark, Canada and Australia, but also for peasants and planters in the less developed world. In this sense, the economic and social and political difficulties are merely exported. This will continue as long as poor and small Community farmers are helped not by specific schemes but by general price support at levels above all economic reality.

As regards these problems what is lacking is not merely international negotiation and international agreements – the absence of which is sometimes a mere excuse – but forward thinking by the Community about the importance and the implications involved in choosing a given support system, adopting specific levels of intervention and protection or taking particular attitudes in international talks.

Thus, when the Community, at the time of the 1968 negotiations on the International Sugar Agreement, demanded an export quota of 1.2 million metric tons – four times more than its previous average exports – what democratic political institution in Europe drew up a balance-sheet of the real long-term costs and advantages which satisfaction of such a demand would entail for the Community?

Again, in 1970, the Community decided to establish a system of 'deficiency payments' to support its internal tobacco production. This meant annual subsidies of about $2000 per hectare, which are bound to increase in the future owing to the growing disparity between labour costs in the Community and in the principal tobacco-exporting countries, most of which are less developed countries. By adopting such a system, the Community has chosen to help its poorer producers of tobacco through an uncontrolled policy of support leading to a relative or absolute increase of tobacco production. Does this choice really reflect its true interest? It seems unlikely, because the economic and social situation of the Community's tobacco producers remains basically unsatisfactory despite the scale of the aid they are receiving; and because it fails to give export possibilities to those tobacco producing countries that are competitive. The Community is helping to deny them a chance to develop their economies and to take their place in the world trading system.

It would be easy to multiply such examples. One such is the Community's policy for rice, which artificially makes it, of all things, a net exporter. Another is its wine policy, which is at present promoting a costly expansion of European vineyards to produce high-priced and often low-grade wine, while virtually closing off imports from Mediterranean countries. The countries of North Africa and in particular Algeria are therefore being forced to uproot vines which, well suited to their soil and climate, are competitive as well as popular. This in turn is leading to widespread unemployment among Algerian farm-workers, at a time when the Community is finding it more difficult to recruit the large quantity of seasonal manpower which the grape-harvest requires. It is true that the burden which such policies impose on Europe, and the relative welfare loss resulting from the maintenance of marginal agricultural activities and the practice of dumping on world markets, are not in themselves unbearable. They may even have some advantages in the very short run. But it is clear that this does nothing to minimise the human cost of the changes which the Community will sooner or later have to bring about, to help the development of the poorer countries, or to reduce the tensions in the world trading system.

For all these reasons it is necessary to examine the ways in which the common agricultural policy can be reformed in order to meet the real interests of the Community – that is, gradually, to integrate Community agriculture in the world context.

Reforming the common agricultural policy

Partly at least, the 'inward-looking' nature and the contradictions of the common agricultural policy can be explained by the necessity and difficulty of achieving, in a relatively short time, compromises acceptable to the agricultural interests and the governments of six countries. Similarly, the absence on the Community level of any machinery for social policy, regional policy, industrial policy, and until recently structural reform in agriculture, quite naturally led the Community to try to solve most of its acute problems with whatever means lay to hand: in other words, by price support and a managed market.

The fact that there are no rules for trade in agricultural goods which are universally respected by the international community also contributed to this situation.

In these respects, both the Community context and the international context have changed.

The enlargement of the Community gives a new dimension to the problem of international trade in agriculture. Three countries enjoying low farm prices, and in some sectors imposing limits on production, will be included in a high-price agriculture economy with large, if not limitless, public guarantees. Unless there is a major change in the orientation of the common agricultural policy the enlargement of the Community will naturally lead to substantial rises in the weighted average of the agricultural prices prevailing within the Nine and a substantial increase in their weighted average protection. The logical result would be an increase in output while at the same time holding demand down. This in turn would lead to both a relative and absolute decline in the agriculture imports of the Nine. The upshot would be a further retrogression in the international division of agricultural activity, since less efficient producers would take the place of traditional and efficient suppliers.

Three products may serve to illustrate this point:

The considerable increase to be expected in the price of grain in the United Kingdom will lead to an expansion of grain production coinciding with a falling demand for feed-grains. The operation of Community preference will enable the original Six, at least in the early years, to sell their wheat and barley surpluses advantageously in Britain. Since there is thus virtually no cost to the budget, the incentive to change the uneconomic policy which has caused these surpluses to accumulate will be reduced;

Although the Community's definitive sugar policy has not yet been established, and although it has undertaken to 'have as its firm purpose' to safeguard the interests of those developing countries which traditionally supply sugar to the United Kingdom, it is nevertheless expected that increased semi-economic production in Britain and the Six will leave little place for the traditional exports of efficient producers like Australia, while reducing export outlets for the less developed countries of the Commonwealth;

Dairy products from New Zealand (and to a lesser degree from Australia), although produced in very economic conditions, risk being displaced in time by increased production in Denmark, Britain, Ireland, and no doubt, France, all of which are less efficient producers than New Zealand.

These, which are not isolated instances, show very clearly the possible consequences of including the world's biggest agricultural importer within a Community which is effectively isolated from the rest of the world by the operation of the levy system and internal market subsidies.

When one adds together the increase in the cost of food, the increased difficulty for the Community's industrial exports, the welfare loss involved in maintaining manpower and capital in low-productivity agriculture, and the unfortunate effects of the common agricultural policy on income distribution, it is easy to see the disadvantages of continuing to apply the common agricultural policy in the same way as today in the Community of Nine.

The balance sheet becomes even worse when one remembers that the reduction of markets and/or of world agricultural prices affects less developed countries which, unlike the United States, are generally unable to reconvert their farm production towards expanding markets (as in the case of soya), to obtain commercial compensation in other fields, or to give the producers income guarantees in time of crisis.

In fact, the steps to be taken to avoid the damage which the common agricultural policy is inflicting on world trade are fundamentally the same as those needed to prevent economic and social imbalance within the enlarged Community.

There are other reasons, too, for a considered reorientation of the common agricultural policy. They include:

The growing weight and the increased economic and commercial responsibility of the Community, which coincides with rapidly growing pressure by the less developed countries which are seeking to escape from their present plight. This pressure itself is partly based on a better understanding of the economic domination, if not exploitation, which is perhaps unwittingly exerted by the richer countries;

The prospect, over the next few years, of a series of highly important decisions in which the Community will be involved (the revision of the International Sugar Agreement, the revision and possible extension of the Yaoundé Association, and above all, the opening of trade negotiations in GATT in 1973). The success of each of these depends on the Community's being ready to make trade concessions on a number of products subject to the common agricultural policy and of importance to one or other of its trading partners, and on the acceptance by the Contracting Parties of a jointly agreed discipline as regards subsidies to agriculture;

The growing realisation, based on experience, of the impossibility for the present price and market support policy to attain the stated economic and social objectives while at the same time enabling agriculture to fulfil the new social and environmental functions which in certain regions it could assume.

It should now be easier for the Community to meet these challenges than it was during the time when the common agricultural policy was first established. On the one hand, since March 1972, the Community has had a policy and machinery for reforming agriculture by encouraging farmers to leave the land, to modernise their farms, and to improve their skills or re-train for other occupations. The Community has also decided to encourage the creation of new industrial jobs in needy agricultural regions and to provide itself with the means of pursuing a European regional policy. Thus, it should now be easier to make the changes which are inevitable if the Community is to be more open to (or more competitive with) agricultural products from the rest of the world. At the same time, the recent acceptance by all the Community's member states of the basic principles of the common agricultural policy – single price levels, financial solidarity, and Community preferences – enables the Community, and basically those of its members which are most firmly attached to this policy, to envisage with much greater equanimity than before the prospect of using the machinery that has been set up, to pursue a different policy from that which resulted from day-to-day compromises.

Towards a coherent policy

It is not difficult to describe what a 'good' agricultural policy for the Community would be: the efforts made since 1968, and which began to bear fruit with the publication of the Mansholt Plan for reforming the structure of European agriculture, have shown that the real difficulty lies in deciding how to move from the present policy to the policy that is desired. The fact is that past and present policies have led agricultural producers to make investments which themselves are a source of rigidity and an obstacle to change.

On the institutional level, the absence of a real political structure which would make possible a fundamental debate on the broad lines of policy has made it hard to take firm and long-range decisions.

This weakness in the Community's political structure carries with it the further risk that pressure groups may distort the carrying out of any future reform of policy. Those products which have been 'sacrificed' in the interests of international trade have frequently been, not the most inefficient, but those lacking the support of an influential lobby. The political temptation to make the wrong decisions in agricultural policy is all the greater because their results do not become evident for some years, and in some cases for a very long time.

None of the changes proposed here is itself a challenge to the system: it is merely a question of applying the system in a different way.

During the decade to come, price policy alone will not be capable of meeting at one and the same time the income needs of less favoured producers in all the agricultural regions throughout the Community and the elementary needs of consumers and taxpayers, to say nothing of the Community's external interests.

If the Community seriously wishes to meet these various needs, it will have to cease relying so exclusively on the very general weapon of price and market policy as a means of dealing with the specific problems of certain groups, regions and even member states. Instead, it will have to deal with these specific difficulties by specific means – social policy, structural policy, and different kinds of indemnities or subsidies. In political terms, it will have to make some distinction between legitimate income demands of specific groups of farmers and general demands. Farm incomes should no longer be determined solely by agricultural prices and selective subsidies should be given to those who need them. In today's Community no price policy could by itself provide adequate income to farmers who live on small holdings or who are working marginal land in peripheral regions, or be acceptable to farmers whose prices are lowered across the board because their national currency has been revalued (which is the very difficult problem faced by German farmers), and be satisfactory in the medium and long term for the rest of the Community's population.

What level of farm prices should be established in the Community? Two approaches are possible, both of them are pragmatic: either a level fixed with reference to the costs of well-managed and well-organised Community farms, or a level based on the domestic prices of countries which export the products in question. In the short term, both of these two approaches give the same result: essentially they mean that the Community should significantly lower its price for grains, sugar beet and oil seeds. At the present time of rapid inflation, the adjustment required could be largely achieved within five or six years by simply freezing prices for these products.

At the same time, it would be necessary to bring the price of wheat closer to that of feed-grains (barley and maize).

Meanwhile, public intervention on the markets for these products could well be practised less rigorously, in order to achieve more competition between the different regions in the Community.

These reductions in real price would no doubt have to be accompanied by partial, temporary, and tapering financial compensation for specific groups of producers, since the change would lead to short-term income difficulties for small and medium-sized farms and financial difficulties for larger farms which on the basis of the present Community prices have undertaken large-scale investments such as the purchase of land and equipment. Given the possibilities for the farmers to react to a new policy, the financial aid could be inferior to the amount of the direct loss resulting from a price reduction and should not be directly proportional to the area under cultivation: an upper limit should be established for each farm.

These price reductions would immediately lead to considerable economic and financial gains. Surpluses of wheat, barley and sugar would be eliminated, in a few years there would be a large increase in overall demand for grains and an absolute or relative drop in the price of animal products. The shortage of beef would be alleviated. The consequent savings should be used as a matter of priority for a series of measures to consolidate and accelerate agricultural reform. For both a lack of sufficient resources and present high prices themselves limit the effectiveness of the Community's recent steps in this direction.

The economic gains from a re-ordering of prices and market policy could rapidly reach some 2000 million dollars a year. With their help, it would be possible to increase substantially the inducements at present offered, particularly to elderly farmers, to leave the land; this in turn would give greater scope to those who remained. Similarly, these sums would allow greatly to increase the Community's action in regional policy and its provision of industrial job opportunities in the peripheral agricultural regions.

The Community should establish a permanent system of

direct compensation for those agricultural regions that are naturally poor or underpopulated (for example, hilly and mountainous regions) but in which it is necessary to preserve extensive agricultural activity for non-agricultural reasons, such as the conservation of the environment, the maintenance of a minimum population, and the provision of economic activity. At present, these regions are not only less favoured, but actually threatened by the competition of areas better placed.

At the same time, other distortions should be eliminated, in particular those that exist on the market for fats. The price of butter should be brought closer to that of butter substitutes (oil and margarine) either by a tax on these products or by a subsidised reduction in the price of butter itself. In the same way, it would be logical gradually to establish greater equality in the degree of Community protection afforded to grains and grain substitutes (in particular, soya-based feeds). This, which would involve taxation or protection on imports of oilseeds at the world price, would have to be co-ordinated with the proposed reduction in grain prices. It would eliminate one of the major contradictions in the European agricultural policy by plugging a serious gap in the European marketing system.

A different policy should be followed for such things as low-grade wine production, tobacco, and olives, in which Community production is becoming more marginal although its prices are not excessive in view of the low income which even efficient Community producers can obtain with these products.

Here, the main feature of reform should be direct incentives to crop substitution, used systematically to eliminate marginal production and encourage adjustment to the Community's competitive position in the world.

This, of course, implies that the Community should as a matter of course take external considerations into account in its annual decisions on prices and market support. If it does not, it risks maintaining, consolidating, and even bringing into being new marginal production. In this respect, the existing system of automatic levies and export subsidies hardly facilitates matters, since it completely isolates Europe's farm prices and markets from the world agricultural economy. Only deliberate decisions taken over the years by the political institutions of the Community (Commission and Council) can ensure that Community prices bear any relation to long- and medium-term price trends in countries outside the Community.

For some cases, the Community could take the world situation into account, as suggested above, on a purely unilateral basis: it would be to its advantage in any case. However, the conclusion of a multilateral agreement regarding the levels of protection and support to be given to agriculture, and the regulation of trade practices, would make such a policy more effective, less difficult to achieve and politically more acceptable.

This is one reason why the Community should encourage the conclusion of such an agreement, which might include jointly agreed rules regarding export subsidies, co-ordinated management of stocks in both importing and exporting countries, which serve to cushion the price effects of good and bad harvests, an agreement on the maximum levels of support to be given to agricultural products in the various countries. These support levels, which for agriculture are the equivalent of customs duties for industrial products, should be measured according to criteria jointly agreed, in order to achieve a common denominator for the different measures of support practised in the countries concerned.

The commercial concessions made by the Community under such an agreement would be in no sense unilateral. By introducing strict limits to the support it accords to agriculture, particularly in the field of grains – which would be to the advantage of the United States – the Community would have every right to demand access to the American market for dairy products and some other processed foodstuffs, and, perhaps even meat in the future, fields in which the United States are relatively less competitive and in which the Community could have a part to play. Such concessions would also make it easier to gain acceptance for the introduction of the system of protection against oilseeds already suggested.

It would be foolish to ignore the difficulties involved in achieving such international agreement. But, during the coming years, the Community will be engaged in multilateral negotiations within GATT. It is here that such a policy should be pursued.

In the present state of anarchy, the prospects for establishing world order of this sort may seem faint. But for the European Community, as for the other members of the international community, the measures suggested here are nothing more than a means of pursuing their enlightened self-interest and organising world interdependence in a field which is vital to them all.

5 Europe's Energy Imports

Jack Hartshorn

Europe's dependence

In 1972, the Six and the new members of the EEC imported about 60 per cent of their total energy requirements. In money terms, this probably accounted for some 15–20 per cent of their total imports. Demand for energy in the Community is now forecast to grow as fast as, or slightly faster than, the economy in general. Energy imports will at first grow faster; but if the present good fortune in the North Sea continues their rate of increase should slacken after 1975. Even so, by 1980 we shall be lucky if we are not still importing well over half the Community's energy requirements; and by 1985, the proportion may still be 45 per cent. In sheer volume, that may mean importing nearly as much as our whole energy consumption today. It is not easy to guess how much energy will then represent in our total import bill. True, the volume of energy imports might not rise as fast as that of the Community's total imports. But the price of imported energy, which throughout the sixties fell while all other prices rose, is now generally expected at least to keep pace with general inflation; and there is little in the market situation to prevent it rising much faster. In any case, energy will remain one of the largest single elements in EEC foreign trade. And oil, which makes up nearly all the energy moving in world trade, has rightly been called the most political of all commodities. The Community's dependence on imported energy may become a factor in its foreign political relations, as well as in foreign economic policy.

The long-term objectives of Community energy policy have been re-stated many times since their first formulation in 1962. As recently as 1969, the definition was 'to seek secure supplies at prices that are relatively stable and as low as possible'. The EEC Commission, at that time, was at pains to deny that the two objectives of cheapness and security of supply were incompatible. But it did admit that neither can be pursued as an absolute. Nor has its pursuit of either objective ever involved any measures as fundamental and specific as, for example, US oil import controls. Its recommendation of a relatively open market for imported energy in the early sixties was not a positive choice between available alternatives. Rather, it was the acceptance and rationalisation of a decline of indigenous coal production and a shift to imported oil that was already well advanced, and seemingly inexorable. In the sixties, oil happened to be much cheaper than would have been necessary simply to undercut coal. That was a windfall, not a success of policy. By 1972, however, the Commission was persuaded of 'the clear emergence of a sellers' market for the majority of energy products, which has forced upon all concerned a change in their conceptions regarding costs and prices'. And at the Summit conference in October 1972, the energy policy objective was accordingly qualified somewhat: 'guaranteeing certain and lasting supplies under satisfactory economic conditions'.

Facing this sellers' market, the EEC Commission is now recommending some acceleration of nuclear investment; the development of all the gas and oil that can be found in and around the Community; and some increase in the use of coal for power generation. (That increase, however, might be in imported coal rather than in Community production.) Taken together, these measures might reduce dependence on imported oil by five percentage points by 1980, and perhaps twice that by 1985. But the forecasts quoted at the beginning of this chapter take account of all the savings in oil imports that the Commission hopes for from these measures. Our reckoning, moreover, credits the North Sea with a good deal more production by the early eighties than the Commission has yet assumed. Even our figures, admittedly, are somewhat lower than the most hopeful forecasts about the North Sea made by some very optimistic analysts. Nobody can prove that such optimists are wrong. Everybody hopes they are right. But it will take until around 1975 to drill even the most interesting structures in the North Sea. Until then, evidence will remain inadequate. And it would be imprudent to found Community energy policy on euphoria. The Commission cannot afford too much optimism about possible self-sufficiency when it assesses Europe's future need to import energy.

In absolute terms European dependence is enormous. The Community imports more energy than Japan and America put together. Proportionately, Japan is far more dependent: it imports over 80 per cent of all the energy it uses, with less apparent chance than Europe of reducing that percentage. And the United States, recently almost self-sufficient, is now facing with dismay a rapid increase in energy imports during the seventies. Forecasts vary widely; but some suggest that by 1980–5 the US may have to import 50 per cent or more of its oil, and up to 30 per cent of its gas too. That might mean some 25–30 per cent of its total energy consumption.

For Europe and Japan, the forecast that by the eighties America may need to obtain 35 per cent of its oil imports from the Eastern Hemisphere is of particular relevance. For nearly fifteen years America has been deliberately restricting its oil imports. This has limited its demand upon the exporting areas in the Eastern Hemisphere from which the Community and Japan draw all their imports. But even by winter 1972, the rise in American imports was becoming one of the strongest single influences in the growth of demand upon those exporting regions – and on world oil prices.

America's new needs

In the United States this degree of import dependence is seen as an 'energy crisis'. In part, this is a matter of national attitudes. The United States is a super-power whose foreign trade represents no more than about 5 per cent of national income. It is always uneasy about depending on imports for the few industrial materials in which it is not largely self-sufficient. Moreover, the American standard of living involves, and is essentially based upon, an almost profligate use of energy in all forms and for every purpose. Signs of less abundance in energy, even when confined to certain fuels and probably transitory, present a shock and a challenge to confidence in

America's continued, exponential prosperity. And the need to depend on imports for any sizeable proportion of energy supplies – particularly from areas of strategic instability where American political and economic interests may diverge – worries the US more than it does traditional importers like the European countries.

Apart from anything else, America's new dependence represents a failure of deliberate energy policy. In the late 1950s, the introduction of import quotas for oil reflected a basic governmental decision that, with a battery of regulations and fiscal aids for internal energy industries, the United States could – and therefore should – maintain a very high degree of national self-sufficiency. No American government since has ever departed from that basic policy (though some subsidiary policies towards particular fuels, notably gas, may have been inconsistent with it). But with proven reserves of oil and gas declining, oil production passing its peak, and gas production levelling out, the basic policy is clearly not for the present achieving its purpose.

In the seventies, additional American demand on Eastern Hemisphere oil will oblige the Community to concentrate more upon Middle Eastern sources of supply, whereas in the sixties it sought to diversify its oil imports. Then, it had some success: the rapid development of North and later West African oil reduced European dependence on the Middle East from about 80 per cent of oil imports in 1960 to about 47 per cent in 1970. But during the present decade total African production seems liable to grow much more slowly. And it is on precisely this African oil, with its lower sulphur content, that American demand may call first. One result is that the Community has once again to rely on the Middle East for over half its total oil supplies.

In any case the shift to African sources during the sixties, it is fair to say, proved something of a mixed blessing for the EEC. Competition from Libyan producers was the biggest single reason why Europe was able to obtain cheap crude oil during most of the decade, right up to 1969. On the other hand, it was Libyan militancy that set off the Tripoli–Teheran series of negotiations between the Organisation of Petroleum Exporting Countries (OPEC) and the oil companies in 1970 and 1971, as a result of which OPEC government revenues per barrel of oil rose by some 40–50 per cent in one jump, with a schedule of agreed increases to follow up to 1975. So Europe's diversification of supplies, eventually, had a double-edged effect on the price of imports.

In the seventies, moreover, the advent of American and indeed Japanese competition for African oil will make it costlier for Europe to keep down the sulphur content of its atmosphere. Middle East crude, which for the present must be regarded as the basic energy supply of the world, has for the most part a high sulphur content. To meet the sulphur restrictions that the US and Japan already impose, and which are beginning to be set in the Community countries as well, this Middle Eastern oil will need desulphurising. This will involve a genuine increase in oil's technical cost, which the industrialised economies will have to accept during this decade if they want clean air – quite apart from the mainly political increases that producing governments may impose on them, or the higher costs they may impose on themselves in developing new production 'at home' or in other 'politically safe' areas of the world.

Energy costs

Many experts fear – though it is not certain – that the foreign exchange costs of importing energy will rank higher in the Community's balance of payments in 1980–5 than in 1970. The volume of such imports should be growing more slowly than we hope European trade can. But imported energy prices could easily rise so fast as more than to offset the slackening in volume growth.

However, it is not only the balance of payments that will be affected by price trends for imported energy. Energy costs, in the Community's developed economy, account for only 6–8 per cent of total industrial costs, although in some basic industries – steel, cement, glass, etc. – the proportion may be as much as 10–20 per cent. A study made in the mid-sixties for the EEC Commission concluded that in export-oriented industries, energy costs tended to represent a higher proportion of total costs than in industry in general. Energy's contribution to industrial costs appears not to have risen during the sixties. But during that decade, as noted before, the basic price of energy in Europe was falling, while all other costs rose steadily. Now that the prices of all forms of energy could easily rise as much or more than other prices, this may no longer be so.

The changing price structure may also affect the relative competitiveness of European and American industry. Average prices for energy in general are lower in America. But as long as America maintained a high level of expensive oil production at home, the low prices enjoyed by Europe and Japan for imported crude must have contributed something, at least, to their competitive strength in world trade. In the more united world energy market of the future, with the US importing a substantial share of its energy, any such relative advantage may disappear.

Upward pressure on prices

Various factors, of differing importance, are now tending to raise oil prices. The first, proclaimed and obvious, is the increase in the 'host' government revenues of the exporting countries. In 1970–1 these rose by 40–50 per cent. In early 1972, they were raised by about another 9 per cent to offset devaluation of the US dollar; and in early 1973, the same thing happened. Such increases cost Europe and Japan nothing; but they might, unrealistically, have hoped to secure sizeable cuts in their oil prices from the revaluations of their currencies against the dollar. At the beginning of 1973, and also for 1974 and 1975, however, increases representing around 5 per cent on ruling export prices for crude were scheduled at Teheran; and up to 1975 the extra premiums that certain host governments receive for low-sulphur crudes will be rising from about 6 cents a barrel to about 12 cents.

In the case of nearly all Middle Eastern crudes, such increases in host government revenue could be passed on cent for cent to the Western customers. All supply contracts made since have included 'government revenue clauses' stipulating this. In the case of some Mediterranean crudes, the companies involved were not, in general, able to pass on

the full increase in their 'tax-paid costs', and Libyan production was reduced because it has become less profitable.
(Fluctuations in freight rates have played a large part in this.)
Fairly soon, however, the rising market value attached to
low-sulphur energy might make Lybian crude as profitable as
before – unless government action there, in the meantime, has
once more worsened the concession terms. But another crude
supply for which companies were not fully able to recoup
the 1971 increases in government revenues – the Northern Iraq
crude piped to the Eastern Mediterranean – had its output
cut even more severely. That is what led to nationalisation of
the Kirkuk fields in mid-1972.

Before 1975, the OPEC governments and the international
companies are due to negotiate about the future of host
government revenues per barrel (set by formulae for 'posted'
and 'tax reference' prices) from 1976 on. It is generally
expected that both sides may seek to agree on another five-
year schedule. If the formula for escalation of these revenues
per barrel were to continue as for 1973–5, they would rise
another 25–30 per cent beyond the 1975 level, to say 75 per
cent higher than in 1970. But the governments are liable to
press for more than that. In 1970–1, OPEC complained of
rapid inflation in the prices of the goods its member nations
buy from the Western customers with the proceeds from their
oil. In the summer of 1972, the Shah of Iran re-emphasised an
earlier OPEC demand for a 'basket price escalation', which
would raise host government revenues per barrel at least as
fast as the price of imports from the industrialised countries.
And since the Teheran agreement inflation in the West has
been accelerating.

It may seem unrealistic to cite such planned additions to
tax-paid costs and assume they can be passed on to consumers,
without allowing for the state of the world market for oil. But
up to now, it has not proved particularly unrealistic. For
some crudes from some sources, as we have seen, market conditions did not allow the 1971 increases to be passed on fully. Oil
companies could not avoid paying the extra royalty and tax:
so they had either to 'absorb' part of this, and reduce their
profit, or to cut back production. Ultimately, the extent of
recoupment depends on the market. But in the Middle East

production went on rising apace, in spite of the increases passed on in prices. And for a time, the companies' profits on production there (which by 1969 had fallen to about half the levels of a decade before) even increased in 1971. Customers were ready to pay more than the rises in tax-paid costs that the international companies were obliged to cover. Then, by the year's end, world economic growth slowed; the prices of refined oil products fell sharply in Europe and Japan; and the total 'integrated profit' achieved between the well and the service station, for some of the international companies, slumped disastrously. By the end of 1972, again, demand had picked up in the US and Japan and somewhat more slowly in Europe. But these fluctuations in European oil product prices, for example, were occurring above a basic crude oil price in the Gulf that was still 60–70 per cent higher than in mid-1970. Increases in tax-paid costs were preventing the natural ebb and flow of prices in the final markets for oil. But they have raised the effective floor level above which these market fluctuations take place.

The balance of bargaining

Consumers and their governments in Europe, in 1970–3, were perhaps shocked more by the manner in which these price increases were suddenly imposed than by their size. Large as the rises were, crude oil prices amount to only about 15–20 per cent of the final prices European consumers pay for refined products. But importers felt that the international companies had had to capitulate to OPEC demands. They felt there had been a fundamental and irreversible shift in the balance of bargaining power – towards the host governments and away from the omnicompetent international middlemen whom Europe has relied on since the war to supply ever-expanding supplies of relatively cheap energy. Uneasiness about further possible exactions contained a tinge of suspicion. How hard need these companies really oppose increases for which they can so confidently pass on the bill?

This uneasiness about the balance of bargaining understandably persists, even among officials who now profess to be content that the days of artificially cheap energy are over. And a significant change in bargaining power has indeed occurred (though some observers who felt this would mean an immediate displacement of the international major companies from production in the OPEC countries seem to have been rather premature). The host governments assembled in OPEC have achieved a loose, but so far effective, relationship for exerting joint negotiating pressure, in which first one and then another government can spearhead successive claims. The others then offer the support of concerted threats. This was the pattern of the price negotiations in 1970-1 where, moreover, some 'leap-frogging' was achieved. The latent threat of joint action also lay behind the pattern of the participation discussion in 1972, in which the governments of the Arabian Gulf have secured shareholdings of 25 per cent, rising quite fast towards 51 per cent, in their main concessions. Leap-frogging, again, may recur when Iran secures a different kind of settlement which the Shah has been encouraged to believe is a far better deal.

At all events there has been a concentration of power in these governments' bargaining. It may coincide with and fit into some further concentration in the market structure, too. OPEC apart, it always seemed possible that there might be less severe price-cutting in the seventies than in the sixties. No new petroleum exporting area of the relative importance of North Africa in the early and middle sixties seems yet identifiable for the present decade. And even in the few areas of rapidly rising output, production does not seem to be as much in the hands of smaller companies, likely to be obliged to cut prices, as it was in Libya in the early years of oil there. (Nor are concession terms in any significant export area now as encouraging to the price cutter as Libya's were then.) In any case, the probable shift of emphasis back to the Middle East tends to increase the share of crude production handled by the major integrated companies. In that region, these companies usually operate jointly; and 'downstream' they have better-established access to markets through their own integrated channels. Independent non-integrated producers, who may find it worth while to cut prices simply to gain access to final markets, play only a small role in the Gulf.

Business behaviour for governments?

As host governments become shareholders in these joint producing operations, they are spliced into a pattern that they
may not initially want to disturb. It is fascinating but unproductive for a Westerner to devise a multiplicity of scenarios
postulating future business behaviour on the part of host
governments which might seem – to us – economically, politically 'logical' – for them. Both Iran and Saudi Arabia have
insisted, for the present, that in their new role as oil sellers
the governments in the main exporting countries of the Gulf
will *not* be interested in undermining prices on the world
market. Consumers who argue that these new shareholders will
be forced to cut prices to dispose of their oil, or should 'logically' do so in order to 'maximise their revenue', are simply
assuming that these producers, in a position of considerable
bargaining strength, will immediately choose to throw this
away for their customers' benefit. It is a somewhat foolhardy
approach to bargaining.

For the remainder of the seventies, moreover, the European
Community would be prudent to assume that the host governments' increasing initiative in these concessions will somewhat
reduce the integrated companies' profits per barrel, particularly
on production up to current levels. (Beyond that level, as
shareholders, the Arab governments will be making their full
proportionate investment in the expansion of Gulf production,
while Iran, under its own special 'new deal', may in theory at
least become the sole investor.) As the companies' unit profits
fall, they will naturally seek to recoup this reduction as insis-
tently as if it derived from increases in the host governments'
fiscal revenues per barrel (although consumers are not necessarily as ready to accept this.) The integrated companies have
been accustomed to financing much of their 'downstream'
investment out of retained profits shown in Gulf production:
tankers, European refineries, distribution, and even a good deal
of their exploration in the North Sea. From now on they will
have a declining share of the upstream profits on production to
finance this. More of the capital will have to be found from
other sources. How much they *can* offset the reduction in their
profits will depend, no doubt, on the world market over the

coming years. But for some years at least, they must do their best to make up a good deal of this reduction through an increase in crude prices, or perhaps preferably in their profits downstream.

Shortage or squeeze?

These increases in world oil prices reflect a political (and geographical) tightening of the structure of the market, not a shortage. The only real shortage of oil one can expect on the world market during the seventies, perhaps, is a transitory shortage of naturally low-sulphur fuels, self-induced by the rich countries that are now more worried about pollution. That shortage will last only until the capacity to desulphurise high-sulphur fuels catches up; and desulphurisation, as we have seen, will somewhat increase the technical cost of using the abundant supplies of Middle East crude.

But apart from this temporary shortage, the oil supply situation in the Eastern Hemisphere has not radically altered since the years of overhanging surplus in the sixties. Output from some countries in the Middle East (though not all, and probably fewer than before) could readily be expanded at technical costs not much higher than at present. Nobody can say how much, or for how long. But it would certainly be enough to meet the expansion of demand from the area's traditional customers throughout the seventies, as well as the additional imports that the US will be seeking. The technical costs at which this Middle East production – but this alone – can be expanded, in any case, are now relatively even less significant than before. Even if they doubled, they would be only about 15–20 per cent of the fiscal revenues that the host governments get. Supply costs may or may not be rising: host revenues are, with companies and customers alike apparently unable to check them. For the present, the host governments seem in a position to increase the taxes still further. Participating in the profits will no doubt, over time, tempt some of them into 'shading' profit margins to get a little extra business. But that still need not deter them from what really pays – keeping up the fiscal pressure.

A continuing potential surplus of supply may not seem the

solidest foundation from which to push up prices. Yet paradoxically, this potential weakness is matched by even greater, and present, weakness on the buyer's side. For during the next five years or so, no alternative fuels – including oil elsewhere – can be obtained in volumes sufficient to meet expansion in world demand, virtually regardless of price. Certainly, there are fuels to be had at competitive costs. Nuclear energy is allegedly already cheaper than oil for generating electricity; and the Community can probably obtain some coal from Australia, South Africa and the United States at landed prices competitive with oil.

North Sea oil and gas can be developed quite profitably at prices aligned on Middle East oil delivered to Europe; more gas can be imported as well, particularly from Russia. But extra supplies of all these fuels to Europe will take some years to build up. More important, they do not, even reckoned together, seem likely to become rapidly available in the quantities required to match the expansion of demand in the world energy market. Middle East oil indubitably can.

That is why those alternative fuels, while competitive in particular locations, seem unlikely during this decade at least to set any practical ceiling to world oil prices. The basic price level will be determined by the prices that Middle East suppliers, corporate and governmental, can get for the only suppy of energy that can meet the expansion of world demand. Whatever local gas or oil is available will be able to find a ready market (and may even be guaranteed one) at prices aligned to those of oil imports. Imported gas, too, seems likely to align to that price level.

The Community is already subsidising local coal, and providing low-interest loans for nuclear power. So far, none of the gas or oil discovered in the North Sea has needed this. Most of the new fields have been very large by world standards, with low sulphur content and very high well productivity. Moreover these new supplies are thousands of miles nearer Europe than the far cheaper Middle Eastern crude. So in spite of very high investment costs, the oil appears to offer quite high profits. The rate of return on investment, even with lower European royalties and taxes, is unlikely to match the return on large Middle East fields, even allowing for investment in tankers as well as in production itself. But this Community oil will be politically far safer – for companies as well as consumers.

The only other fuels that importing countries are likely to consider politically safe may be from other developed countries. Oil in deeper waters; synthetic fuels from shales, tar sands and even coal. Several kinds are practicable; but none are likely to be low in cost, or they would probably have been developed before. If the Community chooses to develop 'politically safe fuel' at home or abroad to improve its security of supply, it must be prepared to pay a premium for safety, just as it must for low-sulphur oil.

Are imports secure?

Since 1945, Europe's supplies have been twice interrupted by the closing of the Suez Canal. After the Six-Day War in June 1967, some of the Arabian countries chose to apply a boycott on nations importing Arab oil, and suspected of collusion with Israel. But the main disruption of supplies, in both cases, arose from shortages of tanker capacity, precipitated when the oil suddenly had to be moved round the Cape.

Today, the world has sufficient tanker capacity, although the Suez Canal remains closed, and a small proportion of crude is being moved along 'short-haul' routes. This tanker balance may last well into the mid-seventies, leaving the world oil trade less vulnerable to a renewal of Israeli-Arab hostilities. The development of more pipeline capacity to the Mediterranean later in the decade, however, and of corresponding pipelines from the Mediterranean to Central and Northern Europe, might possibly increase somewhat again the vulnerability to interruption. Even so, the international companies are planning to move a very large proportion of Gulf exports to Europe in giant tankers round the Cape.

The main risk to security of supply against which European governments have sought to 'insure' themselves is the strategic instability of the region surrounding Israel. Furthermore, some countries in the Middle East have a history of internal political instability – though *coups d'état* have seldom led to any immediate interruption of oil exports, upon which new as well as old régimes' income largely depends. The use of 'oil as a political weapon' has been much discussed, but of late usually disclaimed by Arabs in positions of power. In any case, with the one half-hearted exception of the 1967 selective boycott, it has never been tried.

Restricting exports in order to raise government revenues, also, has only been tried once, by Libya in 1970–1: then it was very effective indeed. It has not yet been repeated by other OPEC governments. But that may have been only because collective threats 'to take all action necessary' have, on each occasion since, been enough. During the negotiations with the international companies, in 1972, host governments such as Iran and Saudi Arabia were careful to assure importers that their supplies would not be affected by any unilateral action that might be taken against companies holding concessions (concessionaires). That kind of reassurance left the importers uneasy.

'Oil insurance' against insecurity of supplies, in Europe, depends partly upon compulsory 'strategic stocks'. These may now be built up to 120 days' current consumption; and the EEC Commission is studying the use of underground caverns, which might provide very economical large-scale storage. It has also considered the possibility of establishing some reserve tanker capacity: for example, by adjusting load line regulations on tankers to reduce the amount each can normally carry.

The development of strategic stocks in the Community is only part of an emergency supply system co-ordinated by the Oil Committee of the OECD. This system includes plans for the re-allocation of world oil movements to make the most effective use of the tanker fleet, and in the interim, i.e. until spare productive capacity can be brought into operation, drawing upon strategic stocks and rationing petroleum as necessary. The only thing now lacking from that system, unfortunately, is its linchpin – the aforesaid spare productive capacity. In the late sixties, Europe had the offer of about 2–4 million barrels a day (100–200 million tons a year) of oil from 'shut-in' fields that could be brought into production in the United States, Venezuela and Canada within a matter of months of a supply interruption. At the time, that represented perhaps 30 per cent of European imports. Since 1970, this spare capacity has no longer been available; North America is using all the oil it can produce. Admittedly, before 1980 North Sea oil production should be as large in quantity as Western Hemisphere spare capacity was during the late sixties. The North Sea production, while saving imports, will however not be spare capacity. Furthermore, by 1980, this volume of production will represent only 15 per cent of Europe's oil demand. Between now and then, Western Europe will be exceptionally exposed to any emergencies in import supply.

Those are the Community's short-term anxieties about insecurity of supply. To these a medium-term anxiety has been added. This anxiety concerns the possible danger that not enough oil production capacity might be developed to meet rising demand. Now that host governments participate in production, the importing nations cannot help wondering whether the concessionnaire companies will still retain sufficient incentive to invest in the huge development of additional production capacity needed for this decade and the next. If not, will the host governments be ready to take over the whole responsibility? To carry out this responsibility requires expertise and managerial experience in supply logistics and development planning at a very high level, which would take time to develop and might be very difficult to hire. Even in host countries where the cash flow required is readily forthcoming, it is not easy to make all the investment decisions involved, which have to interlock with planning downstream.

This problem of organising the necessary growth in production may not arise for a time, if the constantly evolving relationship between host governments and integrated international companies wears on. There are adequate profit incentives for both kinds of shareholder, the host governments as well as their concessionnaire companies. But this does not necessarily rule out confrontations that can upset the relationship beyond repair (even if neither side, on balance, were to benefit). In the rapid evolution of bargaining power during the last few years, consumers watching from the outside can be pardoned for misgivings. The Commission is also concerned about securing the capital for oil investment in Europe, which the integrated companies may be less able to self-finance. Thi can hardly be said to affect the security of crude supply. Prosperous industrialised economies should not find it impossible to finance within their own borders the processing of the fuel they choose to import. But it is a further uncertainty arising within a previously established relationship, on which Western Europe has hitherto been able, if not always wholly content, to rely.

Reliance on the internationals?

During the seventies, the existing relationship between the Community and the international major companies will no doubt evolve, just as these companies' relationship with their hosts upstream is changing radically. In Europe this is a fairly close relationship; one of measured but cordial trust on the part of the Brussels Commission, but much more guarded on the part of some member governments. Since the war the international companies have organised a huge and complex pattern of energy supply for Europe, to the great advantage of both. The companies have a considerable overlap of interests with the governments of both importing and exporting countries, as well as some areas of conflicting interest. Their common interest with some host governments may be reinforced by the new joint shareholding in the selling of crude. Importing governments may welcome the further stability this might offer for their prospects of supply. They cannot entirely welcome its implications for prices.

Within the Community, member government's attitudes toward oil prices are likely to vary. No government likes to spend more foreign exchange on energy imports. But Britain, the Community's largest energy producer, already has a much lower dependence on imported oil than the average for the Community; and by 1980 the North Sea will have reduced this dependence even further. Britain also enjoys, for the present, considerable overseas earnings from the British and Anglo-Dutch international major companies, which sell much more oil to other importing countries than Britain has to import. The Netherlands, similarly, has a sizeable stake in one international major, and is moreover becoming a large exporter of natural gas, for which it can obtain a premium over general energy prices aligned on imported oil. It is hardly realistic to assume that the interests of these two governments in the level of world oil prices (so long as price increases are not wholly pre-empted by the host governments) will be quite identical with those of a pure importer like Italy, or even an importing country with little energy of its own except a coal industry in decline, like Germany.

France is in a special position. At home it has very limited production of gas, coal and oil. Abroad, it has now minority shareholdings in the Algerian oil nationalised in 1971. It is also the parent country of the smallest international major company with interests in the main Gulf concessions. But that has never persuaded France to adopt 'reliance on the majors' as a national policy. On the contrary, since the war, France like Italy, has actively sought a bigger stake in oil abroad, to reduce reliance on foreign companies. The Algerian *débâcle* did not dull its taste for 'government-to-government deals'. After the 1972 nationalisation of the Northern Iraq fields, France hastened to make a new agreement with Iraq for continued supplies of this crude. Italy also, through its state owned gas and oil company ENI, has explored widely in the Middle East, under agreements aimed at a closer relationship with host governments than the traditional concession. Its exploration has had only gradual success; and in Libya it too has now had 50 per cent government ownership forced upon it. Still Italy remains strongly critical of Europe's dependence on the international majors, and on their concerted bargaining with OPEC governments.

In recent years, even the Federal Republic, though a liberal host to the major companies that supply most of its oil, has become restive about its degree of dependence. The government has precluded further takeovers of the few remaining German oil companies, and backed these financially in exploration outside the Community. France, Italy and Germany are poles apart in some of the internal details of their oil policies. But all display the same uneasiness regarding complete reliance on the foreign integrated suppliers whose role in production, so long envied, now seems to them less secure.

Ambitions of the European companies

Even without the radical shift in the majors' bargaining position that began to show in 1970–1, these European national efforts to gain an independent footing in the main exporting regions would have continued. No doubt these governments – along with Japan – will be eager to seize any chances if the new arrangements open fresh new loopholes. The once new styles of partnership and service contracts that these companies used to offer may nowadays look less attractive than the older concession agreements revamped with participation. So the European 'national preference' companies may switch the emphasis of their approach towards long-term purchase contracts for 'participation crude'. For nationalised oil, they might still offer technical assistance in production – if this is welcomed. Any idea that the Iraqis will 'need' Western technicians to help them produce Kirkuk crude may be another myth like those 'indispensable' Suez Canal pilots. But it might be another matter if additional pipeline capacity were needed. Offers of oil (and gas) purchases linked with other investment projects might be welcome. But the expansion of oil production in the Middle East has so far normally been self-financing several times over. By the late seventies, moreover, oil investment inside Europe itself will be making heavy demands upon the finance Europe can muster for oil. By the eighties, the net flow of oil capital may be from some OPEC nations to Europe, not the other way. Many opportunities of technical co-operation and joint investment linked with exports of crude (and gas) will no doubt arise. But it is most unlikely that the exports thus arranged will be cheaper, let alone politically safer.

Essentially, these extra opportunities for European national preference companies will depend on whether they can offer more attractive terms and conditions, as 'offtakers' of host government crude, than the international companies. Within their own national markets, through government backing, the national preference companies may be able to secure a larger share of the business, without the price-cutting that other independent buyers might have to engage in. That is where the national preference comes in (and what the major companies complain of as 'unfair competition'). To the OPEC government supplying crude, this may make such European national companies more attractive than other independent customers, although European consumers may not find the prospect of less price-cutting so attractive. But these national preferences apply only at home. The international companies, on the newly revised terms, offer a comparable ability to dispose of OPEC crude without undue price-cutting, through their own networks of integrated supply – but on a much wider scale. The revision of terms during winter 1972–3, applied to the lowest-cost oil production in the world, probably offers Middle East governments higher unit revenues, fiscally and as profit-sharing participants, than any of the production developed under new-style concessions. For under the participation arrangements, the international companies are now committed to pay the governments prices close to those ruling in the world market for their 'participation crude'. So there is no immediate incentive for them to sell it cheaper to anyone else. The majors' tenure in the Middle East, and the extent to which participation crude will continue to be sold through their integrated channels, will not depend upon the fine print of the agreements being revised during early 1973. Both will largely depend upon their commercial performance as the most effective world-wide offtakers of Middle East crude – measured from the host governments' point of view. National preference companies may be able to offer more advantageous marketing here and there. But the majors are formidable competitors in downstream markets worldwide – and it is by this standard that the host governments will be measuring performance.

Downstream participation too?

There used to be one further inducement that national preference companies from Europe and Japan could offer which the international companies would not. Several OPEC host governments, including Saudi Arabia and Iran, remain anxious to 'participate downstream' in the refining and marketing of their oil. (Other OPEC governments have cooled somewhat towards the idea, now they see that extra revenue can be squeezed, with much less investment, out of crude production alone.) Today, Western attitudes towards such downstream participation are changing considerably: one recent German initiative was based on offering Iran's national oil company joint ownership of a refinery in Germany, linked with a crude supply contract. Up to now, much refining and marketing investment in Europe has been self-financed by major companies out of profits on Gulf production. Under the new participation arrangements, the crude will still flow to Europe in increasing quantities, through one channel or another. But only 75 per cent of the production profits, later declining to 49 per cent, will accrue to the major companies involved. Financing the same investment in downstream re-fining and marketing with far less of the profits available to the majors will raise quite new problems. This and the high investment needs of politically safe oil, rather than the conventionally astronomical figures of 'total capital requirements for the oil industry' regularly paraded by the industry's bankers, are the only really severe financing problems for the international oil industry in the seventies and beyond.

If those upstream profits can no longer be tapped, then Europe will have to finance its downstream oil industry from its own capital markets. Some of the capital available there may, in any case, come from the deposits of oil-rich governments; so their 'cash flow' upstream may be tapped in this indirect way. Nevertheless, before the end of the decade Europe may be seeking Arab and Iranian participation in its downstream investments, not offering this as a favour. It is possible – but most unlikely – that the national preference companies will be the only ones offering this. Some of the international majors, at any rate, are likely to be doing the same. And if those upstream partners are prepared to offer some participation downstream, access to their far larger integrated operations may well seem the more attractive.

Government-to-government deals, and the promotion of a larger share for national preference companies, are the national policies of some EEC member governments. They do not constitute a Community oil policy. Proposals to promote them on a Community scale have never succeeded. For example, the rest of the Six were never prepared to give Algerian crude the 'Community preference' that France at one time sought for it. Nor did attempts to offer a special status for 'Community oil companies', restrictively defined, come to anything. Now that both Britain and the Netherlands are members, any question of backing at Community level for direct or indirect efforts to supplant the international majors as partners in production can probably be ruled out – as long as such a role for the majors remains acceptable to their OPEC hosts upstream.

Such detachment would not survive if, as the result of a further Middle East War in which the United States were identified in Arab eyes with Israel and American concessionnaire companies were forced out, the majors' producing position were to be rendered untenable. By one means or another, a continued flow of crude would have to be secured. For the same reason the Community would not wish to become committed to any confrontation, concerning the concessionary relationships of any particular companies, that would put oil supplies in hazard.

Community policies towards oil imports

The Commission now feels that there is a clear case for some direct contacts with the host governments, even while the established supply pattern seems secure and efficient. Such contacts should be selective, and focused on issues where the Community's economic interests as an ultimate customer are directly and demonstrably involved. For example, the Brussels Commission's feeling that it might have been represented as an observer in the Teheran negotiations seems entirely understandable – though whether it could have contributed any extra bargaining power then is highly doubtful. But for the Commission to have identified itself with the international companies in the participation argument might have been quite unwise. Even in 1972, the commissioner in charge of energy questions had already suggested 'information meetings' with some of the OPEC member governments (possibly within the 'mixed committees' set up with some such countries entering into preferential arrangements with EEC) comparable to those that the Commission's Energy Directorate conducts with a wide range of companies. The Commission may also seek some representation in the OPEC-company discussions, due fairly soon, to schedule tax-reference prices from 1976 onwards. These prices may be the strongest influence on European oil prices for the rest of the decade. In these negotiations, the Community's representatives might at least have a watching brief for predictability, and realism in any proposed indexation of future tax reference prices. Looking beyond this, the Commission has suggested an EEC commitment to offer 'technical and eventually financial assistance, as well as opening its market to the industrial and agricultural products of these countries'; and also of mutual 'rules and guarantees applying to commercial activities and investments' between the Community and the oil exporting countries.

However, none of the evolving new arrangements in international oil – host government participation in the major's concessions, a larger role for national preference companies, the possibility of downstream participation, or direct consultations with OPEC governments – offers the Community much leverage on crude oil prices in the short term. That might arise from unforeseen changes in supply and/or demand. For example: far larger local finds of gas and oil, easy to develop quickly, than even the optimists yet expect – or alternatively, a much slower growth in the Western industrialised economies, and hence in their energy needs, than any government would probably care to contemplate. Both are possible; but they cannot be taken as probable. Alternatively, it might arise from unforeseen changes in the market structure. There may still be breaks in the upward price trend if the few Gulf producing nations able to expand low-cost production rapidly and *ad lib* choose, or are fooled into, internecine cutting of prices and even of their fiscal revenues. Also, possibly, if the integrated structure of the international companies were to be severed, by choice or government action. Both these developments, too, are possible; but for some time at least, not probable. In any case, only two groups of governments could impose such a severance on this integrated international operation. First, certainly, the OPEC governments if they chose to nationalise. Secondly, perhaps though not certainly, the parent governments of these international companies (for example, as Professor M. A. Adelman has suggested, by a radical change in their fiscal treatment of tax paid in OPEC countries). Neither group of governments seems likely, for the present, to choose such action, or the confrontation it would probably involve.

Europe, obviously, is not the only interested importer. Japan has already established direct contacts with OPEC and some of its member governments, and is promoting its national companies' exploration very widely. The United States has considerable diplomatic influence in the Gulf, in addition to the direct involvement of its own oil companies: and now, also its increasing concern as an importer. European and Japanese interests as energy importers are largely parallel, though competitive. That is not yet quite true of the United States – though as its imports from the Eastern Hemisphere mount during the present decade, its interests are coming more into line with theirs. Furthermore, the US has special political commitments in the Middle East with which it might be imprudent for other importing regions to become involved – though conversely, it has also more influence on the possibilities of restoring peace there than any other government outside the region. Nor does the US view with any approval whatsoever some of the Community's political initiatives that might affect oil imports, such as the Mediterranean policy. The Commission already has regular discussions with the US government over oil; and it has decided to do the same with Japan. Within the OECD Oil Committee, moreover, the planning of emergency supply arrangements, for what this is now worth, will go on; and there may be possibilities for co-operation there over long-term developments of politically safe energy, such as the joint subsidy of 'unconventional oil' development such as tar sands and shales.

But it is not certain that the commercial interests of these three industrialised regions in importing energy yet overlap quite sufficiently for them to face OPEC with the 'international buyers' cartel' some Americans have begun to advocate – nor indeed quite how such a united front of importers would plan to impose its diplomatic influence on fiscal and price bargaining over foreign oil. Each of these industrialised importers will have to make up its mind just how much it wants energy to be cheap. Japan's desire for this may be nearly unmixed, but not quite. America's is very mixed indeed; its national interest in developing more of its own expensive energy, indeed, probably still predominates. And the Community, too, seems now to be giving political security of supply a clear priority over cheap energy – if, indeed, any prospects of that remains.

6 European Security

Sir Bernard Burrows

Since the defeat of the European Defence Community in 1954, and more particularly since France decided to leave NATO, there has been some hesitation about discussing Western European defence. This hesitation is compounded by the uneasiness of the German situation, more exposed than that of some other European countries and more delicate in its international implications. No serious discussion of the external problems facing the European Community, however, could leave out the problems posed by Western Europe's defence.

Fears have been expressed about the relative size of Western European defence capabilities in a world where technical progress is so rapid. There is growing concern about the possibility of a reduction in United States forces in Europe, with consequential effects upon the credibility of the nuclear deterrent. Underlying both these questions is that of the existing disproportion between Western Europe and the United States in the defence field – a disproportion which is even greater when the efforts of the Western European nations are considered separately.

The existing reluctance to broach the subject of defence when considering the gradual unification of Western Europe is reinforced by the fact that all military establishments are in some degree discredited by Vietnam; and that the theory of defence has become largely incomprehensible to the ordinary man, and unappetising when it is intelligible. Present tactics for the defence of central Europe against major attack involve the early use of tactical nuclear weapons by the West. This is morally repugnant to a considerable part of public opinion and fails to satisfy the need for security, since it could lead to widespread devastation of the territory which the West is defending. It is necessary to consider whether these hesitations are based on a realistic assessment of the threat and whether there is a better means of meeting it.

The security of Western Europe has been assured for over twenty years by NATO. It was the threat of Communist invasion or penetration of Western Europe which gave rise to this alliance. Europe seemed unable to defend itself on its own. Although super-powers were not so much talked about in 1949 as they are today, it was clear that defence against the Soviet Union had to be assured in large part by the United States. Now there are many in Western Europe and in America who have begun to question whether the threat still exists, at any rate in the same form as before, and whether Europe on its own cannot do all that is necessary for its own defence, or at least a good deal more than at present.

Possible sources of instability

The threat to Western Europe is an aspect of the general relationship between East and West. It is also an aspect of the relationship between super-powers, America and the Soviet Union. But more than in many other areas involved in these relationships there has been stability on the frontier in Europe. This is due largely to the existence of the two alliances, NATO and the Warsaw Pact. Stabilisation of this frontier has had as a consequence that Europe has been divided into spheres of influence and that the rigidity of the system to the east of the so-called 'iron curtain' has been perpetuated. The attempts by Hungary and Czechoslovakia to break out of this system in 1956 and 1968 were suppressed by the Soviet Union, without the West being able to do anything. Infringement of the 'iron curtain' has for so long been regarded as the supreme *casus belli* that any attempt to help either of these bids for freedom would have involved serious risk of major war. The dangers to security in Europe derive from the possibility that the present stability might be upset. This might occur in two ways: the Soviet system in Eastern Europe, although demonstrably free from external threat, is likely to become internally more fragile, with growing pressures for political and economic liberalisation. Further attempts to achieve this, particularly if they involve the GDR, would create a situation of tension, and various circumstances can be, and have been, imagined in which there could be a spillover into the West – pursuit of fugitives, pressure on access to West Berlin, involvement of volunteers from the West.

The other possible case is that of a change of status by a state at present neutral. If one side or the other looked like gaining advantage from this, or if a country like Yugoslavia seemed likely to be split into pro-Eastern and pro-Western segments, this could lead rapidly to a confrontation in an area where no accepted East–West frontier exists.

Another threat to the stability of East–West relations in Europe could come from developments outside: There are many areas of instability – South-East Asia, Latin America and especially the Middle East – where super-power rivalry and competition has full play. As China joins the ranks of the super-powers we may expect to see a complicated three-cornered struggle in which the methods will sometimes be proxy war, more often subversion and economic bribery or blackmail. Western Europe has up to now chosen to stay largely outside these events. If foreign policy is harmonised in the enlarged Community there may perhaps be a greater tendency for Europe to play a part, if this can be done without a military presence in the outside world, which Western Europe is most unlikely to be willing to provide. But for our present purpose the point is this: America and Russia could well find themselves in acute opposition over one of these trouble spots outside Europe. Beyond a certain point, tension between them could spill over into Europe, and at least make more difficult the progress towards détente on which so much hope is now set.

More specifically, the acquisition by Russia of positions of influence and of military facilities in countries bordering the European area, e.g. North Africa, may seem to outflank NATO defences. The strictly military application of these positions of strength, as of the more forward deployment of Russian warships which has taken place in recent years, is of limited importance. Ships without air cover are very vulnerable. Military facilities in foreign countries are of very uncertain value, as the West has often discovered. But the real significance of these developments is political.

In all these situations inside and outside Europe the chances of planned military aggression are small. But military strength and military dispositions are a factor in the general politico-strategic relationships of states or groups of states. They are a factor whose weight is felt as tension mounts. They can lead to the success or failure of political and economic blackmail. If in Europe either East or West became too weak or too strong this would itself lead to a risk of instability: the stronger side would be less careful to avoid accidents, and would, if they happened, tend to exploit them for its own advantage. It might more blatantly seek to add neutrals to its own side and even, perhaps, to detach the weaker members of the other alliance.

Reducing the risk

These are the kinds of threat to its security that Western Europe now faces. There are two ways to reduce the risk. One is to seek to remove the underlying causes of tension by negotiation and the improvement of relations. This is basically a political operation, but many of the counters are military – notably the attempt to agree on the limitation or reduction of both nuclear and conventional armed strength, in the SALT and MBFR negotiations. But only if Western Europe feels assured of its own security can it play an effective part in such negotiations. No progress is likely to come unless both sides play from roughly equivalent strength. Western Europe must form a reliable assessment of the needs of the military situation, because this is a major part of the negotiating position, and because much of the detailed subjects of negotiation will be of a military character. Western Europe therefore needs a forum of discussion and consultation on these subjects. But mainly because France has been unwilling since 1966 to take part in discussion of defence policy, and places strict limits on the degree of her participation in the discussion of disarmament, a united European voice in NATO has not hitherto been available.

The other means of reducing the risk to the security of Western Europe is to maintain an appropriate defence posture. In the era of nuclear weapons it has become a truism that the avoidance of war through deterrence is the main object of defence policy. What is not so universally acknowledged is that deterrence, to be successful, must operate at the con-

ventional as well as at the nuclear level. A defence posture
must be seen as a whole. In matters of security the unexpected
often happens. Even though the risk of planned major attack
against Western Europe now seems slight, this remains a
possibility at the end of a process of accident, spillover, blackmail or world tension. In crisis situations requiring delicate
judgement there is ample scope for miscalculation. When vital
decisions have to be taken by individual men, irrationality
cannot be ruled out.

The role of nuclear weapons in deterrence

Clearly, effective defence is still necessary. The difficult
questions are: what sort of defence and who is going to provide
it? The answers to the two questions are connected. Strategic
nuclear forces are the ultimate deterrent or the ultimate instrument of blackmail. During the period of American nuclear
superiority the security of Western Europe depended on the
knowledge or belief that in the event of attack against a
member of the Alliance these forces would be used in massive
retaliation. Nuclear parity has made the situation more complex. The use of strategic nuclear weapons will now inevitably
result in very large-scale devastation of the user country as well
as of the target country. In the event of any attack on NATO
territory would the US automatically take the step of using
its strategic nuclear weapons? Some believe that it would not
do so. The more orthodox view is that the present system of
flexible response, by which any attack or threat situation is
met with the appropriate response at the lowest level suitable
to prevent the attacker succeeding, provides a credible ladder
from the minor incident to the ultimate weapon. There is no
difficulty in believing that if an attack were made with nuclear
weapons, nuclear weapons would be used by the West in reply.
If, however, there were an attack by conventional means, or,
if a situation of tension resulted in a confrontation of conventional forces, then every attempt would be made to contain
and restore the situation without recourse to nuclear weapons.
   Here, however, we come to the main problem of the system
of the flexible defence of Western Europe. The conventional
forces of the West in Western Europe are inferior to those

of the Warsaw Pact in total numbers and, even more important, in numbers of tanks. There are interminable arguments on how to compare the opposing forces and some Western experts deny that the West is in a situation of inferiority. Nevertheless, on the Western assumption that an attack must necessarily originate in the East, it is the attacker who can choose the place and time, and who has the advantage of surprise. He can therefore achieve local superiority even if the overall levels of forces are more balanced than is usually thought. This being so, in the extreme hypothesis of a major conventional attack the current orthodox Western view is that it would very likely be impossible to stop a Warsaw Pact armoured advance with the conventional forces now available to NATO. Therefore nuclear weapons would have to be used. Here the flexible and gradual approach becomes particularly important. NATO has adopted a doctrine for the selective and limited use of tactical nuclear weapons for defensive purposes in such a situation. The object would be partly to have an immediate effect on the battle in progress, partly to demonstrate Western determination to go to any necessary lengths to stop the attack. The use of nuclear weapons would aim to impose a pause during which there would be time for reflection and hopefully for political action. Possibly the attacker might not believe that the West would use its nuclear weapons. The use of nuclear weapons initially on a very limited scale in order to avoid the devastation caused by a large scale exchange of even tactical weapons would show that this belief was wrong, and would indicate readiness to go to further lengths if necessary.

There is at present no clear answer, or at any rate no publicly known answer, to the question of what happens if the limited use of tactical nuclear weapons fails to stop the attack, that is to say, what further stages of escalation and deterrence the West would apply. This very uncertainty is believed to be an important element in overall deterrence. Even a small probability that at any stage in his attack an escalatory process will be set in train, which could end in the devastation of his territory, is likely to make an agressor more cautious, since he will never know exactly how far he can go without running this risk.

This is the best deterrence theory available, but it is by no means perfect so far as the defence situation in central Europe is concerned. The first use of nuclear weapons by the West is morally and politically repugnant. Since the weapons would be used *ex hypothesi* against enemy troops which had already entered NATO territory the damage caused would be to a NATO state. If limited use failed and a widespread exchange of tactical nuclear weapons took place, the damage in central Europe, most probably to the German Federal Republic and the DDR, would to the inhabitants be indistinguishable from a full strategic exchange. Finally, since most of the nuclear weapons on the western side belong to the US and their use therefore requires a US decision, this vital part of the defence system is largely outside European control.

Replacing American by European nuclear weapons?

Much has been written about the possibility of replacing the American by the British and French nuclear forces, or some joint version of them, and of giving these forces a common European character. But these ideas do not stand up to rigorous examination. The British and French nuclear forces, even if combined, would not amount to more than a small fraction of US or Soviet nuclear strength. There seems virtually no prospect that Britain or France would be willing to spend the very large sums which would be necessary to match the nuclear forces of the super-powers. There is equally little prospect of any real sharing of control of nuclear forces between Britain and France. The French regard the *force de frappe* as the ultimate expression of national sovereignty. The British force is 'assigned to NATO', and partly dependent on US information and supply. Apart from divergent national attitudes there is a real difficulty about sharing control of a decision which may have to be taken at exceedingly short notice. The setting up of a joint command is no answer, since the decision to release nuclear weapons will always be reserved to the highest political authority, and will not be delegated to military commanders. Time for intergovernmental discussion might not be available.

The same reason rules out any idea that the control of nuclear weapons might be exercised by Western Europe as a whole. Two statesmen might be able to consult together fairly quickly on a hot line. No known system permits of speedy consultations between the leaders of nine countries. A further important obstacle is that the Non-Proliferation Treaty forbids the transfer of control of nuclear weapons from a state which owns them to another which does not. This ban is held to cover the grant of a share of control. No European nuclear force is therefore possible until there is a European state, or at least a tight federation, to own, control and operate it.

The position of Germany forms yet another obstacle to the creation of an effective all-purpose European nuclear force. The economic situations of the United Kingdom, France and Germany strongly suggest that if there were to be a major up-grading of the existing nuclear forces of European countries, a German financial contribution would be necessary in order to ensure that an excessive burden did not fall on the UK and French budgets and so distort both military and economic relationships within the enlarged Community. But, even apart from the Non-Proliferation Treaty, signed but not yet ratified by the Federal Republic, this country renounced the manufacture and possession of nuclear weapons in joining WEU in 1954. Moreover it is commonly believed that a change in the Federal Republic's non-nuclear status would be regarded by the Soviet Union as more provocative and more dangerous than almost any other action which might be taken by the West in Europe, and might thus be one of the very few things which could revive the at present more or less dormant threat of aggressive counter-action by the Warsaw Pact.

If, however, to avoid these dangers, Germany were to remain excluded from an enlarged and potentially independent nuclear force in the possession of other West European countries, this would emphasise the differentiation in status between members of the Community and have a very divisive effect within Western Europe and the Atlantic Alliance – even more pronounced if Germany had to make a financial contribution to the cost of expanding the British and French nuclear forces.

These problems might not be quite so acute with regard to the other European members of the Atlantic Alliance, but for two reasons there would nevertheless be strong resistance to any idea of building up the British and French nuclear forces into a full-scale nuclear deterrent. First, as in the case of the Federal Republic, this would appear to crystallise the second-grade status of the non-nuclear Europeans. Secondly, any major change in the western nuclear situation would bring into the open the general reluctance felt by many West Europeans to be involved in nuclear matters at all. This applies to many sections of public opinion in Scandinavia and Benelux, as well as to some elements of the left in the United Kingdom, Italy and France. In so far as they recognise the need for nuclear deterrence at all, these sectors of public opinion would have a preference for leaving things as they are, with the US as the nuclear guarantor, rather than building up a new nuclear super-force much nearer home with which, whatever the procedures for decision might be, the other Europeans might feel a more direct involvement.

Nevertheless there are certain things which could be done. Before a crisis arises, consultation can usefully take place about the way in which nuclear weapons should be used, allowing the non-nuclear countries to have some influence on the final decisions by the nuclear countries. This is in fact happening in the Nuclear Planning Group (NPG) of NATO, which has, for example, produced an agreed doctrine for the limited use of tactical nuclear weapons. Unfortunately France does not take part in the NPG, and no one knows for certain to what extent French doctrine differs from that of the rest of the Alliance. This will soon become of practical importance, since the French are about to introduce into service their own tactical nuclear weapon, Pluton. If it is issued to the French forces in Germany, this will clearly necessitate consultation at least with the German Government. In order to avoid this France may decide to keep the weapon on its own territory. But, even so, it would presumably be fired into German territory, and would thus create a strong moral obligation of prior consultation about the ways in which it might be used.

It might be more acceptable to France if consultations were to take place among Europeans only, in a European NPG.

Besides the advantage of the presence of France, this would provide the means for establishing a view of common European interests on matters of nuclear policy prior to a discussion in the Alliance as a whole. A joint European view would obviously carry more weight than the views of individual countries.

One other way in which the West European members of the Alliance might seek to gain greater control of their destiny would be through tactical nuclear weapons. These do not present such financial or political problems as the strategic weapons. At present, American tactical nuclear weapons are due to be used not only by American forces, but, after release by the US authorities, also by the forces of other NATO countries. There is no serious technical reason why such weapons should not be made by Britain and France and held by them for issue to the other Allied forces once the decision to do so has been taken by the respective national authorities. For the reasons already stated no joint European decision for the use of these weapons would be possible, but there might be some advantage if the decision to release them were to be taken by several European governments together. Against this it has been objected that tactical nuclear weapons should remain American, since this involves the Americans more directly in the defence of Western Europe. On this view it would be wrong to use tactical nuclear weapons without the Americans being specifically involved in the decision. But others again argue that uncertainty as a positive factor in deterrence is strengthened when there is more than one centre of decision with regard to the use of nuclear weapons.

Reducing reliance on nuclear weapons

Another and more effective improvement of Europe's control over its destiny would be to reduce reliance on the nuclear end of the deterrence spectrum. In the unlikely event of a deliberate nuclear attack on the West there would be no choice other than to make a nuclear reply. The weak point in the present situation, however, is the necessity of early nuclear action by the West in the event of a major conventional attack from the East. The defence posture would be radically improved if adequate conventional means could be found to deal with conventional attack. Why has this not been done? Because to do it by existing methods would demand higher defence expenditure than Western governments are prepared to provide. The tendency is exactly the opposite. Unit costs of defence equipment and of defence manpower grow ever faster. With apparent tranquillity in Europe and the prospect of more intensive East–West negotiation, it is extremely difficult for most countries of Western Europe even to maintain defence expenditure at current levels. Proposals to increase the defence vote are electorally unpopular; proposals to increase the social services at the expense of the defence budget are the common currency of parties in opposition and even of some parties in government.

This resistance to higher defence expenditure is increased by another factor: the NATO military authorities have from the beginning regularly said that considerably larger forces were required for the defence of Western Europe. Equally consistently governments have failed to increase their forces up to the levels demanded by the generals. And yet Western Europe has not been attacked. So there is a certain credibility gap. Until now it could have been argued that the deficiency in conventional forces was offset by the nuclear deterrent. But if Europe wishes to be less dependent on this deterrent, then the conventional element in its defence posture has to be taken more seriously.

Strengthening conventional forces

There are two ways in which this can be done: we can try to find a better system of conventional defence, and the West European countries can improve the efficiency of their defence effort by more co-operation and joint action.

In the orthodox view the only way to stop the advance of a force of tanks is to have more tanks in defence. This, as we have seen, is mostly unlikely to be the case in the event of an attack on Western Europe. But there is a growing body of opinion to the effect that other less orthodox means might have a better chance of success. There are possible new weapon systems, such as helicopters firing guided missiles from the flank of an advance; or the delivery by missile of very large quantities of small anti-tank mines to swamp whole areas of possible advance and deny these routes to the enemy. There are new dispositions by which Western forces would be divided into two elements: a heavily armed highly mobile central reserve, and a new category of local forces designed to provide the basic defence of their own localities. These local forces would require less training and less sophisticated weapons, but their equipment would include a very high proportion of comparatively simple anti-tank guns. They would have profound knowledge of the locality and of the possibilities of concealment, increasing the uncertainty for the attacker. The value of such local forces would be greater in irregular and wooded terrain in which local cover would be available, but if they could be relied upon to seal off certain parts of the front this would leave more limited areas to be dealt with by the more centralised mobile force. This concept is also relevant to the policy of forward defence, i.e. the attempt to prevent any significant enemy advance into the defended territory. In the eyes of those who live near the border, as most of the West Germans do, it is clearly a principle of enormous importance. But the present NATO forces are thinly stretched in attempting to cover the whole of the frontier. Any further reduction would very likely mean a change in the strategy towards greater concentration further back, with the consequence that loss of territory would come to seem inevitable. The development of less expensive local forces as an important element in the defence might prevent this happening.

There may be other ways in which conventional defence can be improved. Anything which can be done in this direction will be a much better way to Europeanise the defence of Western Europe than to concentrate discussion on the enlargement of the British and French nuclear forces, which can never be truly European until there is a single West European state, and which to be credible will in any foreseeable future need the American nuclear forces in the background. There is a greater risk that the United States will reduce its conventional forces in Europe than that it will renounce its nuclear guarantee: Europe should pay more attention to the difficult but possible task of making up for some loss in conventional forces than to the probably impossible and unnecessary one of replacing the US strategic nuclear forces.

Joint European efforts

In addition to modifying the existing conventional defence concept the West Europeans could do a lot to make their conventional defence more effective by combining their defence efforts. The first attempt in this direction was the proposal for an EDC, hotly debated from 1950 to 1954, when it was finally turned down by the French Parliament. The keynote of this plan was a high degree of integration; national control was to be very severely limited and land forces, for example, were to be mixed down to battalion level. There was to be a common budget and joint production of military equipment. Many of the features of this plan were inspired, however, not by a desire for greater efficiency, but by fear of a revival of German militarism. This kind of mixing even comparatively small national units is now felt to be inefficient, at least while national differences remain in equipment and training. More promising are the following three methods of co-operation and joint action: standardisation of equipment, including in some cases joint production; the pooling and amalgamation of services below the operational level, e.g. training, logistics, medical and technical services, transport aircraft; and specialisation, by which a country would no longer try to do a little of everything, but would rely on others for parts of the defence effort which it could not afford or did not wish to provide itself. We will now discuss these different methods in more detail.

Standardisation of equipment has been adopted as an objective by the EDC, WEU and NATO, but very little has been achieved. Joint production has taken place for a few particular projects and between a very limited number of countries. It does not always lead to reduced costs, since economies of scale are sometimes counterbalanced by increased administrative costs and the duplication of production lines. There is urgent need for a new initiative by West European governments in the field of standardisation, which ought to become an essential criterion in the selection of all future military equipment. The prospect of effective joint production would be improved if a programme were adopted to cover a number of projects extending over a number of years. It would then be possible for production of each of them to be concentrated in one country, and compensation would be obtained by balancing one project against another, instead of, as now, by dividing up a single project between the participating countries. This, like many other aspects of co-operation, would require the creation of a European military accounting procedure, which could in time lead towards a common military budget. As an interim step in this direction, Community finance could be applied to joint research into new defence equipment.

Standardisation and joint production would be greatly facilitated if there were agreement between the European countries on the operational concepts and tactics involved in the planning and conduct of the defence of Western Europe. It is, for example, absurd that the British and Federal German armies still have widely different ideas about the role and requirements of their main battle tank, even though they would be fighting side by side in the same area against the same potential enemy. There are many other cases of the same kind. In order to overcome these differences it is desirable that staff contacts should be extended in scope and frequency, and that planners and technicians in the West European armed forces should consult together at a much earlier stage in the development of requirements for new weapon systems. Governments will also have to compromise on previously entrenched national positions in the interests of greater European co-operation and more efficient joint defence.

Common support services are being actively studied in the Eurogroup (the informal grouping of ten of the European members of NATO, of which more is said below). They provide a fruitful field for increasing co-operation. However, full benefit is unlikely to be obtained until there is a greater degree of standardisation of equipment, until operational doctrine is harmonised, and until a common financial system simplifies the complicated accounting procedures which would today be required to deal for example with the repair of a truck belonging to one country in the workshop of another.

A certain degree of specialisation exists in practice, in that

many of the Western European states do not try to fulfil every
kind of military function with their own defence forces. Apart
from the obvious case of nuclear weapons, possessed by only
the UK and France, very few have long-range bombers or
ships larger than destroyers. Few are equipped or trained to
carry out military operations except in their own particular
areas. In fact, none of them could fight a war without their
allies. Nevertheless, if the fact of this interdependence were
recognised and exploited, instead of being concealed by talk of
national sovereignty, a great deal more could be done to
increase efficiency by sharing out the tasks. As an extreme
example, why should two neighbouring countries not decide
that one of them should have no air force and the other no
navy, and that each one would specialise in one of these arms
and supply the needs of the other? As an initial step the military air transport requirements of several of the smaller states
might be pooled and be operated by a combined force from a
single base.

Political objections are raised against this concept on the
ground that no state can trust another to such an extent as to
put national security in its hands. As stated above, this has in
practice already happened to a large extent. It is unrealistic for
the Europeans to maintain the fiction of an independent
national defence capability. There may be many practical difficulties, but at least the subject should be explored thoroughly,
with the sole object of increasing defence efficiency.

Burden-sharing

The problem of equitably sharing defence costs among the
members of NATO, and especially between the European
members and the US has been much and hotly discussed. It is
an extremely complex, many faceted and divisive problem for
which there is not *one* simple, logical and definitive solution.
The two main aspects of the matter are, first, the budgetary
costs of the US defence effort related to Europe and, secondly,
the foreign-exchange costs resulting from the stationing of US
forces in Europe. These two elements require separate discussion.

The basis of the Alliance is the conviction that the military power of the US is essential to the security of Western Europe – and that Western Europe is essential to the security of the US. The idea that the presence of US troops in Europe or the US nuclear guarantee are dispensable to American security negates the basis on which the Alliance rests and constitutes a threat to its continuation and credibility.

There can never, therefore, be any question of Europe's 'buying' its security from the United States, because payment itself would destroy the credibility of the product bought. It is, however, a legitimate demand in an alliance which is vital to the security of all its members that the cost of defence be shared equitably among them. But translating this general statement into precise figures that can give guidance to policy is extremely difficult. In the case of the US it is impossible to reach any objective and compelling conclusions as to what proportion of the US defence budget is spent on the defence of Europe as distinct from America's other defence commitments. What part of the US expenses on logistics, manpower, reserves, naval strength and strategic nuclear forces must be considered to serve specifically the security of Europe? All US defence expenditure taken together constitutes a considerably higher percentage of GNP (even excluding military expenditure for Vietnam) than that of any of the European members of the Alliance.

But the GNP of the United States is nearly 50 per cent higher than that of all NATO Europe. Should the principle of progressive taxation apply to members of the Alliance? Furthermore, fewer US troops in Europe might lead to decreases or increases in US budgetary expenditure, depending on whether withdrawal would be accompanied by an absolute reduction in US strength, or whether the troops in question were kept in being in America. No satisfactory answer to these questions has been found, or is likely to be found. As the International Institute for Strategic Studies said in its *Strategic Survey 1971*:

In short, there are so many different criteria of comparison, and they give such diverse results, that within broad limits the exercise is unprofitable because open to too many interpretations. It is only possible to say that, on most counts, the NATO European countries seemed to be providing a reasonable share of the collective defence in 1971; on some counts surprisingly more than the United States, on others notably less.

However, as the same survey points out, the problem of burden-sharing is essentially a political problem – what can and should Europe do to provide arguments against the mounting pressure of public opinion and in the US Congress for unilateral reduction of troops in Europe? For this reason the Eurogroup decided at the beginning of the seventies to increase the European effort in NATO.

In 1971 the Eurogroup adopted a concerted programme of improvement to their forces amounting to the sum of 1000 million dollars over five years. While this expenditure 'visibly' affects the relative share of Europe and the US in the common defence, the most effective way of strengthening the European effort in NATO would certainly be the adoption of the above-mentioned measures for standardisation and joint production of equipment for common support services, and for further specialisation in military functions. Joint procurement, however, may lead to a reduction of European, and especially German, purchases of US military hardware, which offset about a third of the total foreign exchange cost of US troops in Europe.

An earlier (December 1970) commitment of 1000 million dollars over five years by the Eurogroup is helping to reduce both the budgetary and the foreign exchange costs to the US. This European Defence Improvement Programme (EDIP) will strengthen NATO infrastructure (aircraft shelters, a new integrated communication system). In fact, though the US continues to pay the largest single share of NATO infrastructure costs, this share has declined from 40 per cent to 25 per cent over the last twelve years.

The foreign exchange costs of keeping US troops in Europe has, with the deterioration of the US balance of payments, become a contentious issue in its own right. In 1970, the net foreign exchange cost, taking into account offset purchases of military equipment – mainly by the German Federal Republic, was just over 1000 million dollars; this is not a very large sum in the overall US balance of payments. But the inability of the present monetary system to achieve global adjustment has led to a dangerous tendency to consider individual items on the balance of payments in isolation. There is no economic argument for looking at just the foreign exchange costs of security commitments, any more than there is for looking at bilateral trade balances rather than global ones, or for trying to balance inflows and outflows of long-term capital. If the adjustment mechanisms in the monetary system function well, only the overall balance-of-payments position of a country matters. Much less will be heard about military balance-of-payments costs if a reformed monetary system facilitates future adjustments.

But it would be dangerous to count on this happening soon. The balance-of-payments problem, with the recurring debate on military purchases and other offset measures has proved divisive in the past: divisive between Europe and the United States, divisive between Germany and its allies. It would therefore be in the interest of Europe if an arrangement could be found through which this issue could be taken out of discussions on defence and settled through an agreed formula. One proposal[1] suggests a buffer fund to which all members of NATO contribute, which would make offset payments to countries with military foreign exchange costs when these countries are in balance-of-payments difficulties. This and similar proposals have so far not found official support. But, as the International Institute for Strategic Studies points out,[2] a settlement of the balance-of-payments problem through an Alliance Fund could 'have the virtue of turning a potentially divisive issue into a contractual bond between allies during the "era of negotiation" '.

Force reductions

In all probability, East–West negotiations and problems of arms limitation and force reductions (SALT II, MBFR) are

[1] See Timothy W. Stanley, 'Atlantic Security in the Seventies', North Atlantic Paper (London, September 1971).
[2] *Strategic Survey 1971*, p. 25.

going to be permanent features of the political scene during the rest of the decade. No one can predict how strong the forces that seek to diminish the American commitment in Europe will become. But the existence of these vocal forces in the US has already weakened the negotiating position of the West in any force reduction negotiations with the East. Europe cannot be certain that the interests of the United States will always seem the same as Europe's in these negotiations. Europe's security, therefore, can only benefit from the era of negotiations on one condition: that the nations of Western Europe begin to act together in matters of security, including these negotiations. All our nations, France included, share the conviction that American forces in Europe should not be withdrawn, and if possible not even significantly reduced. All of them see a relation between the presence of US conventional forces in Europe and the credibility of the American nuclear guarantee. The Nixon Administration has up to now successfully resisted pressure in Congress to reduce the numbers of American forces in Europe. One of the more effective arguments against unilateral reduction is the hope that there may be mutual and balanced reductions both by East and West. But if the USSR continues to delay its agreement to negotiate on this subject, the pressure for American troop reductions will increase. The most likely outcome is a reduction which would do something to satisfy some of the American critics, but not so great as to disrupt the defence system in Europe, provided that the Europeans act to meet the resulting deficiency. A common West European defence policy along the lines indicated above is the best way to prevent a dangerous reduction of the US military presence in Europe. Strength attracts strength. If a more effective co-operation between what now still are separate West European defence efforts did not prevent a major reduction of American forces – then an even more closely united Western European defence system would be the only way to maintain security. From whatever angle one looks at Western Europe's security – the impossibility of paying for ever more costly defence, an optimistic or pessimistic view of the future of the US commitment to the defence of Europe, a hopeful or an apprehensive attitude towards negotiations with the East – in all these cases a more united West European defence system is the only way to prevent what we fear and achieve what we hope.

Machinery for European action

How could Europeans plan and execute a common defence policy? Much will depend on national attitudes, notably that of France. Since 1966 the French forces in Germany have no longer formed part of the integrated NATO defence structure. It is probably too much to hope that this attitude could be entirely reversed in any short time-span. Regaining French co-operation for a more united European defence effort would be the greatest single advance that could be made. The difficulties, however, are great. French military and political authorities tend to take the line that it is only worth talking about the organisation of European defence if the Americans have withdrawn, or at least on the hypothesis of American withdrawal. They do not wish for this withdrawal, but take a defeatist line about the possibility of influencing American policy or strategy while the Americans are still present in Europe - although there are some signs that this attitude is changing. The West Germans, on the other hand, hesitate to plan defence on a European basis for fear that this will drive the Americans away. They therefore favour the use of only such institutions as already exist, namely the Eurogroup which operates inside NATO, and they show most interest in methods that lead to an increase in Europe's financial contribution, and which are directly related to the persuasion of American opinion in favour of the maintenance of the American military position in Europe.

Other national attitudes are less clear cut. Subject to internal political considerations, the Italians are more genuinely attached to the idea of European defence co-operation than most other West Europeans; and a more European aspect given to defence organisation would be generally helpful with Italian opinion. The United Kingdom, under its present government, is generally in favour of the development of the Community as far as the traffic will bear, which means in practice as far as the French can be persuaded to go. The use of some kind of nuclear co-operation as a factor in such persuasion is not to be excluded, but for the reasons already mentioned is very unlikely to play so prominent a part in the relationship as is sometimes supposed.

There are likely to be particular problems with regard to the other new members. Opinion in Denmark, in a delicate state about Europe generally, has never been enthusiastic for military preparation. It is easier to go on being a member of NATO than to join in a new defence initiative on a European basis. Ireland is the only new member of the Community which is not also a member of the Atlantic Alliance. But the Irish Government seems to accept whatever implications follow from becoming a member of the Community. Nevertheless, the problems of Irish membership of a European defence organisation necessarily closely related to NATO, would require skilful handling.

A West European defence system can only be set up by decision of governments. This short sketch of national attitudes does not suggest that the decision will be easy or is near. Nevertheless, there are urgent pressures to which public opinion and governments will have to respond more quickly than is now generally realised. The threat of American reduction or withdrawal is perhaps the most obvious catalyst. But hardly less pressing is the constant diminution of resources for defence on a national basis owing to inflated costs and the competition of other expenditure. The habit of working together in an enlarged Community, and in particular the search for monetary and economic union and for harmonisation of foreign policy, the preparation for the Conference on Security and Co-operation in Europe and the continuing dialogue on financial and economic relations with the United States will tend to push the Community into the closely related field of defence policy.

What institutions would be required for a better organisation of European defence?

The Eurogroup, to which reference has already been made, is an informal body existing since 1968 and composed of ten of the European members of NATO; but not France, which declined an invitation to participate. Its functions are to consult about matters which may later come to be discussed within the Alliance as a whole, in order to identify a common

European interest, and to study and implement measures of defence co-operation between its members in the interest of greater cost-effectiveness. It has also consulted about the financial measures already mentioned, which are aimed at weakening pressure in the US Congress for a large reduction of American forces in Europe. The Eurogroup has the advantage of already existing and therefore requiring no new initiative. It has the disadvantage that its membership does not match that of the expanded Community, in that its excludes France and includes Greece and Turkey, who are however associate members of the Community. The Eurogroup's intimate association with NATO is usually thought to make it difficult for France to join it.

Western European Union, set up in 1954 on the collapse of the European Defence Community, consists of the original Six and the UK. It has potential consultative and executive functions with regard to European defence. But except in one or two very limited and specific subjects relating to the levels of German and UK forces it has never exercised any defence functions, since it has in fact from the beginning explicitly handed over its defence responsibilities to NATO. As regards a future European defence organisation it has the advantage of being composed of those countries who are most closely concerned with the defence of the central area of Europe and of the western Mediterranean. Serious disadvantages, however, more than outweigh this advantage. It is historically *mal vu* in both the German Federal Republic and France; in the former because it enshrines and supervises the maintenance of quantitative and qualitative restrictions on Federal German armed forces; in the latter because at the time of France's rejection of British membership of the EEC an attempt was made to use WEU as a means of consultation between Britain and the Six instead of the consultation which would have taken place in the Community. More important, WEU has the disadvantage that for many years it has had virtually no operational role in defence. Although useful debates have taken place in its Assembly, governments have paid little attention. Finally, it has no organic connexion with the Community and it is impossible to handle defence policy without reference to foreign policy, and to financial and economic policy. The last two subjects will be handled by the institutions of the European Community, and foreign policy at least in a Community-related framework, that of the so-called Davignon Committee.

The need for co-ordination between these different matters is a powerful motive for finding a Community framework to meet the institutional requirements of European defence co-operation. These requirements are of two kinds. A forum is needed for consultation about the development of a more identifiable and therefore more autonomous European defence system, and for pre-consultation among Europeans of matters which also need to be discussed Alliance-wide with the US. The other requirement is for an executive agency or agencies, initially of a very simple kind, capable of carrying out such functions as the European governments may entrust to it, for example joint training, the operation of joint medical services, and joint research into weapon development. There are valid arguments against using the Commission for these tasks. But, as already indicated, there are even stronger arguments against separating defence from the Community framework. A Committee, similar to the Davignon Committee, might provide a first forum for consultation. A secretariat similar to that proposed for political affairs is urgently needed and might provide the embryo of an executive agency. A secretary-general would be needed, with limited executive functions as head of the various co-operative agencies already mentioned. Gradually, functional responsibility for such activities could be handed over from the Eurogroup to the new Community-related institution.

In the light of the difficulties over the nature and location of the political secretariat it may seem utopian to postulate a more powerful secretariat for defence. The problem of the relationship of a Community-related defence institution with NATO poses other difficult problems. Irish non-membership of NATO might not be a serious obstacle, but the French attitude would need to be clarified. France accepts the continuing necessity of the Atlantic Alliance, of the American nuclear guarantee and of the presence of US troops in Europe (provided they are not on French soil). French military authorities co-operate in several ways with NATO and have agreed plans for the participation of French forces with NATO forces in an emergency, subject to a decision at the time by the French Government. But the French see a sharp distinction between these attitudes and participation in NATO planning and NATO discussion of force levels and strategy, which they reject. The problem will therefore be to find a system sufficiently autonomous to satisfy France and sufficiently linked to NATO to satisfy the other Europeans and the US. NATO machinery has proved to be flexible and capable of adapting to new institutional requirements, both in the case of French withdrawal from defence planning and when the Eurogroup was set up. This group provides a useful stopgap until all the member states of the European Community are ready to accept the need for defence co-operation as an essential concomitant of economic union and foreign policy co-ordination and recognise the true necessities of the present international situation.

7 The European Community and the United States

Emanuele Gazzo

In seeking solutions to the problems posed by the changing world political and economic scene, and by its own emergence on this scene, the European Community must look as a matter of priority to its relations with the United States. This fact is recognised as much by those whose chief concern is for Europe to acquire its own 'personality' as a gage of its independence, as by those who believe above all that Europe's destiny is inseparable from that of America.

In fact, the European Community's relations with the United States are different from its relations with any other part of the world. They alone are marked by interdependence both in security and in economic affairs. The first two chapters of this volume have shown the relatively narrow limits of choice open to the Community in the political and economic sphere. They have also shown, by implication, that the 'special' relationship between the Community and the US is not a transitional phenomenon (and certainly not a now irrelevant remnant of the past), but will exist for the foreseeable future. It is important, to keep this long-term reality in mind and not to put too much weight on issues of the moment ('the problem of the dollar'), however pressing these may seem. Certain points raised in these earlier chapters have particular relevance when considering European–American relations.

Politically:

The European Community cannot accept a position of subordination to one or other of the super-powers. Such a policy would never be agreed upon by all the member states.

On the other hand, the Community could not in the foreseeable future become a super-power itself. That would imply the possession of a nuclear deterrent directed against all points of the compass, which would raise insuperable practical and political obstacles.

The European Community could not adopt an attitude of political neutrality. It cannot opt out of the conflicts in the world, which may threaten its security, its supplies and its trade. Neutrality might be a possible policy for one European country or another by itself; for the Community as a whole, it is not.

In economic matters:

Europe's prosperity rests on its being a part of the international economy. This international economy is profoundly affected by US economic policy, both domestic and foreign.

The Community has the choice either of defending itself against the impact of these policies on its own welfare, or of seeking to influence them by means of a structured dialogue with the United States. The member states, separately, cannot successfully pursue either objective.

If defensive reactions become the dominant mode of dealing with the US, certain member states will not accept their resultant isolation from the world economy. In such circumstances, the Community would break up.

Co-operative solutions in most areas offer the best chance of control over our economic fate. In many instances, moreover, global solutions are the only ones which make technical sense, as international economic activity escapes the control of either the US or Europe (and Japan for that matter), acting separately.

The strains of economic interdependence will cause a rift between the two continents, unless certain forms of joint economic management take the place of the present traditional bargaining. This means that the search for solutions which are viable in the long run must take precedence over short-term advantage.

In reality the Community has only two options. Either it

condemns itself to impotence and disunity by seeking, if only verbally, to attain objectives which imply an adversary relationship with the United States; or it will, whenever possible, seek to apply in its relations with the rest of the world the same method of collective action whereby its own unity is being built.

Europe's choice in this matter will not only affect its own future but might well be a key factor in deciding the direction which world affairs take during the present decade:

> Together with Japan, the European Community and the United States will determine whether the world economy is to drift back into beggar-my-neighbour policies in which each attempts to export its own problems, or whether it continues to move towards an open system.

> Decisions taken by the European Community and by the United States in the security field will be crucial for the further progress of détente, which is impossible without the continued certainty that the security of Western Europe is not at risk.

The relationship between the European Community and the United States is therefore crucial if progress is to be made towards what in the first chapter has been described as a world based on 'contractual relations'.

If the European Community and the United States are to contribute towards this goal, each much recognise the other's independence and equality. This is a precondition for constructive solutions to the problems posed by their interdependence. There has been considerable misunderstanding about these terms.

Interdependence is inescapable: decisions taken on either side of the Atlantic inevitably affect the situation on the other. Properly organised, interdependence on the basis of equality leaves both parties considerable independence. It is this that should be the goal. In some areas, Europe and the United States will need to undertake joint action; in others, they may agree to diverge.

In order to secure this balanced relationship, the member states of the European Community will have to extend their own union into all those fields in which they seek equality with the United States, not only on commercial and monetary policy, but also in matters of technology, security and foreign policy. The United States, for its part, must be prepared to share the responsibility for decision-making in those fields in which a uniting Western Europe is capable of speaking with one voice. The European Summit of October 1972 has brought nearer the moment when the Community will be able to act in most areas of foreign economic and monetary policy. As regards foreign policy, especially outside its regional vicinity, the Community will only be able to move towards co-decision-making to the extent that it is able to discharge the burden of co-responsibility.

If equality is a precondition for mutually acceptable interdependence, then at first sight it would seem that such a relationship cannot exist in the security field. But America, too, depends for its security on Europe. The domination of Europe by the other super-power could completely upset the balance on which United States security rests. Only if the United States one day ceased to understand this interdependence would the Europeans have to face the choice of either accepting dependence (on the United States or the Soviet Union), or of attempting, at staggering economic and political cost, to provide that part of the nuclear deterrent now supplied by the United States.

The value of the security link to both partners is reduced if it is questioned. Such questioning would be implicit in any attempt by the US to deny interdependence and mutual self-interest, by using the security element to gain advantages in the economic field: the huge disparity between Europe and America in the nuclear field can only be accepted if their interdependence in security remains unquestioned.

Similarly, if interdependence in the economic field is denied on either side of the Atlantic through policies which take no account of the other partner's interests, the security link will not remain unaffected: unilateralism on the part of Europe would strengthen the hands of those in the US who plead for American disengagement from Europe. American disregard for European interests would cause Europeans to doubt the reliability of the American partner, and lead them to seek new ways of safeguarding their security interests.

The interaction between the two kinds of interdependence – in security and in economic affairs – therefore easily becomes a source of instability. This instability can be reduced in so far as both sides, at all times, retain a clear view of their 'global' interests. These are fundamentally joint interests which should leave no place for feelings of frustration or superiority on either side.

But the pursuit of a policy based on these interests is made difficult both by the current climate of opinion in the United States and by the unfinished structure of the European Community.

The changing attitude of the United States

Alexis de Tocqueville, when he visited the United States, was more profoundly struck by the differences between Europe and America than by the resemblances. The Americans he met seemed to wish to sing the praises of their own society, praising the superiority of a new civilisation as against older, declining, or even decadent societies.

A century and a half later, some Americans still have not lost their belief that their society is fundamentally superior. In a speech made at San Clemente, on July 4, 1972, President Nixon claimed that the United States were 'the best and strongest nation in the history of mankind'. The United States' role in two World Wars and especially in the last 'post-war' period gave them a profound belief in the inevitability and virtue of America's mission. But it is interesting to note that Tocqueville himself, who so greatly admired American democracy, fully approved of American foreign policy – because, he thought, it was passive rather than active. He quoted the famous letter from George Washington which urged Americans not to tie themselves to Europe or to any part of it and not to let themselves be drawn into factions – advice that was encouraged and backed by Thomas Jefferson. This shows that already at that time some Americans held a 'missionary' ambition and a desire to play the part of a 'policeman' outside the North American continent, even if their voices were not heard. Tocqueville believed that an abstentionist policy was wise, and that it owed its wisdom to the fact that foreign policy, unlike the rest of American policy-making, was based on 'aristocratic' principles: most of the powers in question were in the hands of the President, who was able to avoid the 'irrational emotions' of the people, which might have drawn the nation into the worst kinds of foreign adventure. There is an interesting parallel here with the current criticism of American post-war foreign policy, as expressed by such observers as John Kenneth Galbraith, who claim that America aims at leadership in all fields – strategic, tactical, and economic – a leadership modelled, according to Galbraith, on 'second-class imperialism'. In this analysis, foreign policy is marred by the excessive concentration of power in the hands of one man and of the establishment grouped around him – a system in which presidential errors are diluted and attributed to the administration. This leads, he has suggested, to the 'democratisation' of the mistakes and the 'aristocratisation' of any successes.

American policy *vis-à-vis* the rest of the world, as William Rogers has said, is 'a mixture of continuity and change'. But it is difficult to say exactly how far the change will go and how much continuity will remain. The United States have known a brief period of world leadership, during which they had two converging motives: to preserve American interests and to assure a measure of world order. Then, the pursuit of these goals was made easy by a Manichean view of the world which enabled them unreservedly to support the good against the wicked and the weak against the strong. The fact that this period is over is symbolised by President Nixon's visits to Peking and Moscow, where he shook the 'wicked' by the hand. At the same time, the weak no longer seem to enjoy a guarantee of protection and survival. This change is evident also in America's relationship with her friends, who were once protected and accorded favours, but who now are seen as critics and even as rivals on the economic and, perhaps, the political scene.

These changes in American foreign policy are also the inevitable fruit of profound changes in American society – including the growing influence attached to qualitative rather than quantitative factors, whether in criticism of economic growth and of the space programme or in re-evaluation of the

'American way of life'. Although this is not the place to examine these changes in depth, they increasingly influence those who are called upon to devise American foreign policy. Their effects can be seen in four or five areas:

A shift in priorities. It is now generally accepted that the solution of America's social problems (the cities, racial integration, drugs, unemployment) should take up a large part of the resources previously devoted to world commitments, to ventures such as the space programme, and to the support of a foreign clientele which is felt to be neither particularly grateful nor very reliable.

A new attitude towards foreign countries. The American way of life has lost its 'mythic' quality, resulting in a greater openness towards other ideologies and cultures.

A growing reluctance to leave foreign policy solely to the executive and a growing desire to introduce an expression of democratic will and control.

The growing awareness of the ecological consequences of growth, which is fostering a sense of co-responsibility and may lead Americans to seek new forms of collective action.

Changes in the attitude of Europe

Enlargement will have a profound effect on the Community both as regards the formation of its common policies and as regards the strengthening and development of its institutions. Great caution is therefore necessary in predicting its character and behaviour during the seventies.

The Community will have to deal with the problems of organising a new internal balance; a balance to be established between nine countries, and one that must replace the equilibrium achieved not without difficulties between the interests and priorities of the original Six. At the same time, new and difficult problems have to be solved: those posed by the transformation of society, spurred by the increased flow of ideas, persons and goods.

A further complication arises from two different tendencies with which the Community will have to learn to live. On the one side there is the tendency to be intransigent and slightly protectionist, and to lean towards technocracy and centralisation. On the other side there is a tendency – especially now that the Community is enlarged – towards free trade, towards mistrust of all excessive centralisation. The first tendency seeks above all a European identity. The second, rather indifferent to this quest, will be strengthened by the growing involvement in the affairs of the Community of neighbouring and often neutral European countries.

Given these differing tendencies, the weakness of the existing institutions may well become more obvious. It may become even more difficult for a Council of nine governments to take decisions on highly political subjects. The Commission may tend more and more to become a technical body which the governments will use as an intermediary and little more. The rule of unanimity, if applied as at present, will threaten to paralyse both the Council and the Commission. The Parliament, if not directly elected, will be in danger of becoming more and more a forum whose debates interest only specialists but have no impact on public opinion.

In the Community of Six, there was reason to fear the formation of a Franco-German bloc such as de Gaulle dreamed of, and by means of which France would have ruled the roost. In the Community of Nine, there is grave danger of returning to the classical game of the balance of power.

As a result of these internal contradictions, of the weight of existing structures, and of the weakness of the Community's institutions, the Government of Europe, in so far as it will exist at all, will be weak and therefore slow to take decisions; it will be incapable of dealing with sudden crises or of undertaking crisis management. This will be all the more so in so far as the institutions of the Community lack a body responsible for planning political action with a view of all the problems, internal as well as external, posed by the Community's existence.

In the economic field, not only different conceptions oppose each other, but the national systems themselves are different, rooted in ancient tradition and therefore difficult to change. Furthermore, large-scale resources are still devoted to maintaining anachronistic sectors of economic life while other resources are wasted on developing sectors of advanced technology in which the aim is often to re-invent for prestige reasons what already exists.

However, the gradual removal of economic frontiers should make possible a very profound and large-scale overhaul of these existing habits, and should help to eliminate at least the major contradictions without resulting in drab uniformity. The clash of different vested interests, ideas and traditions may also help make it possible to find and accept solutions which are in the general interest.

Nevertheless, in view of these differences in political and economic opinions, traditions, and interests, the Community will be very vulnerable and the handling of its external relations very difficult.

What is still lacking is a genuine political framework within which a fruitful confrontation of different ideas and objectives could take place. Europe has many a 'Forum': it still does not possess a 'Capitol'. There is no 'mediation'; there is no means of educating European opinion and thereby forming a European will, on any subject. The juxtaposition of a series of national wills and national conceptions, even if sound in themselves, often does not result in the emergence of a European viewpoint.

The unsolved institutional problems of the Community are thus not only an internal matter. Institutions are a precondition for the conduct of a common foreign policy, a goal which has, for the first time, been made the subject of official declarations by some heads of government during the Summit of October 1972. That conference has not solved the institutional problems. But by setting far-reaching targets for Community action in the future, it has made institutional progress nearly inevitable.

The mere fact of having asked the Community institutions to work out a global concept for the coming trade negotiations is important: it leads the Institutions to formulate a 'Community interest', which, because of the Community's greater weight and larger responsibilities, is different in kind from that of any single member state. Where each of the member states separately will pursue mainly economic interests, the Community as such must develop a broader, political concept of the collective interest.

This, however, is only a first step. As long as real powers of decision-making lie in the national capitals, the Community will find it difficult to be recognised and effective as a negotiating partner for the US. A divided Community will enter the coming dialogue with the United States from a position of weakness.

The Community, however, cannot avoid this dialogue. Without some agreement on the relationship which it should seek with the United States, the Community itself would find its internal development blocked and ultimately destroyed. There is no possibility that an agreement could ever be reached among the member states to turn the Community into an anti-American bloc. It is equally impossible that an agreement could be reached which would subject Europe to the hegemony of the United States.

As President Pompidou expressed it at the October Summit:

Our links with [the US], the world's foremost economic power with which eight of our countries are united within the Atlantic Alliance, are so close that it would be absurd to conceive of a Europe constructed in opposition to it. But the very closeness of these links requires that Europe affirm its individual personality with regard to the United States. Western Europe, liberated . . . thanks to the essential contribution of American soldiers, reconstructed with American aid, having looked for its security to the American alliance, having hitherto accepted American currency as the main element of its monetary reserves, must not and cannot sever its links with the United States. But neither must it refrain from affirming its existence as a new reality.

Agreement can only be sought and found along the lines already indicated: steps to strengthen the independence and the identity of Europe, and new manifestations of Europe's specific role in many fields of activity, must be accompanied by corresponding readiness to move towards 'negotiated interdependence'.

The Atlantic agenda

The capacity of Europe and America to engage in a structured dialogue will soon be put to a number of tests. Several issues,

chief among them monetary reform, demand immediate attention. Furthermore, important international negotiations
already scheduled on trade, East–West relations, and relations
with developing countries (which will themselves be an issue
in monetary reform, in trade talks, and in the renegotiation of
the Yaoundé Convention, starting in 1973) will require
Europe and America to define the terms of their future relationship.

The foregoing analysis of the two protagonists has shown
that neither is well prepared for this test. True, the United
States shows signs of upgrading its concern for European
matters, after some years of relative neglect, and of seeing in
the forthcoming negotiations with Eastern Europe a chance
to consolidate the peace and to adapt its relations with Europe
to fit new circumstances. But this emerging political vision is
not yet matched by an equally clear view of economic priorities, as political pressure to seek short-term advantages vies
with an older tradition of responsibility and restraint.

Monetary reform is the most urgent issue to which the Community and the United States will have to address themselves.
No other issue raises so sharply the principal question of their
relations: the delicate balance between independence, interdependence, or defiance. A successful solution of monetary
problems would ease tensions in international economic relations as a whole and, as suggested in the chapter on European
Defence, in the security field as well. Fortunately, there are
signs of convergence in official thinking on both sides of the
Atlantic. Greater flexibility of exchange rates between the
major economies, and some international discipline even on
surplus countries to keep realistic parities are now increasingly
accepted. As to the shift away from dollar and into SDRs
(with a residual role for gold) as reserve assets, the only major
disagreement now seems to be about the speed with which this
shift can take place, and the ways in which international
liquidity creation is to be managed.

But until these monetary issues are settled, the climate of
trade relations between Europe and America risks getting
worse before it gets better. The United States is in as tense a
mood as it was on August 15, 1971. External pressure from a
continued unsatisfactory balance of payments, and internal

pressure from protectionist forces in US trade unions and (non-multinational) industry, may lead to further unilateral action or uncompromising bargaining. The Community, apprehensive of the effects of enlargement, may hesitate to call in question common policies, the '*acquis communautaire*', even where the further pursuit of these policies may prove politically and economically damaging at home and abroad. True, both sides periodically reaffirm their commitment to an open world economy, but these statements, measured by their actions, sometimes sound rhetorical.

There is therefore a real danger that the test of coming negotiations may not be a fruitful one, but rather the sterile attempt to find out which of the two economic powers is an irresistable force, and which the immovable object. A co-operative approach to the problems of economic interdependence is the only one which can give the economic and social results which both sides seek to accomplish. But, paradoxically, the best hope for a more moderate and conciliatory climate in economic relations between the US and the Community may come from a rediscovery of the larger political context which has brought such moderation in the past.

Such a rediscovery may be stimulated by the series of inter-related negotiations with Eastern Europe and the Soviet Union referred to above. New rounds in the Strategic Arms Limitations Talks (SALT), exploration of the possibility of arriving at mutual and balanced force reductions (MBFR), and the Conference on Security and Co-operation in Europe (CSCE), all raise very fundamental issues, not only between East and West, but within the Alliance. Such basic negotiations tend to focus the attention of statesmen on long-term interests rather than short-term quarrels. The year of the enlargement of the Community may therefore – in spite of the difficulties – initiate a creative period in the relations between the United States and the Community.

Even if used to good purpose, this creative moment need not lead to the setting up of an elaborate new institutional structure in which to carry out the transatlantic dialogue. This is not the time for global blueprints. The most 'modern' of the institutions we now have, the GATT and the OECD, were slow adaptations rather than instant creations. But their evolution was only possible because there was an underlying political and intellectual consensus on the direction in which progress was to be made. The decade ahead, as has been argued elsewhere in this book, requires substantial progress on the road towards joint economic management among the industrialised countries. Much would be gained if a consensus on this goal were to guide what must, in the nature of things, be temporising negotiations on only parts of the economic agenda: monetary reform, non-tariff barriers or agriculture.

High on this agenda must also be a joint look by Europe and America at the problems of the less developed countries. Without a joint approach, there will be great reluctance by these two most important trading partners of the LDCs seriously to open their borders to the manufactured products of those countries: each would hesitate to carry alone the 'burden' of adjustment which such a step would involve. To mitigate such adjustment through a selective opening of frontiers to favoured regional partners – as is the case with the Community's preferential agreements – is certainly a second-best solution. Special economic links carry the risk of creating a political clientele. Such links are not only unsatisfactory in themselves; they also create divisions within the industrialised world and undermine the possibility of a joint approach by the developed to the problems of the less developed countries. Without a universal trading system, no effective development policy is possible. The untying of aid and the strengthening of multilateral aid machinery, which would provide substantial efficiency gains while avoiding the exploitation of the receiver's weakness, both require a non-discriminatory system.

Apart from these major issues a host of other, by no means minor, problems concern the industrialised world as a whole. These, too, would benefit from an attempt by the United States and Europe, in consultation with the other participants in the world economy, chief among them Japan, to discover areas of joint interest, and to advance these by co-ordinated action.

One of these is oil supplies, where the new US role as a major importer, the new strength of the producer countries, and the changing role of the major oil companies, are becoming a cause of uncertainty and concern for makers of public policy. Competition for the safest or cleanest oil, for privileged relations with one or the other producer area makes little sense in a world where each economy depends on the welfare of the other.

In areas where public policy makers want to exercise a measure of public control over oil companies and other multinational business, joint action will often be necessary to achieve this. A technically simple step, but one involving all the sensitivities of sovereignty, would be an exchange of information, and later common standards, on disclosures by such companies. Another area of industrial policy, the control of pollution, requires that the major trade competitors put roughly equal financial burdens on their industry. Here, too, talks on the timing and severity of standards could be pushed further than present efforts by international bodies.

In none of these areas can there be progress unless the major participants, Europe and America, with Japan, have a meeting of minds. This does not mean that they are to dictate policy to the others, but rather that they should remove what would be the most intractable obstacle to international agreement: disagreement among themselves. This has worked well in the Community of Six: agreement between Germany and France often paved the way for major advances. One should beware of formalising this tripartite leadership. At the same time, the search for agreement, and the pursuit of common economic objectives cannot be carried out in an entirely *ad hoc* fashion. A revitalisation of OECD as a forum for 'pre-negotiation' – the search for the facts *and* the technicalities and for policies to deal with problems – might be useful. This, however, demands flexible formulae which do not make such pre-negotiations dependent on the co-operation (and veto) of all members of OECD at all times.

Any such possibility of Europe's helping to shape the world economy of the future as an equal partner of the United States, of avoiding the *Diktat* of the forces of the international economy or of the policies pursued on the other side of the Atlantic, depends on the Community's ability to act as an entity on a much larger scale than before. This means not only an extension of the technical areas where the Commission has the right of initiative and negotiation. It means also an agreement by the member states on the broad lines of policy in a number of fields where 'foreign' and 'economic' policy are involved at the same time. Only with the support of such 'framework' agreements on broad lines of policy can the institutions of the Community find the freedom of action that is needed to carry out its new complex tasks.

8 East-West Relations

Michel Tatu

Although a generation has elapsed since World War II the European Community has still not worked out a common response to the challenge it faces in the division of Europe. Yet this issue is the touchstone of its ability to play a political role. What sense is there in speaking of its world responsibilities and its status as one of the world's great powers if it does not tackle the problem of its relations with its Eastern neighbours, and works out a coherent policy in this field, in terms of both security and co-operation? It is all the more natural that it should do so, in so far as the existence of the rigid Soviet bloc, the threat which that bloc seemed to represent and, more generally, the impasse in East–West relations after the war, were among the origins of Western Europe's first efforts to unite. Today, the sense of threat has greatly diminished; but the Community would not be what it is without an awareness of that 'other world' across the East–West frontier.

Let us look in turn at the context of East–West relations in Europe, at the objectives that the Community might set itself in its approach to the East European countries, and finally at what concretely might be done in the course of the next few years.

This not the place to give an exhaustive description of the situation on either side of what is still, unfortunately, the 'Iron Curtain'. A number of factors, however, influence the relations between Eastern and Western Europe.

The situation in Eastern Europe

Here, two main facts stand out. The first is the vast disproportion between the strength of the Soviet Union and that of the popular democracies. The second is the contrast and the time-lag between all these countries and those of the West.

Economically, the East European countries are some ten or

fifteen years behind Western Europe. True, the Soviet economy is very powerful, and capable of remarkable achievements in certain fields, as a result of the flexibility which it paradoxically derives from its system of central control. Thus, for example, the concentration of its resources has made possible the development of fearsome military power and the maintenance of high standards in related sectors such as space and the atom. Elsewhere, however, the system shows all the faults of such excessive centralisation: a lack of initiative, errors in planning, arbitrary prices, etc. One result has been that during the 1960s the economies of the USSR and its allies failed to undergo the technological revolution experienced in the West; and they are finding this failure very difficult to remedy, notably in the development and use of electronics.

The same is true of the standard of living, where despite slow progress the gap dividing East from West is widening rather than narrowing. It is particularly great in such matters as the efficiency of services, the development of leisure, freedom to travel, and the abundance of information, all of which account for much of the progress made in the societies of the West. It is true that these disadvantages have recently been offset by another factor. Not having enjoyed the benefits of the 'consumer society', the countries of the East have also been spared most of its disadvantages. Despite industrial pollution, the problems of urban overcrowding and psychological tension, indeed many of the ills affecting the quality of life, are much less acute in the East than in the West; there, the demand is still overwhelmingly quantitative. But this in turn leads to further widening of the gap between Eastern and Western society. While Communist societies have lost much of their force of attraction for Western revolutionary youth, the opposition in the East, disconcerted by the ideology of Western rebels and unable to grasp the nature of the *malaise* and other problems caused by over-development, is beginning to wonder whether the West will long retain the attractions which it has hitherto seemed to offer.

Politically, the single-party system which exists *de facto* or *de jure* in all the Eastern countries, and the absence of all organised opposition, have kept their institutions and ideas well apart from developments in Western Europe. At the top, priority is given to the perpetuation of party rule, and to the ideological norms from which it is supposed to derive its legitimacy. Economic growth and a higher standard of living are certainly sought after, but only as a second priority. This is the reason for the slowness and difficulty of achieving economic reforms which further this second objective but threaten the Party's monopoly of power. Similarly, the rejection of all ideological and political pluralism prevents any true interpenetration of culture or the free movement of men and ideas.

At the grass roots, the monopoly which the Party enjoys in all spheres has produced a virtually atomised society in which the different social groups have no organic means of expression of their own. At the same time, these societies are in general more homogeneous than in the West, owing to the great levelling of incomes effected by the original revolution. True, a new stratification has emerged since then; but between the highly privileged classes at the top – Party and government leaders, scientists, official artists and writers – and the mass of the people there are very few middle classes. As for the 'technocrats', despite efforts to 'integrate' them in the GDR, Hungary, and Roumania, they seem likely to remain for a long time on the fringes of real power.

The Soviet Union

These characteristics are shared by all the countries of Eastern Europe; but they are still more marked in the Soviet Union, the 'mother' of all the various Communist systems. Its internal conservatism is necessarily more accentuated, if only because it is the guarantor of the various 'daughter' systems elsewhere. What is more, since Khrushchev's attempts at 'modernisation' undivided power is once more in the hands of the Party *apparat* and its representatives, and in particular the ageing but still active generation of leaders trained in the Stalinist school. There is very strong pressure, therefore, not only to maintain the Party's prerogatives, but also to perpetuate its traditional 'style' of leadership. This implies the maintenance of some degree of tension, or at least of opposition, *vis-à-vis* the West and the democratic system. The latter are no longer necessarily held to be 'aggressive' in the military sense of the term, but they have to serve as a kind of artificial enemy, an opponent which it would be dangerous for Soviet society to be associated with. True détente, therefore, which would involve interpenetration between the two societies, is impossible so long as the present generation of 'apparatchiks' remains in power.

And yet the situation is slowly evolving. The policy of 'dialogue' with Western Europe and the United States must surely, in the long run, eliminate the old conditioned reflexes. In more general terms, the ideological tone, the faith in the virtues of the Soviet system, are now no longer what they were under Stalin and even under Khrushchev. White-collar workers, who have already taken on many bourgeois characteristics, are attracted by Western products, the Western way of life, and the efficiency of Western management. Conscious of the defects of their own economy, Soviet leaders are seeking more and more to exploit Western technology and know-how, and to this end they have concluded some important cross-frontier contracts. The population at large, in spite of censorship, is better informed about reality in the rest of the world. Now that repression had been reduced to what is considered 'necessary' – and no longer includes, as under Stalin, what is superfluous – a kind of public opinion can be said to exist. Even the organised opposition, which finds its expression in such clandestine writings as the *samizdat* publications, is no longer negligible. But despite these developments, there are still important limits on the development of East–West co-operation.

In the economic field, exchanges with the West will always be marginal by comparison with the size of the Soviet market. More than any other country in the world, the USSR is in a position to be almost self-sufficient if need be: its foreign trade is only a tiny fraction of its GNP. For the same reason, even the most ambitious projects for co-operation with the West are only a drop in the ocean: they offer less hope than elsewhere of leading to a reform in the structure of the Soviet economy. What is more, so long as the present political system survives, any desire on the part of Moscow's leaders for trade with the West will always take second place to their fundamental political preoccupation – that is, to maintain all the prerogatives of the Party.

In the field of ideas, it is not even certain that genuine liberalisation would lead to a *rapprochement* between the USSR and the systems of the West. The old dispute between 'Westernists' and 'Slavophiles' is still not dead: among present-day opponents of the régime, alongside the 'democratic movement' which believes in the rights of man and in Western forms of liberty, there is a movement no less strong known as 'Russite', which calls for a return to tradition and to a Greater Russian nationalism strongly tinctured with chauvinism. In other words, even after the present generation of Soviet leaders has passed, there may well be a new move to the Right, in particular through the emergence of a more efficient but still 'hard-line' régime, backed by the 'technocrats', the army, and the nationalists.

Finally, the Soviet Union is not merely a European but also a world power. Its military strength is now for the first time as great as that of the United States; its ambitions are on the same scale and often employ the same methods (naval power, the conclusion of pacts, the installation of bases, etc.); and it faces similar security problems outside Europe, mainly *vis-à-vis* China, which oblige it to pursue an active policy in Asia. In this respect, by comparison with the United States, the Soviet Union faces the disadvantage of greater burdens, but enjoys the advantage of being able to operate in several different theatres at the same time. Thus, whereas the United States is geographically distant from Europe and from Asia, the USSR can present itself now as a European power, now as an Asian power: in this way it can claim that most of the world's trouble-spots (the Near East, the Indian sub-continent, etc.) affect it directly because they are 'close to its frontiers'.

In this situation, it would be vain for Europeans to seek to ensure their security by means of bilateral disarmament, or to hope that negotiations with the Soviets on force reductions could lead to a real diminution of Soviet military power. The Kremlin is certainly interested in negotiating mutual balanced force reductions in Europe, in order to consolidate Western détente – the more so since these negotiations offer every prospect of accentuating the differences of view among its Western partners. But it will always be able to argue that it needs greater strength than anyone else in order to meet its obligations in other theatres.

Even so, Western Europe, which is a formidable concentration of industrial power on the threshold of the Soviet Union and which, although strategically exposed, is a pole of attraction for the popular democracies, cannot but be a priority area of Soviet foreign policy. To think that in Russian eyes it was no more than a 'backyard' to be neutralised in order to make possible greater concentration on the 'main front', i.e. China, would be to underestimate Europe's importance. The policy of all-round détente which was launched in Europe by Brezhnev in 1969, and of which the Berlin agreement of 1971 was both the symbol and the pledge, is a response to a number of pre-occupations, not all of which are defensive or conservative.

The consolidation of the *status quo* in Eastern Europe – meaning the recognition not only of existing frontiers but also of the present régimes between the Elbe and the Bug – is certainly the first priority in Soviet thinking, and the precondition for all other objectives. It has been largely achieved already by means of the German Soviet and German–Polish Treaties signed in 1970 by the Brandt Government and ratified by the Federal Republic in the summer of 1972; but similar recognition has yet to be obtained from the whole European 'concert of powers', and this will in particular be sought at the Conference on Security and Co-operation in Europe. Beyond such consolidation of the *status quo* in the East, the Soviet Union has further objectives more directly centred on Western Europe.

It wishes, first, to encourage the present trend towards American disengagement, to slow down (as far as possible, for here Soviet ability is limited) the movement towards political and military unity in Western Europe, and to enable Soviet industry to profit from the West's technological resources. A Europe economically advanced, but politically disunited and militarily weak, is what most appeals to the Soviet leadership.

It is further anxious to influence the foreign policies of Western Governments in such a way as to neutralise any anti-Soviet tendencies, and foster on their part a policy of systematic friendship with the USSR. Soviet relations with France are in this respect held up as an example in other capitals, making it possible both to use France as a pole of attraction, and to oppose her to her partners (Great Britain, the Federal Republic, Italy, etc.) when the latter are more refractory. This attitude of 'the outstretched hand' is in any case more tempting to the 'bourgeois' Governments in so far as it in no way encourages the local Communist parties to follow an actively revolutionary line, as was the case in the post-war years, and so does not encourage internal crises. The aim is to influence governments rather than forces of opposition, and foreign policy rather than domestic affairs.

A third Soviet aim is to secure a footing in West European organisations by means of the permanent machinery which is seen as one outcome of the Conference on Security and Co-operation in Europe. Represented in this machinery, Moscow would have a say in matters concerned with the European Community, its enlargement to other countries than the Nine, its economic and monetary union, etc. Once again, although the United States is to be invited to attend the Conference the Soviet Union can count on enjoying a more favourable position from which to interfere in West European affairs, either directly, as a fully-fledged European power, or through the intermediary of its Eastern allies. The same machinery should also be an effective platform from which to put obstacles in the way of Western Europe's political and military unification.

These objectives seem mutually contradictory, or at least logically inconsistent. In the East, the aim is to consolidate the *status quo*, to strengthen the cohesion and integration of the members of the system, and to limit its penetration by Western influence. In the West, on the other hand, the aim is to loosen the bonds among the members of the EEC and between them and the United States, to hinder further integration, and to facilitate the penetration of Soviet influence. But in reality this contradiction is in no way at variance with Soviet interests, and it therefore in no way embarrasses the Kremlin. Nevertheless, it involves a gamble, in so far as it implicitly concedes that the West, formally at least, enjoys possibilities of introducing its influence into Eastern Europe similar to those which it intends to exploit on its own account in the West. The disunity of

Western Europe, the multiplicity of its centres of decision-making, and its lack of a common doctrine, give the Soviet Union a good chance of succeeding in its gamble: but the game could become too risky if the various Western allies, and in particular the members of the Community, were to show greater unity and greater decisiveness.

The other countries of Eastern Europe

With the exception of Yugoslavia, which had the 'luck' to be excluded from the 'family' in 1948 and has no plans for returning to it – and with the exception also of tiny Albania, which later on used the Yugoslav screen and the protection of China to secede – the six countries in the area between the Elbe and the Bug and between the Baltic and the Black Sea which is covered by the Warsaw Pact all rely on Soviet protection and all have political systems officially modelled on that of the USSR. Nevertheless, there are important differences between them and the Soviet Union, and they are more open to Western influence.

They were latecomers to the Soviet system, and its most extreme version, the Stalinist variant, covered only a very short period – scarcely eight years, from 1948 to 1956. The old generation of leaders in these countries has earlier memories, especially of the pre-war bourgeois system, while the new generation has lived through the traumas of destalinisation, the Hungarian uprising, and the dramatic events in Czechoslovakia and Poland. Public opinion, following a deep-rooted historical tradition, is for the most part oriented towards the liberal values of the West: there are few representatives of the Right-wing, anti-Liberal tendencies already noted in the USSR.

At the top, these countries' leaders certainly give priority to the system and its maintenance in power, but everyone knows that the real judge of whether or not their régime is orthodox is the Soviet Union. The result is that, within the limits of elementary prudence dictated by circumstances beyond their control, these régimes can be much more flexible than that of the Soviet Union.

In the economic field, none of these countries can afford to live in a state of near self-sufficiency, as the Soviet Union can. All are very largely open to the rest of the world. Owing to the small scale of their economies, to the traditional upbringing of their managerial classes, and to the less dogmatic attitude of the Party leaders, trade with the West has much more effect on the standard of living and on organisational methods here than in the USSR. Not only in Yugoslavia but also in Hungary, in the GDR, and in Bulgaria, there has been considerable 'debureaucratisation' in the field of foreign trade, facilitating contacts with Western firms. But there are, of course, limits to this development, and not merely for political reasons. The drive for industrialisation in the 1950s led to the establishment in these countries of industries that were ill-adapted to natural conditions, and largely dependent on Soviet raw materials. In addition, their time-lag *vis-à-vis* the West, and their lack of competitiveness, make very acute the problems of exporting to the West and securing hard currencies. For the most part, therefore, these countries are obliged to trade among themselves. As a result, three types of external trade coexist alongside each other:

'Semi-colonial' trade with the Soviet Union, inverting the usual order of things in a colonial relationship, in that the East European countries buy raw materials and other unfinished products from their 'mother country', and sell it finished products and capital goods. It is true that the Soviets also supply their allies with some industrial products, and that they are trying to increase this trade under the various programmes of specialisation and division of labour that have been applied during the last few years. But the biggest category of Soviet exports to the other East European countries remains that of raw materials – which causes friction, since the Soviet Union not only charges different prices to its Eastern and Western customers, but also has for some years demanded that its allies should contribute to the more and more costly investments that are needed to extract and transport the raw materials in question (in particular, Siberian oil).

More 'normal' trade among the various 'small' popular democracies: the exchange of finished or semi-finished products on the basis of division of labour between economies of comparable size. Although naturally better balanced, this trade is not completely 'normal' owing to the rigidity of the bureaucratic structures involved, the artificiality of the prices quoted, and the inconvertibility of the national currencies. Some of these difficulties may be reduced by internal reforms, and possibly also under the 'Complex Programme' for greater integration in COMECON adopted in 1971.

More 'modern' trade with the countries of the West: exporting the best products of agriculture or industry in exchange for imports of advanced technology. This is also the trade that has the most 'modernising effects, in so far as its development leads to greater flexibility in the bureaucratic structure, greater autonomy on the part of enterprises, and more efficient management. But it is seriously limited by the shortage of hard currency and also, in a lesser degree, by trade barriers in the West, such as the common external tariff of the EEC and especially its levies on imports of agricultural products.

Finally as regards trends in opinion, the most striking characteristic of the East European countries is their nationalism. Paradoxically, these countries have in effect succumbed to the domination of the greatest power on the continent, which is also one of the most backward and least 'progressive' in the true sense of the word. Whereas American influence quite naturally spread in Western Europe after the War, owing not only to the military but also to the economic, technological and even cultural predominance of the United States, the Soviet Union in almost every case exported its own system by force of arms, without decisive cultural or economic superiority: the economic, technological, and intellectual capital of the countries which it took under its protectorate was in general higher than its own, as was – and is – their standard of living.

Soviet domination is thus essentially military and political, i.e. blantant. It is all the more so owing to the Soviet leaders' totalitarian view of power and influence. For them, military occupation and top-level pressure are not enough: they also expect from the countries under their domination some manifestation of 'eternal' friendship, obligatory reverence for 'Big Brother', and so on. The result is strong – and anti-Soviet – nationalism, all the greater for being daily provoked.

Although officially condemned and repressed, this nationalist feeling nevertheless has repercussions even on a political level. In Roumania, the Gheorghiu–Dej régime simply assimilated it into official policy – as has that of Ceaucescu, thereby acquiring a legitimacy it would otherwise have lacked. In Yugoslavia and Albania, resistance to Soviet interference has been made a cardinal feature of official doctrine in both cases, whatever the other differences between them. These are the most spectacular examples; but all the Eastern régimes, in a greater or less degree, can be said to be seeking to preserve their national identities and to have had at one time or another to restrain the excessive pretensions of Moscow. Some, like Kadar in Hungary and, apparently, Gierek in Poland, are trying to achieve greater freedom of action for internal reforms at the cost of stricter alignment in their foreign policy. Other countries, like Roumania, like the GDR under Ulbricht, or like Poland in recent years under Gomulka, seem to want greater external freedom of action at the cost of a 'hard-line' policy at home. Only the present Czechoslovak régime has had to give up all vestiges of independence both at home and abroad, which is why it is so unpopular. Indeed, it will not be solidly established until it can show that it is trying, if only in a single policy field, to resist Soviet interference. This in itself is a strong temptation for Husak or for whoever comes after him.

The Soviet occupation of Prague in 1968, moreover, led to a development of nationalist feeling almost everywhere, since it confirmed what was already implicit: i.e. that the barrier to freedom and reform, in the last resort, was not so much the local Communist system as the physical or moral presence of the USSR. Where true independence has been achieved, as in Yugoslavia, changes have been possible that have led to a high degree of freedom. In most other East European countries, a satisfactory *modus vivendi* between the Party and the people is certainly conceivable; but the prerequisite is to solve the problem of relations between the Party and Moscow. The Soviet leaders are aware of this nationalism, as they are aware of

how exposed their allies are to Western influence. This is the
weakest point of their system, and one which also faces the
Western powers with a delicate problem in working out their
policy *vis-à-vis* the East.

The Western approach

Hitherto, the member states of the European Community have
pursued independent policies *vis-à-vis* Eastern Europe. The
only solidarity that has been recognised – and that not always –
is Atlantic solidarity. The only agreement at a purely European
level was, first, to do nothing that would harm the existence and
maintenance of the Common Market, and secondly to try to
reduce East–West tension, or in other words to encourage
détente. But the various West European countries are far from
having the same interests and concerns; and at least three tendencies can be distinguished.

France has no problems of a national scale to discuss with
the East. Contrary to fairly widespread belief, she has not even
any particular affinity with the East European countries, despite the fact that they have for centuries looked towards
French culture. The various Eastern alliances formed by Paris
over the last century have no very deep roots. Concluded for
tactical reasons – most frequently, for fear of Germany – they
have ended either in disappointment (as with Russia at the
turn of the century), or in impotence (as in the case of
Poland), if not in betrayal (as of Czechoslovakia at Munich).
Today, especially, with no particular danger threatening,
France's East European policy is rather a kind of luxury, from
which benefits are expected that often have very little to do
with the region in question – as for instance to counterbalance
American influence, to 'contain' Germany, or to be involved
in the great affairs of the world: the aim, in other words, is to
enlarge the freedom of action of the nation-state by means of
the traditional balance of power. This was above all the
policy of General de Gaulle; but elements of it will continue
to be latent so long as Eastern policy is not closely co-ordinated by all the Community's member states.

Great Britain is somewhat in the same situation, for she has
barely any interests in Eastern Europe outside the field of

trade. Although more clearly oriented towards Western Europe, the United States, and the Commonwealth, she is able to deal with the USSR and its allies in a somewhat detached manner, and either to practise a policy of détente or to take a harder line (as when 105 Soviet diplomats and civil servants were expelled from London), without markedly affecting her own interests.

The German Federal Republic has greater affinities with her Eastern neighbours, for geographical reasons and because of her traditional influence in Eastern Europe; but above all it is the East that holds the key to her main national problem: German reunification. Whether the Eastern policy pursued by Bonn be rigid and conservative, as it was under Adenauer, or conciliatory, as under Willy Brandt, it is never opportunistic or a matter of indifference: it is always the result of a fundamental choice. In the case of Willy Brandt's *Ostpolitik*, the renunciation *de jure* of the 1937 frontiers, and *de facto* of the reunification of Germany, is only justified in a context where the principle of nationalism has lost its primacy and been replaced by something more important. In the last resort, supranationalism in the West should be the logical counterpart of the national amputation accepted in the East. It would be vain, no doubt, to ask Germany's partners to accept supranationalism for this reason alone. But the fact remains that since the German problem is the main area in which the improvement of relations with the East can have concrete and favourable political consequences for a West European State – the Federal Republic – solidarity with that State should have priority over all other considerations, and in particular over the transient and opportunistic advantages that in other countries sometimes masquerade behind the policy of détente.

A third approach is more difficult to associate with any given country. This is the pacifist approach, with all its possible variants, ranging from underestimation of the military aspects of security to pro-Soviet idealism, from a taste of self-criticism to a negation of all Western values, from anti-Americanism to reliance on the United States assuming all the burdens of defence. Although mostly a matter of public opinion and prevalent among the young and on the Left, certain elements of this approach may now and then influence the attitude of governments, especially in the small countries, where the temptations of neutralism are stronger. In fact, this attitude is based more on internal considerations and on introspection – concern for the quality of life in the West – than on an overall examination of the situation in Europe, and especially in the countries of the East. Anxious to reach conclusions that fit the point of departure, which is essentially concerned with affairs at home, those who adopt this attitude often ascribe to the Governments of Eastern Europe concerns and intentions that they do not have.

Although confined to those who hold them and scarcely reflecting the facts, these opinions will nevertheless affect East–West relations in Europe if they develop. In the last resort, any serious internal crisis in a Community country, or any fundamental challenge to the *status quo* in the West, would have at least as important an effect on East–West relations as would a crisis in the East: Soviet leaders would not fail to take an interest in it as a source of new opportunities. More generally, however, no Eastern European policy of any importance can be pursued without a minimum of stability and consensus among West-Europeans, not only on the problems of the East, but on relations with the United States and on the role of Europe in the world.

So far, there has been close solidarity among the allies on one point only, although an important one: the negotiation of the agreement on Berlin and the support of Willy Brandt's *Ostpolitik*. As soon as the dialogue with the East becomes the affair, not only of the four NATO powers involved in these negotiations, but of all the members of the Community and of the neutrals, it will be necessary to go very much further.

The aims of the European Community: security and beyond

In this general context, what should be the aims of the enlarged Community's policy regarding Eastern Europe? Briefly, they should be concerned on the one hand with security, and on the other with what 'lies beyond security'.

Rightly or wrongly, in the years immediately following World War II, the military security of Western Europe was believed to be under threat. The Soviet leaders were credited with aggressive intentions, but it was not realised that they lacked the resources to carry such intentions out. The American nuclear monopoly made the Atlantic 'umbrella' almost totally credible, while the USSR's conventional military strength was in reality much less powerful than was thought. Today, this situation is reversed: everyone recognises the military strength of the USSR, both conventional and nuclear, and hence the diminished credibility of the American guarantee; at the same time Moscow's intentions are now thought to be less aggressive. But is it reasonable to base one's security policy merely on the potential adversary's intentions – which may change – rather than on his capabilities, which are being maintained and developed?

The answer is obviously 'no'; and with it begin all the inextricable problems of West European defence. This is not the place to examine in detail all the various imaginable options: the establishment of independent defence on the part of a European super-state, full reliance on the United States and NATO, purely 'moral' defence, etc. These questions are dealt with in Chapters 1 and 6 of the present book. Suffice it to note that the choice which is made, whatever it is, will profoundly affect the character of East–West relations in Europe. The Soviet leaders would very probably prefer a 'diminished *status quo*' involving the maintenance of Western Europe's military inferiority and the gradual erosion of the American guarantee and of Europe's links with the United States. In their eyes, present tendencies seem to be moving in this direction, which is why a more threatening attitude on the part of the East can be considered very unlikely in the foreseeable future: the result would be that the United States would return in force to Europe and/or that the countries of Western Europe would make a joint military effort – both of which the Kremlin is anxious to avoid. Equally, the development of political and military unity in Western Europe, accompanied by substantial rearmament, would lead to a period of tension with the East; but if this period could be lived through without too much difficulty, relations could later be normalised on a new basis. Intermediate solutions, such as Franco–British nuclear co-operation, multilateral co-operation in conventional defence, etc., would lead to similar reactions, whose intensity would vary, however, according to the degree of 'provocation' that Moscow thought was involved.

Beyond security

European security cannot be considered merely in military terms. It is also a political matter, and depends very much on what happens in Eastern Europe. And here too the aims of the West Europeans need to be defined more clearly, since a number of ambiguities surround the notion of détente.

In principle, and granted that the security of Western Europe has been and still is more or less assured, West Europeans ought to desire the preservation of the *status quo*, not only in the West but also in the East. Political stability is an essential ingredient in security, and it was realised or sensed at the time of the Hungarian and Czechoslovak crisis in 1956 and 1968 that a revolution in one of the countries of Eastern Europe was not necessarily to the advantage of Western Governments, even if it reflected the liberal aspirations they share. The mere fact that such revolutions make the Soviet leaders nervous is in fact disquieting for everyone. At the same time, however, conservatism of this sort runs counter to the ambitions of the peoples of Eastern Europe, as well as to the Western Governments' legitimate desire to encourage the free movement of men and ideas. The solution, if such it be, lies in gradual evolution; but the difficulties must not be underestimated. In the first place, the history of Communist régimes is seldom smooth: it moves by fits and starts, through a series of crises of succession (the death of Stalin, the fall of Khrushchev, the struggle between Novotny and Dubček, etc.). In the second place, the influence that the West can bring to bear on events in Eastern Europe is virtually nil, since the dangers that threaten the authorities there are internal, not external. All the more reason, therefore, to bear in mind the continual latent risk of serious and even violent crises – without, of course, giving up the effort to encourage the gradual and peaceful evolution of East–West relations.

Which should take priority – the improvement of relations with the USSR or with the popular democracies? It is natural – although such an attitude can only be tactical – to answer that Western Europe must seek détente with all these countries at the same time, indiscriminately. In reality, the policy of independence pursued by certain East European countries, such as Yugoslavia or Roumania, makes it often necessary to choose: any given agreement or decision may please Moscow and displease Bucharest, or *vice versa*. This is all the more so at times of crisis: the passivity of Western Europe in face of the mounting pressure on the Dubček régime in the weeks before August 1968 was in itself a political choice.

In purely selfish and conservative terms, it would seem natural to accord priority to the Soviet Union, the strongest power on the continent and the only one which is capable of threatening Western Europe. In so far as the Kremlin is the guarantor of the *status quo*, and in so far as the *status quo* serves the security of Western Europe, it is the Kremlin that seems to warrant support. The Soviet leadership, moreover, has sufficient control over the foreign policy of almost all its allies to oppose any unilateral détente which was not to the advantage of the USSR. Détente, it has often been said, begins at Moscow.

The objection to this argument is that it contradicts the ideals of freedom and independence espoused by the Governments of the West, and that in this sense it threatens further to tarnish their image for the peoples of the East. But there is a further objection: that in the long term such a policy is unrealistic. There is no ignoring the fact that the basic source of tension on the European continent is, and no doubt will be more and more, the control which Moscow exerts over her allies, and the anti-Soviet nationalism which is everywhere its result. The apparent calm of the present situation may be seductive: but it will not prevent crises in the future. A more long-term objective, that of 'another Europe', must brighten the vision of the enlarged Community.

What form could such 'another Europe' take? Leaving aside whatever unforeseen and unforeseeable changes may take place within Soviet society, such a 'new Europe' would offer a better future to the hundred million Europeans who live between the Baltic and the Black Sea and between the Bug and the Elbe: it would at the same time fulfil their ambition to be freed from Soviet domination and their hopes of freedom at home, take account of the special situation they have inherited from a quarter-century of Socialist change, and finally help them to overcome their economic backwardness. The formation of a group more flexible than at present, linked with the Soviet Union in a security system similar to that which links Western Europe with the United States, while respecting the legitimate interests of Moscow, would seem to be the optimum solution.

It would be natural for these countries, once they had achieved greater independence, to turn more than at present towards Western Europe; but they would also be well-advised not to become too dependent upon the enlarged Community, which will be economically far more powerful. The establishment of an East European common market as the first step towards a form of confederation, could help to lessen such a risk. It is significant that some Communist leaders, like Dimitrov, put forward ideas of this sort just after the war in the euphoria which followed their coming to power. At that time, naturally, they were promptly rejected by Stalin's 'recall to order', but they were never entirely forgotten. It may be that the 'Complex Programme' adopted by the COMECON countries in 1971 included certain elements that might be exploited in this sense by some of its adherents.

Clearly, the Soviet leadership is too much wedded to its present system of domination to countenance such changes at the present time, and they therefore could only be effected in the long term. Nevertheless, there is nothing rash about bearing them in mind and nothing unrealistic in deciding to avoid any steps which might hinder them. Without calling in question the *status quo* (and in any case the 'other Europe' suggested here would not seek to alter either the existing frontiers or the present régimes), the enlarged Community ought to avoid any action which directly or indirectly might serve to consolidate the hegemony of the Soviet Union in Eastern Europe. For example, agreements concerning any East European state ought to be negotiated and concluded with that state alone, and without giving the impression of seeking prior approval from Moscow. Unfortunately, it is just this impression that has been given on a number of occasions both by the East European policy of General de Gaulle and by the *Ost politik* pursued by Willy Brandt.

In the field of trade, as will be seen later, there are ways and means of assisting the popular democracies without necessarily 'provoking' the USSR. Nor is it necessary to barter recognition of the EEC by Moscow – which *de facto* Brezhnev has already granted – against official recognition of COMECON, at least in its present form, in which the USSR plays the dominating role. Finally, President Nixon's visits to Bucharest and Belgrade – not to mention his visit to Peking – *before* his visit to Moscow showed that if gestures of this kind do not exactly delight the Soviet leadership, they certainly do not prevent a fruitful dialogue with it.

For the same reasons, a more active China policy seems much to be desired. China, after all, is the only Communist country which has openly welcomed the enlargement of the EEC and would like to see it strengthened. There is good reason to bear this in mind, the more particularly since the Community could gain greater respectability in the eyes of the Third World as a result of approval from Peking, well-known as a champion of the peoples of Asia, Africa, and Latin America. China, too, understands the European situation well enough not to object to the Community's intention to enjoy, if possible, good relations with the Soviet Union. It is true that Peking poses as the resolute adversary of Moscow, and that some people fear that an active China policy might compromise the dialogue with the USSR, which, after all is so much closer to Western Europe. But this entirely depends on the spirit in which the dialogue is conducted.

What should that spirit be? Let it be said at once that the notion of détente is unsatisfactory as a way of describing the optimum relationship with Moscow. General de Gaulle spoke of 'détente, entente, and co-operation': but a much better formula is 'dialogue and co-operation'.

This not merely a matter of words. Détente, and more especially entente, suggest that there is a general climate that is thought to affect the whole relationship between two countries. That presupposes a certain community of ideas and a certain similarity of internal structure, such as exist among the various countries of the European Community. But the Soviet leaders – even if they too use these expressions in their speeches – scarcely believe in the notion of 'climate' in general and of détente in particular: we have already observed that the maintenance of their domestic system demands a certain degree of tension, of 'alienation', between their country and the outside world.

To proclaim a policy of détente, moreover, implies a commitment to good relations with Moscow in all fields, right across the board. To accept such a commitment would somewhat restrict one's freedom of action, particularly since in the last resort its success or failure depends on the Soviet Government. It takes two to make a détente, and by threatening at any moment to take a harder line the Kremlin can always force the other country to make dangerous and ever-growing concessions.

That is why a policy of dialogue, pursued as opportunities present themselves and without inhibitions on any subject of common interest, seems by far to be preferred. Such a policy need naturally not exclude wide-ranging economic, technological, and cultural co-operation; it merely implies that a proper order of priorities be observed among the various interests in question, and that the freedom of action of the Western Governments be broadened rather than narrowed thereby.

As regards priorities, one crucial question needs to be answered fairly soon. Should the Community put the improvement of its relations with the East higher or lower on its agenda than the closer unification of Western Europe? Hitherto, the Western Governments have evaded this question, or rather – very naturally – they have acted as if it did not exist. Both policies, it was said, must be pursued in parallel as long as they possibly could, and the choice in the last analysis was in the hands of the East. It was for Brezhnev to decide when and how he would oppose integration in the West.

But there is no disguising the fact that the Soviet leadership would not like to see any progress towards political and, still more, military union in Western Europe. In the latter case, indeed, one could not rule out a suspension of the policy of détente, or even a more lively reaction which might temporarily worsen the security situation. Conversely, in the event of American disengagement, the only alternative to a joint military effort on the part of the West European countries would be for them to conduct their dialogue with the Soviet Union from a position of inferiority, which would lead in the long run to appeasement and capitulation to Soviet demands. That would not be a good solution either.

In any event, as regards political integration, the pursuit of European unity is too important and too promising to be sacrificed to hopes of détente with the East, which are still very vague and uncertain. The prospect of true détente within the Eastern bloc, which alone would make possible a genuine pan-European reconciliation, might conceivably merit serious consideration. But it is impossible to imagine the Kremlin proposing such a bargain; and, even if it did, all the economic, political, and other motives that West Europeans have for affirming their solidarity *vis-à-vis* the rest of the world would remain valid.

In this field, as in many others, relations with Eastern Europe raise the same questions concerning the European Community's future role in the world as are studied in other chapters of the present book. The security problem already raised the issue of relations with the United States. The choice of a global role for Europe raises that of political as well as trade relations with Japan, also an economic power on a world scale and one more committed even than the Community to a growing political role. In Western Europe's relations with the East, it is clear that a balanced dialogue, conducted autonomously by the Community with Moscow and its allies, is only possible if the West Europeans decide to organise themselves in a highly articulated system which is both politically and militarily strong. If they do not, or cannot, co-operation with the East will still be possible, but any dialogue is likely to be more apparent than real, and to avoid the important subjects – as it often has hitherto. The result would be no more than the vague notion of détente already described.

Economic Co-operation and the European Security Conference

These larger objectives should not be lost to view; but equally they should not be allowed to distract attention from more concrete possibilities for Community action in the months and years to come. Two such possibilities are economic co-operation and the Conference on Security and Co-operation in Europe.

The development of East–West trade in Europe has faced and still faces two difficulties: first, the lack of competitive goods for the East European countries to export, and hence their shortage of hard currency; and secondly, the deadweight of bueaucratic procedure in the state-controlled economies. But these two difficulties, which are clearly interlinked, are less evident in some places than others. While all the East European countries ask their suppliers for credits to finance their imports, some of them – in particular Yugoslavia and Hungary – are gradually abandoning the most rigid of their procedures, such for example as the ban on suppliers making direct contact with the user of the goods or equipment being sold. It is quite understandable that the Community should prefer to deal with those countries that undertake such reforms; and this needs no particular urging on its part, since businessmen are glad to operate wherever they find the best welcome.

But since the credits that the West European economies can grant are limited, the Governments of the Nine and the Community would be wise to collaborate in guaranteeing their credits wherever the effect on the economy of the beneficiary and on the standard of living of its people will be most rapidly felt. As has been said, the popular democracies of Eastern Europe are much more receptive in this respect than the USSR, where the influx of Western technology is much more of a drop in the ocean. In choosing among the different possible beneficiaries, the Community should make no secret of the fact that it intends to favour those countries that undertake internal reforms to make their management methods less rigid – not because it wishes to encourage political developments, although genuine economic reforms do have political effects, but simply because a broad measure of 'debureaucratisation' in the East European economies is the necessary precondition for progress and hence for better returns on the investments that West European countries make in granting them credits.

In fact, the notion of trade has already been somewhat overtaken by the development of a more complex form of economic relationship which seems likely to grow in years to come. This is technological co-operation, usually by means of joint industrial projects in which the Western element is often supplied by multinational companies. Such products demand large-scale investments, e.g. the Fiat factory at Togliattigrad in the USSR, the trans-Siberian pipeline, or the Kama truck factory. Curiously enough, this form of co-operation is more suited to the traditional structure in Eastern Europe, if only because the large state-run organisations for once have the advantage of being on a scale comparable with that of the multinational companies of the West. At the same time, it has to be realised that projects on too large a scale have the effect of benefiting the USSR at the expense of credits and resources that might be better used elsewhere.

From January 1973 onwards, commercial treaties with Eastern Europe will have to be concluded by the Community rather than by its separate member states. True, the development of industrial co-operation somewhat limits the importance of this innovation; but from that date onwards the problem of the status of the EEC in the eyes of the East European Governments will nevertheless become more acute. Since the statements made in 1972 by Brezhnev, it seems as if the USSR will not refuse to deal with the Community as such, but will demand in return that it take into consideration the interests of the members of COMECON. It will be observed that there is no demand for formal recognition of COMECON. On the other hand, some East European countries, and in particular Roumania, have on several occasions shown a desire to deal directly with Brussels, and this tendency can only grow. The argument that the popular democracies may be afraid of becoming dependent on a partner much stronger than themselves is scarcely convincing so long as Soviet domination in Eastern Europe remains what it is. By dealing with Brussels, the small countries of Eastern Europe can only increase their freedom of action *vis-à-vis* their main partner, which is and will remain the USSR.

A different danger would threaten, however, if the fact of dealing with Brussels rather than with the national governments were to aggravate rather than facilitate matters for the East Europeans. This is what would happen if the

Commission, deprived of any political function or concern, were content merely to be the guardian of the common external tariff and the common agricultural policy, and limited itself to a conservative and protectionist role. Hitherto, the Governments of the popular democracies have found that the Governments in Western Europe had enough political understanding to undertake the legislative adjustments that were necessary in any particular case; and if the Commission were to disappoint its future partners in this respect they would no doubt once again gradually return to their former ways. They would not fail to exploit the weaknesses of the Community system and ask the member states which in any case are anxious to limit the Commission's power – to negotiate directly with them, more or less discreetly. This shows very clearly that unless the Commission's political powers develop in step with the progress of the Community, the result can only be retrograde.

The case of trade with the GDR, needs to be dealt with separately. Under the 'Protocol on inter-German trade' appended to the Treaty of Rome, the GDR is not considered to be a country foreign to the Federal Republic, and hence to the Community; and its trade with Bonn – ten per cent of its total commerce – is exempt from customs duties.

It could even be said that the GDR, which was already held to be 'the seventh member' of the original Common Market, is also a door open to all the members of COMECON, if the Government of East Berlin so desires: the origin of the goods it exports to the West cannot be checked in every instance, and other East European countries are thereby in a position to sell certain products, especially agrricultural produce, duty-free in the Common Market.

In principle, this situation should be terminated with the formal recognition accorded by Bonn to the GDR, the more so since the notion of inter-German trade is incompatible with the principle of *Abgrenzung* on which the East Berlin leadership insists, and which makes the Federal Republic very definitely a foreign country. At the same time, however, East Berlin enjoys a great advantage under the present system, and it may continue if Bonn has no objection to its tacit prolongation. But this will also require the agreement of the Community's other member states: here again, a political gesture is involved, which requires a consensus among governments both as regards their solidarity with Bonn and as regards the longer-term aims of their policy *vis-à-vis* Eastern Europe. It is possible that unless there are political concessions from the East which Bonn regards as sufficiently attractive, the present rules for inter-German trade may be replaced by a preferential agreement of the type already concluded with other European countries.

The Conference on Security and Co-operation in Europe

This is not the place to discuss whether the convocation of this Conference is a good thing or a bad thing: that question has been overtaken by events. In effect, the Conference began when the multilateral phase of its preparation started at the end of 1972. It will be recalled that the Soviet Union has been calling for such a Conference for a number of years, originally since 1954 but above all since 1969, with the evident purpose of drawing nearer to their objectives in Europe – consolidating the *status quo* in the East, and securing a *droit de regard* on developments in the West. But other East European countries, such as Roumania and Yugoslavia, have their own reasons for wanting the Conference: they wish to limit the Soviet hold on their policies and to forge closer links with the West. Since at the same time a number of people in the West, including some of those in Government, are also in favour of the project, which they hope will improve the chances of co-operation with the East and lead to greater openness on the part of the East European countries, it can be seen that the situation is more complex than it appears at first sight. In this context, what action might the enlarged Community take?

The need for a co-ordinated attitude on the part of the Nine is beyond question, despite the argument sometimes advanced that discussion between the blocs should be avoided. In the first place, it is difficult to see any point in talking about the co-ordination of the Community member states' foreign policies if this unique opportunity for practising it is not seized. In the second place, the West is not a bloc and will in any case speak with several voices, owing to the presence of the neutrals, not to mention the United States and Canada. Finally, the argument that by co-ordinating its attitude the Community would help strengthen the cohesion of the East European countries is very unconvincing, since the Kremlin will easily find other pretexts if it thinks it necessary to impose on its allies a single line of conduct.

It is true that the multiplicity of organisations that have studied the problems of the CSCE has led to some confusion. NATO has so far been the main forum for their discussion. But the Davignon Committee and the Commission of the European Community have also done some work on the subject. However, a common position of the member states has not been reached on all points. The work of these European bodies, unlike that of NATO, has had no publicity. It would seem reasonable that Community bodies should be the main centre for West European preparation of the CSCE, with NATO playing the role of an auxiliary and associate rather than vice versa, as has so far been the case. It does not seem essential for the Commission as such to take part in the Conference, the more so because no analogous institution exists on the Eastern side, unless it be COMECON. If the Commission were to attend, the Soviet Union would at once insist that COMECON do the same, and since they are its most important members this would further aggravate the imbalance between their part in the Conference and that of the United States. On the other hand, the indispensable minimum is that a representative of the Community – for example a delegate from the country which at that time has the presidency of the Council of Ministers – should speak in the name of the Community on all questions that may arise concerning the EEC. This minimum is far from satisfactory: the Community ought in fact to take a similar line on all important questions raised by the Conference. For this will be the first test of its will to pursue a common foreign policy, and the first time that its field of application is specifically European. It is impossible therefore to exaggerate the importance of this occasion.

The Conference, which for a long time was described as a Security Conference, hardly merits this title: it would be more appropriate to call it a 'Conference for Co-operation'. Its discussion of security will not in fact go beyond the drawing-up of a very general proclamation about the independence, sovereignty and territorial integrity of European States, and the principles of non-interference. There would certainly be no point in harbouring illusions about the worth of such a text: it will not prevent the USSR from intervening, even militarily, in the affairs and on the territory of the popular democracies, if its leaders believe that their higher interests are in danger. Nevertheless, the countries which might be the victims of such intervention are themselves in favour of a declaration of this kind, since a text, even if only symbolic, is always better than nothing, and may have some moral persuasive force.

At all events, there is some point in dotting the *i*s and crossing the *t*s on the subject of non-interference and sovereignty: in reaffirming, for instance, the right of all countries to choose their systems of social and political organisation without outside interference; and their right to belong to an alliance, but also to leave it and to announce their neutrality. It would be a good thing for the members of the Community to insist on such a statement, even if some of them might fear that it could weaken the Atlantic Alliance: after all, the right to leave the Alliance or its military organisation is already recognised, not only *de jure*, but also *de facto* since the departure of France from NATO. The insertion of such a statement in an East–West declaration would thus alter nothing in the West, but would represent considerable progress in the East.

Since the negotiation on force reductions in Europe has been excluded from the CSCE proper, the latter will deal scarcely at all with military matters. But it would be a mistake to underestimate the importance of the so-called 'collateral measures' which the Conference will study and discuss: reporting and inspecting troop movements in Europe, sending observers to military manoeuvres undertaken by both alliance systems, etc. These measures, which are sought especially by Roumania and other East European countries, would be a definite step towards better security, and would in particular discourage the use of military manoeuvres as a means of intimidation.

Nevertheless, co-operation will be the major theme of the conference. It will be divided into two main subjects: economic co-operation and cultural co-operation, which would be better described as the freer movement of men and ideas; and will probably continue after the conference through the establishment of two permanent *ad hoc* bodies. As has been said, these committees will give the USSR and its allies a certain right to scrutinise the affairs of the Community; but the latter, if it only knows what it wants, should be able to obtain in exchange a right to scrutinise affairs in the East, to use its influence to loosen the constraints of excessive Soviet domination, and to enable the popular democracies to benefit more effectively from co-operation. As far as free movement is concerned, it is natural and desirable that the Europeans should take the initiative unreservedly – although they must realise that such an open attitude will mean sacrifices on the part of some Governments, for example on the granting of visas.

In sum, the Conference on Security and Co-operation in Europe, planned with very different objects in view in the two camps, may lead to some satisfactory compromises. Co-operation, if not security, can only gain from it; and the Community may also benefit – provided, that is, that its members are united and that they seek a constructive dialogue rather than the very vague notion of détente. This is the precondition for any sound policy *vis-à-vis* Eastern Europe, whether of one nation or of nine.

9 The Community and the Mediterranean

Wolfgang Hager

As an emerging political entity, the European Community is going through a process of defining its geographical limits and of establishing the mode of relations it is to have with its neighbours. On no other part of its periphery has the process been as accidental as it has been towards the South. To the extent that conscious criteria guided the Community a decade ago, when most of the legal and economic decisions with which we still live today were taken, these have in part become dated, in part been overtaken by events, and in part replaced by new criteria which stress the Community's wider responsibilities.

The geographical limits were drawn, seemingly sharply, by a Rome Treaty provision (Article 237) limiting membership to European states, and the *de facto* condition that such states be parliamentary democracies. The first test-cases, Greece and Turkey, revealed the need to introduce a third criterion, that of a level of economic development similar to that obtaining in the Community. Accordingly, Greece was offered, in 1961, the half-way house of association; and Turkey, two years later, a 'pre-association' which in 1970 became an association, due to lead to membership in twenty-two years. The Greek association was 'frozen' after the colonel's coup; *de facto* economic rapprochement continued. Turkey, perhaps judged by less stringent standards of democratic probity, continued to enjoy the benefits of association, while dragging its feet on economic liberalisation towards the Community. Spain, which trades three times as much as either of the other two, has only a commercial treaty with the Community: the more realistic the prospect of full membership, the more stringent the political criteria.

If relations with neighbours on the northern shore of the

Mediterranean are thus more ambiguous than a look at the legal statutes would lead one to suppose, those with the other states bordering the Mediterranean – which will be the main subject of this chapter – are only at this moment entering a period of sharper definition. Until now, two association treaties, with Morocco and Tunisia (little more than commercial treaties), co-exist with a whole network of trade agreements with the rest of the littoral. If a proposal submitted by the Commission to the Council in the autumn of 1972 is put into practice, the whole area, from the Lebanon to Spain, is to be linked to the Community in a free trade area, with financial and technical assistance for the developing countries among them.

The implementation of such a project could well represent a turning point for all parties concerned. It would give a definite direction to the future evolution of a relationship which until now has remained fluid, consisting essentially of pragmatic solutions to economic problems. For the Community, the less-than-sharp definition of its southern limits would become permanent; for the new partners, economic and political development would be intimately linked with that of Europe.

This, at first sight at least, is nothing more than accepting the consequences of what is already a near-symbiosis between the Community and the other coastal states of the Mediterranean. Economic exchanges cover a wide range: trade in goods, substantial capital flows, workers, oil, tourism. Common ecological problems – in an area which has been an ecological disaster area for two thousand years – form a further bond.

But if by symbiosis we mean a state of interdependence, the term does not really describe the situation. Rather we find two kinds of dependence, so different in character that the precondition of interdependence – equality of the partners – does not exist. Europe has a substantial security interest in the area. It does not – with the exception of part of its oil supply – depend on the area economically. Its partners, on the other hand, heavily depend on the Community economically, while the Community is largely irrelevant to their security: it is neither a threat, nor a prospective protector.

In the following, both security and the economic relationship will be examined; the aim is to define, however tentatively, a political model which takes account of both.

European security and the Mediterranean

Back in the days of the Pax Americana the Sixth Fleet spared Europe the need to think about what, as a sign of changing times, is now referred to as the 'southern flank'. Indeed, that same fleet firmly discouraged them from doing so, when, in 1956, two formerly great European powers took a last important and ill-judged initiative in the area. The Suez crisis marked the end of the European, and the beginnings of the Soviet presence in the crucial Eastern Mediterranean. Even this was scarcely recognised as important by Europeans, though they continued to observe with sympathetic interest the growing difficulties of Israel and the United States. Only slowly did it become apparent that the area was permanently affected by two simultaneous and interacting weaknesses, which greatly furthered and encouraged the Soviet presence. The emergence of a strong and permanent Soviet fleet in the area meant a qualitative change in Europe's security position.

What were these weaknesses? One, clearly, was the international polarisation of the area around the conflict with Israel: America, in its role of guarantor of international order (which it played in the Cyprus conflict), was committed to the *status quo*. The Arabs were revisionist. Soviet aid allowed them to continue what without it might have been seen as a sterile and self-defeating policy. In the process, from Syria to Algeria, the Soviets were increasingly accepted as allies and friends. This process was helped by, and indeed contributed to, the second endemic weakness of the area: the instability of its political régimes. The resultant emergence of military régimes, half leading and half led by, popular mass parties mobilised towards a single issue, Israel, using arguments of war economy together with a selective socialism, sharply limiting the role of independent politico-economic forces which might have exercised a 'civilian' restraint, did not contribute towards moderation in the internal and external politics of the area. As long as force remains the main political currency, the area is vulnerable to outside intervention.

While its nations live in a state of mutual distrust (Jordan/
Egypt, Libya/Morocco, etc.) the establishment of co-operative
relationships based on the civilian values of welfare for the
population will be difficult.

In security terms, Europe is affected by these developments
in several ways. First, there is the risk of a direct clash among
the super-powers. Though both powers seem to be aware of
this risk, one cannot have the same confidence in their
capacity for conflict management in a volatile region like
the Eastern Mediterranean as one has about Central Europe.
The fact that the Soviet Union chooses to accept this risk
(the US has far less choice in the matter, being tied by long-
standing treaty to the defence of Europe, and morally committed to the defence of Israel) points to the importance given
by that power to a region whose only conceivable interest
is strategic.

The central and particularly European preoccupation relates
precisely to this strategic interest. There are multiple reasons
for the Soviet naval presence. One is defensive: planes from
the Sixth Fleet and missiles from French submarines can
reach targets in the Soviet Union. Another is related to the
Arab–Israeli conflict and neutralises a potential interventionary
threat by the United States, which might be launched to fore-
stall an Israeli defeat. This same 'neutralising' effect has given
all non-allies of the United States more room for manoeuvre,
not less,[1] and only Egypt, because of a much more far-reaching
military dependence, seemed for a time to have lost a degree of
independence to the Soviets.

In general, however, as Curt Gasteyger points out,[2] the
Soviet presence has created that rare situation: a Mediterranean
not dominated by a single power. If this allows the neutrals
to be more neutral, it forces the allies of the West and the
northern littoral to move a few steps in the same direction.
Greece and Turkey, in particular, are worried, as nine-tenths
of their trade is done by sea. Greece's fairly successful efforts

[1] Curt Gasteyger, 'Stabilité intérieure et sécurité extérieure dans la
Méditerranée, paper presented to the Conference on Europe and Mediterranean Africa, organised by the Atlantic Institute and the Istituto Affari
Internazionali, Rome, October 28–30 1971.
[2] Ibid.

to come to terms with its Balkan neighbours,[1] and Turkish eagerness for good relations with the Soviet Union, are evidence of this shift, as are similar moves by Spain, including the granting of supply facilities to the Soviet navy. Partially, this is due to skilful Soviet diplomacy: support of the Turkish claim in Cyprus, the Cypriot claim against the British, and the Spanish claim to Gibraltar, coupled with commercial approaches. But the point is that such Soviet support is increasingly worth having. Furthermore, certain régimes which felt more secure because of the American guarantee now prefer to negotiate a reinsurance which deprives their internal opposition of Soviet support. These moves are instructive, rather than vital, as regards peripheral countries of Europe: they are very limited and help to soften the confrontation. Of greater concern to Europe is the potential or actual loss of bases, such as Wheelus, Cyprus, Malta, or Mers-el-Kébir, as host régimes are emboldened to exercise their sovereign rights. In this, the loss of bases itself makes little difference to the West, but loss to the Soviets would dramatically alter the military (air cover) and political climate in the region.

The real danger, in the short run, comes from possible reactions of member states of the Community itself. Italian fears of, say, a Soviet-supported Communist coup in the Romagna may be fanciful, but the growing feasibility of such a move can influence external policy, either by inducing Italy to seek insurance from the Soviets by accomodating policies, or by satisfying internal opposition by 'neutralist' moves, or both. In any case, one vital element of future Community security is endangered by the fact that one member country experiences a Soviet threat specific to itself and not shared to the same extent by its partners: the chances of a common foreign policy for the Community could be seriously at risk. Political accommodation towards the East, and/or increased dependence on America for its security will be the result of a fragmented Community approach.

The size of the Soviet naval presence is largely independent of bases in the area. Since it has headquarters in the nearby Black Sea, from which it can easily get reinforcements and

---

[1] F.-W. Fernau, 'Griechenland zwischen Balkan und Mittelmeer', *Europa Archiv*, XXVI (October 19 1971) 673–83.

supplies, permanent naval bases in the Mediterranean are a convenience rather than a necessity. Its effectiveness, however, depends in part on the acquisition of air bases from which to give cover to this fleet. At the moment, the Sixth Fleet, most of whose ships are more than fifteen years old, more than matches the smaller but faster and newer (mainly less than five years old) Soviet fleet, with its superior missiles, by virtue of an overwhelming air superiority. Expanded facilities like those now granted by Egypt would alter the military balance. But the acquisition of any kind of base, if only a radar station, would have a strong psychological impact on the region.

This psychological impact would not so much derive only from change in the military balance itself. As in nuclear matters, variations within a stalemate situation are more a barometer of intentions – one could almost say of will – than significant in battle terms. Indeed, precisely because they are floating nuclear triggers, the Soviet and US navies are less 'operational' than others in the area. Furthermore, naval bases, and, more relevant for Soviet purposes, the right to use 'facilities', are only one of many manifestations of Soviet influence.

The likelihood of a Soviet presence, in whatever form, being accepted by the countries of the region depends, to a large extent, on the state of political tension and instability in the region. A reversal of the general trend of newly-independent countries towards non-alignment is a desperate act. It is only taken by a government, such as Egypt, for which the necessities of war outweigh such considerations, or by a government which needs an outside guarantee against internal opposition – as yet a hypothetical but not unlikely case. It is in contributing to a lessening of tension, indeed of desperation, that the Community could, to a very limited degree, make a difference. It will be argued in the following that the Community may, on the contrary, be paving the way for future tensions which would make the Soviet Union a permanently-needed element in the region.

Europe and Mediterranean oil

After security, oil is the second fundamental interest of the Community in the region: indeed it can be understood as another aspect of its general security interest. This is not so much due to the area's importance as a producer of oil: Algeria, Libya and Egypt account for only 5 per cent of world reserves. Most of the Community's oil imports will continue to come from the Persian Gulf. But a substantial part of this Gulf oil – that which is not transported round the Cape – will move through the pipelines and port terminals and along the shipping routes of the Mediterranean.

In Europe, as in other developed regions, virtually all economic life depends on oil. An almost total reliance on outside sources for an essential and even vital commodity is not very satisfactory at the best of times. Dependence on one of the most volatile regions of the world, with transport routes (Syria, Iraq, the Sea) under the partial influence of a hostile power, easily gives rise to an alarmist view of Europe's situation.

These possible dangers are more easily seen in their true proportions if one looks at different contingencies one by one. The most dramatic, and perhaps most likely to happen in most people's minds, would be an interruption of supplies if armed conflict broke out in Europe. Under conditions of conventional war this would matter; but such a war, in Europe, would either be very short or end in a nuclear exchange – or both. Another short-term interruption of supplies might be caused by a near-total loss of political control through revolutionary or civil war in the Arab world. Again, it is hard to conceive of such disturbances lasting longer than reserves, or of being so complete that increased production in areas not touched would not allow Europe to survive such an emergency without major inconveniences. If such disturbances, however, followed a prolonged OPEC 'strike' which had exhausted European reserves, the situation would be more serious. It should be recalled, as stated in Chapter 5, that Europe can no longer, as in the sixties, count on Western Hemisphere sources to make up shortages of supply.

Another contingency sometimes evoked is a long-term diversion of supplies towards the Soviet Union. But given the near self-sufficiency of the Soviet Union, and its limited capital resources, most of the oil would find its way back to Western Europe – at world prices. Barter deals, like the one with Iraq, exchanging equipment for oil, cannot easily be multiplied. The real competitor for the oil of the Middle East is the United States, now becoming a major importer of oil. This may raise a number of problems in the future. Will US oil companies, in the crunch, have to give preference to the US market? Will the US back up its new interests by forms of economic co-operation with oil-producing countries which compete with similar Community efforts? But these are not, by themselves, security problems.

As pointed out in Chapter 5, the participation of OPEC countries in the concessions of the major oil companies might lead to a relative scarcity of capital available for investment in future production and refining of oil. High prices, however, are an inconvenience rather than a major threat to industrial prosperity. This is true as long as bargaining continues to take place rationally. A radicalisation of bargaining – with frequent recourse to the 'strike' weapon – could lead to serious disruptions of economic life in the Community. Against this, the Community as such can do little beyond establishing relations of confidence with its neighbours, while diversifying its sources of energy supplies.

The interests of our partners

The central fact, both politically and economically, is the economic dependence of the countries of the Mediterranean littoral on the Community. The Community often accounts for half their trade and in some cases for two-thirds. Trade in turn represents an unusually high percentage in the total GNP of the developing countries of the region, proof of its vital importance for economic development.

But trade figures tell only half the tale. Other countries on the periphery of the Community, e.g. Austria or Sweden, show an equally high trade dependence on the Community. The difference lies in the high specialisation of the export structure of the Mediterranean countries for the European market, especially in the all-important agricultural products. Here we must distinguish between the northern and the southern littoral. For while it is true that all the countries of the region, including Southern Italy and France, produce similar agricultural products – citrus fruit, olives, wine and vegetables, to mention the most important ones – the history and effect of this production differ. In the South, and notably in the Maghreb, this specialisation was a deliberate creation by Europeans. Being oriented exclusively towards the European (French) export markets, the development of modern agriculture occurred without much regard for local needs. From this resulted a secondary dependence, less well known, on *imports* of agricultural products, i.e. those actually needed for local consumption (cereals, sugar).[1] While Morocco still exports twice as much agricultural produce than it imports, Tunisia covers less than two-thirds of its imports, and Algeria is also running a negative balance. But even countries less marked by colonial experience share in the predicament of having to rely on the agricultural sector for much of their national income. And, unlike more favoured countries in the North (and Israel), they have neither the skills nor the capital resources to allow rapid diversification to other sectors of economic activity.

This dependence on agriculture is a major hurdle for development in the countries concerned. Increased productivity in this sector is both difficult to achieve (wine or vegetable growing are inherently labour-intensive) and often undesirable, if this means using labour-saving techniques which increase unemployment. At the same time, a population growth of 2 per cent and even 3 per cent annually means rising food consumption, hence increased imports from countries of the temperate zone. These imports will have to be paid for by exports of citrus fruit, etc., for which there is a low demand-elasticity, only one important market – Europe – and which are hard-pressed by American, and in some cases, Community competition.

From a technical point of view – and this underlies present Brussels thinking on the unity of the Mediterranean – all countries of the area share the predicament of having to rely on a limited market for a narrow range of products. But, as pointed out above, for the poorer countries of the South the

---

[1] M. D. Pépy, of IRAT, Paris, drew attention to this phenomenon at a conference held by the IAI and the Atlantic Institute in Rome in October 1971.

resultant economic dependence on the Community is different in quantity (the proportion of national wealth and labour force involved), and quality (the availability of alternatives).

Most of the European countries of the area which are not members of the Community will probably choose to see their future in increasingly closer ties with the Community. With the long-term prospect of membership, and given a basic commitment to follow Western patterns of political and economic development, dependence on the Community and the very limited possibilities of influencing its decisions count less. For the countries of the South – and Turkey may well represent a borderline case – the desire to determine their economic fate, and hence their political independence, will increase, not decrease. Algeria's fairly radical break with the division of labour imposed by Europe is an example for the future, rendered possible by a relative abundance of cadres and by revenues from oil. Others will follow. The question is not whether change will come, but whether it will be evolutionary or revolutionary. And the question is whether the Community will impose its own pattern of relations on the area – at the risk of seeing agreements repudiated by future leaders.

There is, of course, another aspect to dependence, often referred to by leaders on both shores of the Mediterranean: domination by the super-powers. Relations with Europe, it is thought, might provide a counterweight, and alternative, to dependence on the Soviet Union in particular. This may be true as regards economic dependence, which plays a role in Egypt's ties to the super-power (markets for cotton, investment projects). But then the argument cuts both ways: excessive dependence on the Community may necessitate, for reasons of prudence and national pride, and to gain bargaining power, a permanent counter-balancing role for the Soviet Union. As to the Community's ability to be a third, and neutralising, force against the strategic domination by the super-powers, this overestimates the Community's capabilities as a power (in the traditional sense), and fails to see that it can only have effective influence as a 'civilian' power. This, however, means establishing relationships which are equitable

and beneficial to our partners, and will continue to be seen
as such.

Community policy

The Community's Mediterranean policy started with a relatively minor act of policy, taken almost absentmindedly, which
led to a number of 'escalations', each of them logical and
necessary, and none of them large enough to warrant much
public attention. But with the plan submitted by the Commission to the Council of Ministers in autumn 1972, suggest-
ing the creation of a vast free-trade and co-operation area in
the Mediterranean, this policy has assumed proportions which
warrant profound questioning by Europeans.

The first step was taken with the conclusion of an association agreement with Greece, in 1961, which was meant as
a transitional arrangement allowing eventual full membership.
This association set a pattern which, without the objective of
full membership, was repeated elsewhere in the region and
which may now be extended, *mutatis mutandis*, to the whole
of it: trade liberalisation on a preferential basis – the Community liberalising faster than the poor partner which was
granted a long, twenty-two year, period of grace – coupled with
loans from the European Investment Bank (EIB) to aid the
process of industrialisation and to bring Greece up to the
level of development of the rest of the Community.

In the Turkish association, which followed two years later,
the difference in economic development pushed the goal of
complete trade liberalisation into the distant future. A five-year
'pre-association', which gave preference to a few Turkish
agricultural exports and $175 million in EIB loans, was
followed by a 1970 agreement of association on the Greek
pattern (customs union after twenty-two years; and the possibility of membership). However, Turkey is dragging its feet
on liberalisation, and is ill-suited to take part in the 'harmonised', single economy the Community is to create with
monetary union. The agreement shows the dangers of
incremental decision-making. A simple trade agreement would
have solved Turkey's problems, if it had not been for two
products, raisins and tobacco. A non-MFN-based concession

would not have been in conformity with GATT; furthermore, the Community had granted a veto on concessions concerning these products to Greece.[1] To get round these problems and in order to give equal treatment to Greece's neighbours, the Community initiated the complicated and doubtful long-term task of making Turkey a future member of the Community.

While the Community was thus extended to the Eastern Mediterranean, the southern shore was also to have its association agreement. The promise of such an agreement for Tunisia and Morocco had been annexed to the Rome Treaty. Algeria, then, was *de jure* French, and thus Community, territory. After a decade of negotiations, association agreements with Tunisia and Morocco were concluded in 1969. These were in effect little more than trade agreements, which the Community undertook to renegotiate after three years to include financial and technical assistance. In honouring its commitment, the Community is led to extending it to the other countries of the region.

These aid instruments were ever more urgently required to complement the commercial policy as the Community began to run out of the concessions it could give, especially in the field of agricultural exports. The orange became the symbol of a basic predicament of the Community's Mediterranean policy: the countries of the region not only compete for the same limited market but also compete with two member countries – France and particularly Italy. Since, in the early days of the Community, with the agricultural policy not yet defined, it was impossible to take a comprehensive view of the problem, there occurred a see-saw of bargains with the interested countries, each trying to restore equitable treatment which the preceding one had put in question.

The concessions to Greece led to Italy's being granted a guaranteed market and prices for its produce. This led to increased Community production and contracted the total market available to others. Israel and Spain, two efficient outside producers, had to be given concessions – mainly for political reasons – which were in the form of tariff preferences. Morocco and others more or less kept their market share by

[1] Stanley Henig, 'The Mediterranean Policy of the European Community: *Government and Opposition*', VI 4 (1971).

even larger tariff concessions (80 per cent) – though quality proved increasingly more important than price, hence the felt need to include technical assistance in future agreements. A complicated network of technical devices – special taxes, injunctions to respect minimum prices – complemented the various agreements and ensured the protection of Community producers. Through these devices exporters gain not so much a commercial advantage, i.e. an increased market share, but rather an 'economic advantage', i.e. higher revenues.

By the autumn of 1972, the Community had concluded, or was about to conclude, agreements with all the countries of the area except Libya, Syria and Albania.[1]

The basic 'benefit' of all these agreements was thus a *de facto* market allocation in agriculture, coupled with the prospect of financial assistance. About half of each country's agricultural exports is covered by concessions. The bulk of other exports, usually oil and other raw material, have no tariff anyway. While 70–100 per cent tariff reductions on industrial exports into the Community are the rule, these play a very small role in the trade of the poorer countries, and are hedged about with quotas and tariff-quotas. Enlargement of the Community (and hence the adoption of Community practices by the three new members) damages present 'beneficiaries' of the Mediterranean policy sufficiently to warrant renegotiation of the terms of some agreements. It is this prospect which is one of the reasons which led the Commission to present its plan for a broader Mediterranean policy at this time.

Reverse preferences

All existing agreements contain concessions for Community exports. With the Greek and Turkish agreements this makes sense if a customs union can really be achieved. For Israel and Spain, political considerations ruled out an association. Both felt that a non-preferential trade agreement would not really benefit them. The Community thus chose a preferential trade agreement, which bent or broke the rules of GATT, but which solved a real problem. A fig-leaf of GATT propriety

[1] Yugoslavia, as it represents economically and politically a special case, is left out of consideration in this chapter.

was maintained by a very long-term commitment to free trade between the new partners. American criticism of the agreements was waved aside as purist and theological, which was true if one considered these new agreements as associations which could not be called that for the time being but in due course would be. Furthermore, American protests had an element of pettiness in them: pressure from the US citrus lobby, which felt damaged by concessions on oranges, seemed to lie behind US talk of high principle and the importance of the most-favoured-nation clause. In the heat of the battle, a serious argument about preferential trade agreements did not take place in the Community. Convinced of its innocence, the Community did not ask for a waiver in GATT.

Once the breach with GATT orthodoxy was made, it seemed that equity demanded the conclusion of preferential agreements with the Arab states (the Maghreb, Egypt, the Lebanon), and with Cyprus and Malta. None of these agreements include aid provisions (except for some technical assistance for the Lebanon) and all foresee more rapid tariff dismantling by the Community than by the other contracting parties. But timetables for tariff-cuts are vague, and the commitment to establish free trade areas is in some cases implicit rather than spelt out as required by GATT.

The new proposals by the Commission are meant to reduce the great diversity of these agreements. Among the common elements to be introduced is a single timetable for dismantling Community tariffs (100 per cent by 1977) and a commitment between the Community and each of the countries to create free trade areas or customs unions with the Community. For partner countries two timetables are envisaged to take account of different stages of development: Israel, Spain, Cyprus and Malta would, like the Community, abolish all tariffs by 1977, and for some 5–10 per cent of sensitive products by 1985. Egypt, the Lebanon and the Maghreb would have to abolish restrictions by about 1990.

These tariff cuts concern trade in industrial goods. The Commission, rightly, stresses however that tariff dismantling can do little by itself to encourage industrial development in the poorer countries. It therefore suggests a number of ways in which co-operation between the Community and its partners in the region could promote economic development: financial grants and loans, technical assistance and social benefits for migrant workers are the most important. Furthermore, the Commission concedes that industrial export opportunities are at present of limited interest to many of the less developed countries of the region, and that concessions on agricultural products, at present covering about half of each country's exports in this sector, should be raised to perhaps 80 per cent of such exports.

A critique

The dividing line between a policy which accepts the responsibility of the rich and powerful towards the weaker countries which depend on it, and the creation of a zone of influence is a subtle one. But it is a distinction worth making if the Community wants to achieve the twin goals of a peaceful Mediterranean, and of a civilian world economic and political order.

Three arguments militate against attempting to create a zone of influence in the area. It will not work: the Community is unlikely to be able to discharge its economic responsibilities; and the attempt, if copied by others, is likely to lead to a fragmented world.

Even assuming that close co-operation as envisaged in current plans would bring substantial economic benefits to the Community's partners, the attempt is likely to be politically counterproductive. One recalls that France in the sixties sought to maintain a privileged relationship with Algeria, *inter alia* by buying its oil at prices substantially above the world level, by effecting massive financial transfers (far beyond anything which the Community is likely to practise in the area as a whole), and by an ambitious technical assistance programme. At the same time Algeria enjoyed very liberal access to French markets, and its workers were welcomed in large numbers. And yet this relationship ended in a protracted crisis, because the division of labour which was, in a sense, written into Franco-Algerian co-operation agreements did not satisfy the Algerian leaders' desire for independent industrialisation – by sowing oil to reap industry, as one Minister put it.

The Community's relations with the developing countries of

the Mediterranean may not become quite as close as that. But the political concept of the proponents of an ambitious Mediterranean policy is reminiscent of this earlier bilateral experiment in co-operation.

For a variety of reasons the Community is unlikely to be able to provide sufficient economic benefits to make very close ties between the countries of the Mediterranean and itself tolerable in the long run. Thus, as regards the most pressing problem, that of agricultural exports, the Community is highly unlikely – given the internal political bargains involved, and the time needed to implement any policy – to alter present arrangements radically in the sense of a better division of labour based on comparative advantages (cf. Chapter 4).

According to Commission experts, the total market for their products cannot be enlarged (regardless of price?). If this is true, a rise in the relative share of imports would necessitate profound changes in agricultural policy. Such changes may come. But they are more likely to occur in sectors like cereals and sugar (where international pressure is heaviest), than in the socially more sensitive sectors which provide employment in some of the poorest regions of the Community itself. The chances are, therefore, that the Community will prefer to give 'economic benefits' in the form of high prices. This, however, would not provide badly needed employment; it would make the beneficiary countries permanently dependent for a part of their budgetary receipts (export taxes) on the vagaries of the Community market; and it would reinforce the tendency towards surpluses in these products which already plagues the region. Furthermore, these outside suppliers would not benefit from the market guarantee given to the farmers of the Community. As marginal suppliers, they already now carry the full risk of harvest variations. This risk could be reduced if the Community allocated minimum annual quotas. But the resultant bargaining constellation – all countries of the region competing with each other for the Community's favours – would not be conducive to inter-regional harmony.

The Community, given the constraints of the agricultural policy, is unlikely in the medium term – and five or ten years is a long time for a developing nation – to open its agricultural markets sufficiently to allow poorer countries to earn sufficient export receipts without special economic favours, i.e. high prices. Since, moreover, there is an increasing need to feed a growing population, the best way of overcoming what is a structural element of dependence is to reduce the importance of agricultural exports and to encourage a shift towards growing foodstuffs for domestic consumption. This is already declared policy in the Maghreb countries, which can point to some initial successes. But local production of cereal and sugar – especially under the labour-intensive conditions which are desirable to reduce unemployment – cannot compete with subsidised production from the temperate zone. Seen against this need, the call in the Commisson's proposal for concessions for the Community's agricultural exports seems disquieting. For the countries of the region, a combination of a high-price policy for fluctuating exports, combined with artifically cheap imports, would mean a perpetuation of dependence.

Uneconomic solutions to the social problems of underdevelopment in the region could mean the need for perpetual economic intervention and special support by the Community. Furthermore, solutions which create welfare clients for the Community in the region may well in time lead to political conflicts. The sums which may be spent on the consolidation of the present agricultural division of labour, should therefore rather be spent on a programme of diversification which would lessen dependence on the Community. It is often claimed that this is technically impossible. No such conclusion should be accepted before a serious attempt has been made to prove the contrary: through research into new grains, new techniques, investment in irrigation, and, most important, through the elimination of present distortions in the price structure: subsidies both for European exports and for Mediterranean imports.

What are the likely benefits for our Mediterranean partners from being linked to the Community in nascent free trade areas for industrial goods? The margin of preference which duty-free access to the Community would bring depends on the level of the common external tariff in the late seventies. This may well be reduced from the present eight or nine per cent average to below five per cent. The granting of zero-tariff access to other countries – present and future Yaoundé associates, and the beneficiaries of the Generalised System of Preferences – already seriously erode the special advantages of duty-free access to the Community market.

Furthermore, Mediterranean industrial exports in such 'sensitive' sectors as processed agricultural goods, textiles, and refined petroleum products are likely, even in the future, to be hedged about with safeguard clauses, quotas, and a 'voluntary' observance of market discipline.

Such a pessimistic forecast seems justified not only by past performance, and by the language of the present proposals, but also by the bargaining context of the proposed negotiations. As in past negotiations on preferential agreements, the real bargain is not between concessions for industrial goods on both sides, but between privileged access for Community manufactures (and investments) on the one hand, and incorporation into the Community's agricultural arrangements, plus financial assistance, on the other. Many of the obligations which partner governments may be led to accept concern sectors of the economy which do not yet exist – infant industries as yet unborn – but which may soon become important through the rapid diffusion of technology. On the other hand, the Community may well be willing to 'trade' a tolerant attitude as regards already existing infant industries against an equally tolerant attitude towards its own, often identical, declining industries (textiles, etc.).

The establishment of a free-trade area between partners of very unequal economic and political strength thus risks limiting considerably the freedom of economic choice of future governments, and is likely to perpetuate the present division of labour between the European North and the Mediterranean South. The Commission argues, rightly, that a lowering of tariffs by our partner countries is a good thing. But the lowering of economic barriers may occur too fast, go too far, and be too exclusive. Like the Yaoundé Convention, the Mediterranean agreements will allow partner countries to extend concessions to third parties, and for intra-regional customs unions, to discriminate against the Community. But neither is encouraged: each of the countries will practise free trade only with the Community, not with its regional partners.

The EFTA agreement offers an example for an alternative approach. In order to gain access to the British market, the Scandinavian countries gave up their long-standing reluctance to practise free trade among themselves. Through the resulting industrial integration the economies of those countries were able to meet the requirements of modern production: specialisation and large production units. A lowering of economic barriers among our Mediterranean partners at least as rapidly as towards the Community would seem a precondition for their independent industrial development and for the promotion of a wider than North–South integration in the region.

Also relevant in this context is the manner in which Community aid is to be distributed. Present plans suggest the granting of hard and soft loans by the EIB, and some concessional aid. The creation of a 'regional development organ' (including funds from partner countries, presumably the oil producers) is not ruled out for the future, but is not included in present plans. Such 'realism' risks making difficult the future development of regional co-operation, since some countries will always prefer to deal with the Community bilaterally, rather than sit down with often distant cousins to solve common problems. It is hard to see how the Community will avoid imposing its view of economic priorities unless the North–South, donor-receiver relationship is avoided from the beginning in favour of a multilateral approach.

But the exclusiveness of the Community's links with its partners exist not only within the region, but for the region as a whole *vis-à-vis* the rest of the world. The opposition of the United States to at least one aspect of the Community's policy, the reverse preferences, may shift the debate away from judging this policy on its merits, and towards a false choice between submission to US demands and the assertion of the Community's interests. The international implications must however be taken into account, and these pose the question of the kind of economic, and ultimately political, world order the Community wishes to promote. This is either a world where each of the major economic powers looks after its own region, with all this implies for Latin America and Asia, or an open world in which the Community as the greatest trading power can prosper and co-operate with its partners among the advanced nations in solving the pressing problems of development. It is also unlikely that equitable, rule-based relations among the advanced countries could co-exist with bilateral arrangements on a regional scale where everyone writes his own rules.

To think of regional blocs only in terms of trade flows would be to underestimate the growing importance of capital flows in shaping economic and political relations among nations. The notion of special investment guarantees for Community firms as part of the total co-operation agreement has therefore intra-regional and global implications. Both US experience in Latin America and Japanese experience in South-East Asia show that investments from a single source, above a certain threshold, become politically intolerable to the host countries. Preferential investment links thus not only risk introducing future sources of conflict within the Mediterranean region, but also hinder the efforts of the rest of the world to diversify their economic links.

It must be recognised, however, that even under conditions of equal access, Community investments in the area will and should rise considerably. Such a development is the precondition for a reversal of the present policy of importing labour – with all this means in terms of social hardship for migrant workers, congestion in our industrial regions, maintenance of uneconomic, labour-intensive industries within the Community – and adopting one of exporting capital (and where possible, managerial and technological know-how, without necessarily majority ownership by Community firms).

The issue of exclusiveness and preferential access is also posed by the suggestions of establishing special investment and purchasing links with the oil producers of the region (and those of the Persian Gulf). Indeed, the notion of creating a 'spirit of co-operation' which would improve the chances of secure and cheap oil supplies is one of the motives for creating special aid and trade links with the region. Taking the most optimistic hypothesis, that Mediterranean co-operation will be seen as a blessing, the economic advantages for producer countries are only a minute fraction of the sums involved in oil deals. Furthermore, there is a risk that competition among the industrialised countries for privileged access to certain sources of oil will create tensions between them, while weakening their bargaining position. The offer by Saudi Arabia, made in the autumn of 1972, to conclude a special oil agreement with the government of the United States shows that the Community will not necessarily come out ahead in this game.

In the above analysis, alternatives to the present and possible future policy of the Community have often been implied rather than stated. The aim has not been to present detailed technical solutions to the problems of dependence or interdependence in the area, but to question, on political as much as on economic grounds, the direction of present policy. An arm's-length relationship, a devolution of dependence, the active encouragement of a diversification of the economic links with the Community's partners – these do not mean turning away from their problems. On the contrary, considerable efforts need to be made by the Community in a number of areas: the opening of its borders to the products of the region, with a minimum of exceptions; internal efforts by the Community to make structural adjustment in its industry and agriculture; the transfer of real resources to eliminate past distortions and to give a starting aid to allow more equal participation in the international division of labour for countries which so desire.

It is important, however, that in assuming its responsibilities the Community does not confuse a seeming short-term interest in acquiring safe market and investment opportunities with either its own or its partners' long-term economic and political interests. Nor should the Community fall victim to a mystique – the millennial unity of the Mediterranean re-established through ever closer co-operation, with its echoes of the 'Manifest Destiny' and the 'Greater East-Asian Co-prosperity Sphere' of earlier region-builders.

One should not overestimate the practical effects of public policy. In the short run, neither a policy of devolution of dependence nor one of seeking closer ties will greatly change the underlying reality of unequal distribution of wealth and power in the area. But the direction in which evolution occurs – this the Community has learned from its own experience – can be as important as the practical changes brought about by such evolution.

Security policy

We started our analysis, and terminate our reflections on policy, by looking at the region as it affects the Community's security. Within our chosen time-horizon – decisions by the mid-decade for the contingencies of 1980 – the Community is doubtless going to act increasingly as a single entity in this field.

How can Europe meet its security interests in the Mediterranean? The traditional, and still partially valid, answer is through the alliance with the United States. With American diplomacy tied by the Middle Eastern conflict, American naval power can do little to prevent the spread of the Soviet presence, but it remains the only effective protection from the military consequences of such a spread. When, during trade talks with the US in January 1972, the Community pleaded for the recognition of its special responsibility for the area to justify discrimination against US citrus exports, the American representative is reported to have brushed this aside with the remark: 'The responsibility is ours. We have a few ships down there.' The remark misses an important point, namely the necessary sterility of the American presence. It can preserve the strategic *status quo* – no small matter – but it cannot transform the economic and political *status quo* of the area which makes it so vulnerable.

Should Europe assume a greater share of the defence effort in the region? When the Soviet force first appeared in strength in the Mediterranean, France reacted by taking its fleet out to the Atlantic. At first sight quixotic, this move had something to commend it. It removed the temptation of countries in the eastern Mediterranean to seek protection against a residual French interventionary threat from the Soviet Union. Mers-el-Kébir has not become a Soviet base. As the Soviet presence increased, France gave up any short-term hope of transforming the eastern Mediterranean into a 'Sea of Peace', and began to collaborate with NATO units on manoeuvres and in aerial surveillance, and strengthened its links with Spain. Since then, the Americans have repeatedly asked for stronger European efforts.

It has been proposed that Europe should strengthen its

naval efforts through NATO by forming the present 'on-call forces'[1] into a permanent 'standing force' with participation by countries at present not engaged in the area, notably Germany. The principal aim of this proposal is to demonstrate Atlantic solidarity, or more precisely, to demonstrate to domestic critics of the American presence in Europe that the Europeans do their fair share. Yet it is just as likely that the actual implementation would demonstrate the limits of that solidarity. Navies, more than any other branch of the armed forces, are diplomatic instruments as much as military tools. For Europe to play the role of the junior partner of the Sixth Fleet is diplomatically counterproductive (and as a concept very dated). The scheme would contribute little towards defence against the Soviet navy, while visibly tying Europe to American diplomacy *vis-à-vis* the Arabs. At any rate, Germany is very cool towards the plan, while the participation of France seems excluded.

What about a common, purely European naval force? This has several attractions, since it would be one of the easiest first steps to achieve in a prospective European defence collaboration, and would demonstrate to the Americans that the Europeans are playing their part. It would allow a more wholehearted French participation while detracting little from the now NATO-supported but largely self-contained Sixth Fleet.

Nevertheless, a large European surface fleet might well do more political damage than is warranted by any increase in the defence capacity to which it could contribute. The combined numerical weight of the West would appear overwhelming, leaving the Soviet Union in the role of the underdog and anti-imperialist guardian; and this at an important moment in Soviet-Arab relations, when the Soviet Union is beginning to acquire what Walter Laqueur calls 'a past' – the accumulated rancour over unsatisfactory relations of dependence.

Europe's efforts should more usefully be employed to stiffen its defences by other means: a very efficient common surveil-

---

[1] 'NAVOCFORMED' was created by a decision of the NATO Council of Ministers in January 1969. Activated three times, it now consists of a destroyer each from Greece, Turkey and the US, as well as a British and a Italian frigate (*Atlantic News*, no. 407).

lance network, using the latest electronic devices; shore-based naval missiles; submarines and planes for anti-submarine warfare and specifically anti-naval hardware in general. Particular emphasis should be given to aircraft. The weather of the Mediterranean is uniquely suited to their deployment. Europe has ample air bases. Aircraft make possible a greater degree of 'conflict management' than guns or missiles: they can threaten without hitting, they can identify targets with greater certainty, and they can be recalled as a missile cannot. Of course, such a force should be Euro-financed, and eventually use planes specifically and jointly developed. Detachments from 'northern' air forces should participate as a demonstration of solidarity. Mixed 'European' squadrons would be technically easy to organise.

What can Europe do to influence the central conflict of the area, the Arab–Israeli confrontation? The answer must be: very little directly. Thus, the present ambiguous neutrality, which allows France to keep friends, and Germany to do its duty towards Israel, is certainly preferable to a common Community stance, which, without being politically effective – the Community is unable to guarantee a settlement – would play havoc with the diplomacy of the member countries. If there is to be a common stance, it should be a joint commitment to resist Arab attempts to export the conflict through threats of boycott, etc., in retaliation for dealing with Israel.

The necessity for the Community to respond to a long-standing Israeli demand for association, and hence to risk direct involvement in the conflict, has been sidestepped by the free trade area plans which would encompass both Arabs and Israelis. A lowering of the Community's economic barriers in both industrial and agricultural trade would obviate the economic need to make special arrangements for Israel. Whether the more substantial political ties with which Israel seeks to lessen its isolation should be formalised, even after the end of the present conflict, is doubtful. But it is clear that economically and culturally Israel's ties with the Community will tighten over time.

By and large, however, Europe should not complicate an already confused situation by adding a further element to the power politics of the area, not least because its cumbersom decision-making structure makes it difficult to conduct subtle diplomacy. If the troubles of the area stem from a surfeit of politics, Europe's contribution should be the introduction of civilian relations based on welfare aims, equity, and rules.

Thus, if it is in Europe's interest to reduce Soviet political penetration of the area, it should not attempt a counter-penetration of the same style, replacing one exclusivist claim by another. It should do the opposite: offer stable economic relations without political strings. The availability of an attractive alternative is the most effective means of reducing the opportunity for the Soviets of making political capital out of such economic and aid links as they have established. Once 'neutralised' in this manner, East European aid efforts can and should be welcomed as a contribution to the development of the area. This, indeed, is the only formula acceptable to countries which only recently freed themselves from Euro-American dominance. Arab diplomats, even those most sympathetic to Europe, insist on this point: only the simultaneous presence of Europe, both East and West, can assure their development while preserving their independence.

But the political role of this Soviet presence, as suggested above, will depend on the perception, by the states of the southern littoral, of a 'hegemonal' position by their great European neighbour. Algeria turned to the Soviet Union for its military needs during the period of Franco–Algerian co-operation. In the future one can easily imagine countries engaged in contentious negotiations with the Community making demonstrative gestures of economic and military co-operation with the Soviet Union in order to gain additional bargaining strength. Thus, the fewer the strings attached to relations with the Community, the smaller the need for a political role for the Soviet Union in the area.

As regards arms exports, however, a no-strings policy by Europe is simply not possible. Yet it is precisely through becoming the exclusive arms supplier that the Soviet Union came close to reducing Egypt to a client state. Events have proved that this dependence, too, has become politically counterproductive. Nevertheless as long as the conflict with Israel persists, Europe is at a serious political disadvantage.

In the future, and in areas less touched by the Middle East

conflict, Europe has an interest in limiting the amount of arms scattered around. To go further to an agreed no-arms export policy by the Community would be an effective demonstration of its civilian character. But this implies that Europe, under all circumstances, prefers to see the Soviets and the Chinese satisfy the arms needs of its neighbours. Clearly this is not the case. This does not mean that it should not be declared European policy to limit such exports to the minimum. A mercantilist export drive in arms is incompatible with a responsible role for Europe. Such self-restraint will be made easier, if Europe can internally provide the market for British, and especially French, hardware, which at present is limited by commitments to purchase US goods. Furthermore, a common policy on arms sales will become increasingly necessary as Europe progresses towards an integrated high-technology industry. Present practices, like the Anglo-French agreement to leave to France the marketing of the jointly-produced Jaguar in politically sensitive markets, cannot continue as Europe is increasingly judged as a unit in the eyes of the world.

Conclusion

In our attempt to sketch the ways and means for Europe's future relationship with its southern neighbours, we have treated the economic and military aspects as ancillary to the political relationship. The most important aspect of this relationship is inequality, a fact which is going to become much more salient in the politics of the region when the conflict with Israel ceases to occupy all attention.

Expressed in somewhat basic political arithmetic, inequality plus proximity equals dominance. While there is little one can do about inequality in the short run, one can lessen the 'proximity': encourage the diversification of links beyond the main north–south axis where they are translated into dependence.

The alternative approach, which seeks to intensify economic and political links, is politically dated. No amount of goodwill and altruism on the part of Europe will be able to prevent a division of labour on the terms of the larger partner. To prove this point one has simply to point to the institutional structure of the Community: internal bargains are so difficult to strike that external factors are only considered if these are backed up by considerable pressure.

Europe's interest lies in the de-radicalisation of the politics of the region. It should not lay the basis for a future conflict of which it would be the object.

A preferential policy by the Community threatens to exclude the rest of the West from the region. While Eastern Europe has an important role to play in the development of the Mediterranean, the question is whether this is done on 'civilian' terms, or as part of a political struggle for influence, with consequent further radicalisation of the area. Europe should make sure that in the choice between independence and dependence it does not appear on the wrong side.

It is also in this context that future military policy in the Mediterranean should be considered. Starting from the assumption that, even in the seventies, large naval vessels are seen as gunboats by those who do not have them, Europe should choose a politically less doubtful means of defence against the Soviet naval presence.

This analysis of the southern shore of the Mediterranean, neglecting the northern arc from Turkey to Spain, has concentrated on the belief that its problems are different in kind, and different in urgency. Briefly, one can see this relationship slowly becoming an internal European problem: an extreme case of regional policy (for which solutions have by no means been found) and a conflict over the internal socio-economic and political régime. This conflict will sharpen with time, as Europe unites, and as relationships with the US, as 'co-partner' of the countries concerned, change. But the basic orientation of Community policy towards closer ties seems not only irreversible and inevitable, but also sound in principle.

10 The Community and the LDCs

Henri Perroy

The enlarged Community will have an influence on the development of the third world that is second to none. It is the principal trading partner, the main banker, and is about to become the greatest aid-giver. Any number of decisions taken in Europe – the opening or closing of markets, the fixing of agricultural prices, labour market policies, monetary and even industrial policies, have an impact on the less developed countries (LDCs) which may be as great as or greater than the intended welfare effect at home: they may have a powerful influence on state budgets, and even on the social structure of a country and thus on the general direction of future development. The Community and the member states act; but such action often lacks both concept and coherence. Few would doubt that, in principle at least, Europe feels its world responsibilities – or rather its co-responsibilities, since it continues to measure its actions by those of the United States. But the precondition for responsibility is the intellectual and organisational capacity to account for one's acts. Does Europe know what it is doing? Do its many right hands know what its many left hands are doing? The complexities of the problem are only beginning to be understood, and common thought is at least as necessary as common actions.

The enlarged Community buys a third of the exports of the less developed countries against 15–20 per cent accounted for by the US. It takes twice as many of their agricultural exports as the United States, but competes with the LDCs on the world sugar market and has even become a net exporter of rice. Its importance as a banker to the third world can be measured by the fact that in the first half of this decade the four biggest countries of the enlarged Community will receive more payments for the service of LDC debts than the US. The

Community employs millions of workers from its southern periphery and parts of the British Commonwealth. The French and British currencies play a leading role in parts of the third world; European decisions on parities and rates of inflation profoundly influence the terms of trade, the balance of payments and the size of the debt of the third world. How many of these decisions are taken with their effects on development in mind? How many international agreements on trade and monetary matters are the result of bargaining among the rich countries alone, or are made from purely internal considerations? Does the Community take account of the LDCs when it fixes high agricultural prices which stimulate production and hence may limit their markets? The evidence points in the opposite direction. Europe lacks a coherent development policy. It has, at best, a number of aid policies, and an association policy which is more the result of the past than a considered policy for dealing with the problems of today and tomorrow.

How to help development

This question has become much more difficult to answer since the brave days of (American) engagement in the affairs of the third world in the fifties. Then, in what turned out to be a much too simple analogy to our own nineteenth-century development, industrialisation was thought to be the key to development. As it turned out, industrialisation posed as many problems as it solved. It touched only a small part of the population, created unemployment as much as employment by displacing artisan methods of production, etc. Then agriculture was placed in the centre of attention when hunger became the issue of the sixties. But the green revolution based on miracle grains – too often encouraging large-scale farming and the use of fertilisers and other capital inputs – led to an increase in social disparities and unemployment where big landowners displaced the small farmer. Now we are putting employment at the top of our priorities. Divergent demands from the developing countries themselves do not make the task of choosing the right policy easier.

The reasons for confusion are perhaps best illustrated by a

country normally considered to be a success story – Mexico. While the country's rate of growth over the last twenty years has been impressive – 6 to 7 per cent annually – its distribution of income has become inequitable. Whereas factory workers' income increased by more than 70 per cent between 1950 and 1960, landless labourers' income decreased by about 15 per cent. Also, unemployment has so increased in the last twenty years that there are today as many Mexicans without work as there were at the lowest point of the Great Depression. Among much of the population, malnutrition is still widespread.[1]

Not surprisingly, a growing number of students of development believe that our past definition of development as growth of GNP covers only one aspect of the problem. For further evidence one can point to the fact that growth in the third world, on average, is now higher than that of the developed countries, but for a large part of the population the problem has become worse. What has gone wrong? At the risk of oversimplification we can point to three interrelated factors which have frustrated development.

The first of these is, of course, the rapid growth of the population, which 'takes away' half the growth of the successful countries, and may lead to negative *per capita* growth for the poorer performers. Looking more closely at the results of population growth one can detect two consequences: the exodus from the land leads to an excessive, even malignant growth of the cities. In our Western experience, this exodus had at least one positive, and in fact decisive impact on development: as the rural population diminished, productivity of agriculture increased to the point where an ever-decreasing rural population could feed a growing proportion of the population engaged in the modern sectors of industry and services. In most of the LDCs, however, population in the rural areas, far from decreasing, is actually still on the increase.

Thus, the problem of employment is posed both in the cities *and* in the countryside: more dramatic and visible in the cities, but as deadly in the countryside where a majority of the population continues to live. Growth alone cannot solve this problem. Manufacturing output would have to grow by 15 per

[1] J. P. Grant, 'What is development?', *Intercom*, 69 (April 1972) 3.

cent annually for the rest of this century just to absorb the increase of the labour force during that period. The fundamental weakness of traditional development policy, indeed, may well have been precisely this stress on industrialisation. Increasing productivity means not only, and perhaps not even primarily, the creation of jobs through investments, but the replacement of labour by capital. With growing technological efficiency attained through (Western) capital goods, this trend is growing. Also, in agriculture, the much-heralded advent of miracle grains which demand extensive use of fertilisers and other capital inputs, has had a negative effect on employment. They increased the productivity per man-hour, and increased the total productivity of the countries concerned. But many experts agree that the positive effects of the green revolution could have been achieved without quite as many of the negative ones. The headlong rush towards capital-intensive production occurred (*a*) because capital was too cheap (owing to overvalued exchange rates, badly oriented development aid and low, sometimes negative, interest rates); (*b*) because certain social reforms did not accompany the green revolution: large landlords were the first to be able to profit from the increased productivity, and were thus able to buy up the small farmer who was lagging behind. Rural co-operatives, using intensive methods over the larger areas required for the new grains, would have done the trick as well.

The important conclusion that many observers have drawn is that the choice between labour-intensive and capital-intensive production in agriculture and industry is not so much a choice between efficiency and inefficiency as a choice of technique. The West, however, knows much more about reducing the share of labour in the production process than about maximising what is the most abundant resource of most LDCs. Examples like Korea and Taiwan, which deliberately encouraged labour-intensiveness by making capital dear (through high interest rates and a realistic exchange rate) show what can be achieved. Western policies often make this choice more difficult.

The second important conclusion is that development policy without a social policy is liable to lead to growth, but not to development which touches more than a small fraction of the population. An important element of such a social policy is concern for an equitable distribution of income. In fact, contrary to earlier theories, an inequitable income distribution may not only be socially undesirable and politically dangerous but is itself a major obstacle to growth. Until recently the opposite was thought to be true. Growth meant savings, and these could only come from the rich. It then turned out that the rich consumed a great part of their supposed surplus – not surprisingly, when one considers that an income twenty times the average in India equals that of a US factory worker. The savings of the very rich were either channelled into the international money market or put to use in unproductive activities like real estate. Furthermore, the concentration of income into the hands of a few has led to a distortion of consumption, and hence of production patterns, in the LDCs – few bicycle-makers but many jewellers.

Development in any real sense can only take place if all incomes rise, including those of the farm. The first step towards achieving this goal is, of course, full employment. Higher incomes, as experience has shown, in general lead to a lower birthrate. This in turn would ease the employment situation. It is this virtuous circle, or rather triangle, which a development policy in the larger sense must help to bring about. We will discuss the two most important elements of such a policy, aid and trade, with this objective in mind – still in general terms before turning to the more specifically European role in the development process.

Aid

Irrespective of the form it takes – gifts of goods and knowledge, or 'soft' loans for investments or imports – aid often means a transfer, not just of resources, but of our model of development. This means that the 'sacrifice' made by the rich is not necessarily related to a corresponding gain by the poor. How can one explain this paradox?

A gift of tractors, for example, encourages a transformation of production patterns in the direction of our own: large-scale, capital-intensive, 'American-style' farming. In addition to the artificial distortion of the market relationship between capital and labour – by making capital cheap – the tractors entail long-term additional costs of foreign exchange for petrol and spare parts. Why do we give, or furnish on credit, tractors rather than ploughs? Because we are good at making tractors, but have almost forgotten how to make ploughs (at least those which don't need machines to pull them). A similar case has also been made for a whole range of industrial capital goods: the weaving looms, the steel-mills, the earth-moving equipment we furnish for infrastructure improvements – all incorporate centuries of efforts to minimise labour. The realisation of this basic distortion has led to a growth of research into the development of 'intermediate technology'. But the (re-) discovery of labour-intensive ways of production will remain academic, as long as aid remains what it often is today – a form of export promotion.

There is no point in refusing to accept the generous intent of much of what we call aid. The mistake is made in the implementation: the translation of a transfer measured in monetary systems into the actual goods and services provided. At this moment, the real purpose, development, is too often obscured in favour of the promotion of exports. A symptom and consequence of this attitude is the fact that most bilateral aid is tied to purchases from the donor country. The purely financial loss in the effectiveness of such aid has been estimated as 30 per cent of the nominal amount of the aid. The more insidious effect is in the kind of product that is given or furnished on credit. An additional element working against relevant development aid is the tendency of bureaucracies, in both the donor and the recipient countries, to concentrate on single, large programmes, say hydro-electric dams, which are familiar and manageable. The fact that the underdeveloped countries themselves demand this form of aid is not unrelated to another form of aid, commonly called technical assistance.

This is a field of particular relevance to Europe, since fully half of the technical assistance from OECD countries comes from a single member country, France. But are the skills that Europe teaches the right ones for development? Are the economic models we offer appropriate? The mere introduction of an accounting measure, GNP, can distort perceptions of what constitutes success and failure.

Together with inappropriate models of efficiency, the West offers inappropriate models of education. Formal education based on a certain notion of literacy developed for the European bourgeoisie can lead to the following results: in Senegal, 38 per cent of those who had completed seven or more years of education were unemployed in the late sixties, against only 11 per cent among the illiterates.

Potentially harmful effects can also be observed in the forms of transfer where governments have little or no influence, and where relations seem to be based more closely on purely economic criteria of mutual benefit. This is the case with export credits, offered by private firms (but often guaranteed by the State) to finance their sales of capital goods. This form of transfer is recognised as one of the main sources of the growing debt of the developing countries – to the point where there will be a net outflow of public capital from the poor to the rich in a few years. Debts, in our experience, are of course useful motors of development – the financing of US growth in the nineteenth century through borrowed British capital is an often-cited example. In the world of LDCs this truth, likewise, does not hold good. Investments made by receiver countries with the borrowed funds are not always profitable. This is partly inevitable for long-term projects planned under conditions of great uncertainty. Part of the blame must also go to aggressive sales methods by Western firms, often backed by their governments, which the poorer countries find hard to resist. The result is often a combination of two vices: the neglect of development in the wider sense through maximisation of foreign input, and the neglect of even purely economic criteria of efficiency, which is leading to the bankruptcy of much of the third world.

Trade

It has become commonly accepted in the last decade that trade is far more important for development than aid: four-fifths of all the receipts of foreign exchange of LDCs come from trade. And, in contrast with aid, the LDC can dispose of this revenue as it sees fit. But trade, as presently operating, does not ensure a stable flow of foreign exchange on which to build a long-term development strategy, since the prices of many of the goods of the third world fluctuate widely on world markets, or face uncertain prospects owing to protectionist practices in the industrialised world.

The role of commerce is not only to provide foreign exchange, but to achieve a better allocation of resources through the international division of labour. Its full realisation through worldwide free trade would pose many problems for the LDCs, if only because comparative advantages are constantly changing through technological advances (e.g. the substitution of synthetic for natural raw materials). But the point is that we ourselves refuse to let the law of comparative advantage play when it would favour the LDCs. Labour-intensive industries, and processed or unprocessed agricultural goods, are among the most highly protected industries. Thus shoes and textiles have been largely excluded from generalised preference schemes, and where textiles have been included they have been hedged with tariff-quotas and other non-tariff barriers. In agriculture, of course, protection comes not so much from tariffs, but from levies and the support given to the production of our farmers.

In these circumstances the LDCs are led to pursue two policies, both of which harm development. They may try to diversify their exports into less protected products. This, however, means capital-intensive production, where their comparative advantage, and hence our protection, is lower; hence less employment, and the growth of industries less relevant to domestic needs. Or the LDCs, too, may refuse to accept the international division of labour and engage in a policy of import substitution. This means a waste of resources if production costs are higher than those of imported goods. It means a shift in the 'internal terms of trade' of the country in favour of industry and against agriculture. It means substantial additional imports of capital goods – partially defeating the original purpose of import substitution.

Thus, for industrial products, it now seems that liberal trade (both ways) would benefit less developed countries, and that the 'infant industry' argument does not hold in its traditional form. Instead of protection through high tariffs, a direct financial starting aid seems to answer better the legitimate wish of the LDCs not to be condemned for ever to be hewers of wood and drawers of water. This choice, of course, is not for the developed nations to make, but for them to make possible.

For certain industries of great capital-intensity, where location is almost discretionary, but where competing prestige interests lead to overproduction (as in the case of coastal steel), some form of joint industrial planning may offer a more certain way to equity than the law of comparative advantage.

What is the contribution to development of agricultural trade, the sector which is the main source of export receipts especially for the more populous countries? Here the answer is even more complex; since different problems – deteriorating terms of trade, price fluctuation and employment considerations – arise in different ways for three major groups of products.

For tropical products which are produced only in LDCs (coffee etc.) the basic problem is one of overproduction, slowly growing demand, and hence falling prices in relation to imported goods combined with sharp fluctuations in prices. Here a form of economic management allowing both stable prices and diversification away from these products (a diversification made difficult by the falling prices) seems the only solution.

A second major category is that of products which compete with synthetic products in the developed world (natural fibres, rubber). Here comparative advantage favours the synthetic products (because of our high protection for transformed natural products), and in the long run diversification away from these products may become necessary. In the medium term, comparative advantage could be restored, if the pollution cost of the substitutes is taken into consideration, not only in production, but also in disposal (biodegradability), and if the *de facto* protection for substitutes were lowered.

The most interesting problem is that of foodstuffs which are also produced in temperate zones or which compete with similar products in the rich countries (cereals, sugar, fats, citrus fruit). In this sector we refuse to let the law of comparative advantage operate, since we limit markets and subsidise the production of our farmers. But even if we made a radical shift in the direction of opening our markets to the cheapest producers, the positive effects on development would by no means be assured. In a world of truly free trade in agriculture, the developed countries of the temperate zone (US, Canada, Australia, etc.) rather than the LDCs would prove the most efficient producers. This means that LDC export revenue could only be guaranteed by a general discrimination on the part of Europe against other exports; with all the difficulties that this implies for a harmonious trading relationship with, above all, the US.

But even this option would not necessarily be conducive to development: production for export, as experience has shown, may lead to a shift towards capital-intensive production. Exports mean bulk orders of standardised products, favouring plantations rather than small holdings. And, since capital-intensive production is now almost always more efficient than agriculture based on even the lowest-paid labour, the need to compete on world export markets may entail a shift in the wrong direction. This, however, is less true for inherently labour-intensive industries like wine-production and rice.

A development-oriented policy of agricultural trade thus presents social as much as economic problems. If Europe were to open its markets generally to foodstuffs from the LDCs, it would risk, as we have seen, increasing unemployment both in Europe and in the third world. One thing we know for certain: the disposal of our surpluses (sugar and cereals) as food aid or in the form of exports disturbs not only world markets, but also the internal markets of developing countries, lowering the price, and hence the incentive to produce.

Considering all three groups of agricultural products together – tropical products, agricultural raw materials, and foodstuffs – one must conclude that this is not the sector of trade from which we can expect dynamic impulses for development.

This means that industrial trade must take up a growing share of the exports of developing countries. But there are fairly narrow limits even to this: our own ability to absorb the production of the third world and to adapt our industry and work-force; and the fact that export-led growth will in all probability help those that are already strong, the so-called 'threshold countries' – South Korea rather than India, Brazil rather than Chad.

If, as is likely, our efforts to open our borders to the exports of the LDCs fall short of what is required to solve the most pressing problems of development, we are forced to take a second look at that unsatisfactory alternative, aid. But, as the preceding analysis has suggested, we must do so with a salutary doubt in mind. Much of our machines, our advice, our rules, only makes sense in our world of 'machine-led' growth.

It is perhaps because of this doubt that, in the following sections on Community policy, the stress will often be put on minimising harm rather than achieving a breakthrough towards development. Even in this limited perspective there is much that needs to be done. But, curiously enough, if there is a sacrifice on our part, this is rarely a financial one. The main and difficult task before us is one of discipline.

Errors and omissions

A comprehensive discussion of Community efforts in the development field would have to include the individual efforts of the member states, the bilateral trade agreements of the Community, its global commercial policy, including the Generalised Preferences, the Mediterranean policy (discussed in Chapter 9) and the African association agreements. Here we will chiefly deal with this last, and most comprehensive, experiment in Community development policy, as well as with the specifically development-orientated part of commercial policy, the Generalised System of Preferences.

The African association agreements are the first, and most solidly based, foreign policy act of the Community, having been written into the text of the Treaty of Rome setting up the European Economic Community. This step has been correctly described as 'a limited multilateralisation of the colonial interests' of some member states.[1] In spite of the granting of independence in the early sixties, in spite of the inherent beneficent effects of 'multilateralisation', and in spite of the

---

[1] Gordon Weil: *A Foreign Policy for Europe* (Bruges, 1970) p. 137.

more enlightened role of the Commission, as compared with the 'mother countries', the historical origins of the Yaoundé Convention have deeply marked the Community's relations with its African associates.

When the Common Market was established, the African colonies of France presented a technical problem. Directly administered from Paris, their economies were part of the economy of France, yet they could not become part of the new Community. At the same time, the symbiosis between motherland and colonies entailed a number of highly artificial instruments of economic management which had to be taken into account. Foremost among these were agricultural arrangements, by which France granted guaranteed markets, at prices substantially over the world price level, to the traditional export staples (cotton, peanuts, etc.) of its colonies. Rightly, France insisted that these colonies could not be 'weaned' from this system overnight. But certain governments, and especially the Dutch, insisted that the *surprix* system be replaced by a more simple arrangement. As a compromise, the gradual abolition of the *surprix* system was coupled with a system of agricultural preferences. The change from the high 'colonial' prices to a level closer to that obtaining in world markets was to be made possible through a diversification and modernisation programme, financed by the European Development Fund (EDF).

In the event, the associates were caught between too much liberalisation and too little modernisation. For some products, like cotton which has a zero tariff, Community preferences provided no shelter from international competition. For others, a successive lowering of the common external tariff, which helped to reduce the discrimination against other LDC producers, reduced the value of the original preferences. Also, a liberal policy on soya from the US (an animal food whose by-product is vegetable oil), seriously damaged markets for African palm-oil and peanuts.

While the Community was asking its Associates to play by the rules of free trade, it violated these rules when European agricultural interests were threatened. Thus it imposed a levy on manioc imports (which competed with maize), and on rice, stimulating uneconomic Community production to the point where the Community has become a net *exporter* of this commodity, thus competing with LDCs on third markets.

In this situation, the success of the efforts at modernisation and diversification made by the EDF became crucial. Less than a third of the 730 million dollars allocated under the first Convention (1964) was earmarked for this purpose, the remainder going to infrastructure and price stabilisation expenditure. The total transfer was less than that under the French colonial system – a circumstance which forced the Associates to *tax* key exports in order to ensure sufficient budgetary receipts.

By 1969, as planned, agricultural prices had come down to world market levels, and the remains of the *surprix* system could be abolished. But, if this has left these African producers no worse off than other LDC producers, they continue to share the uncertainties which dependence on a few staple export products brings (fluctuating and falling prices). This dependence is due to the less than unqualified success of the diversification programme. Thus, the Ivory Coast, with the help of the EDF, vastly increased its production of palm oil, while a number of countries in and outside Africa also increased production of vegetable oil. Senegal, realising the need to diversify away from such production, chose, among other things, cotton – together with Malawi, the Ivory Coast, Togo, etc. At that time Chad and the Sudan were already finding it difficult to market their cotton. The examples could be multiplied. Diversified surpluses are little better than dependence on a single crop. It can also be questioned whether Community aid should be used to compete with efforts of other developing countries to increase their own agricultural exports.

It is of course always easy, with hindsight, to find fault with the policies adopted by the responsible authorities. After all, when the Community became involved with Africa, these countries were still colonies. After independence, the conflicting demands from the Associates themselves may have made an effective strategy more difficult. But one can at least ask oneself whether, in fifteen years, more could not have been done to achieve two different kinds of diversification: away from export crops to food for home consumption (36 per cent of total Senegal imports are of food); and towards agricultural transformation industries and other forms of industrialisation (about 1 per cent of EDF expenditure went to this latter purpose). In spite of some progress – half of Senegal's vegetable oil exports to the Community are now processed locally – most exports are still 'raw' materials. The Community has thus been laid open to the criticism of being unwilling to break the traditional – and colonial – economic structure between home country and dependency, and of having been too receptive to pleas from European plantation owners in Africa for modernisation aid, at the expense of a true development strategy. The reluctance to create, in Africa, industrial production liable to threaten certain Community industries may also have played a role.

Apart from the – now weakened – agricultural link, the Yaoundé Convention contains more general commercial provisions. It establishes no less than twenty free trade areas between the Community and the Associates. By 1968, when the Community's Common External Tariff began to apply, there were no tariffs on exports from the Associates, although, as pointed out earlier, levies continue to be applied to some agricultural exports. In return, the Associates had to agree to a gradual dismantling of their tariffs and quotas, though retaining the right to protect infant industries, as well as to levy customs taxes for budgetary purposes – a right they extensively make use of, and which applies both to Community and to third country exports.

One can look at the implications of this free trade area approach from a number of viewpoints: its international effects, its economic effects, its implications for African unity, and its implications for the long-term political relationship between Europe and Africa. In all these cases, the possibility that the Yaoundé system will be extended, wholly or in part, to most of Africa as a result of British entry into the Community, makes such an examination particularly urgent: Nigeria, should it join, would by itself double the population thus linked by specialties to the Community.

The legality of the Yaoundé Association agreements is no longer questioned in GATT. They more or less fulfil the criterion for granting a waiver to free trade areas: the liberalisation of substantially all trade. Should we therefore dismiss continued complaints by others, and especially the United States, as being 'discriminated' against by the special concessions granted to the Community? The immediate effects of such feelings on the other side of the Atlantic is growing cynicism with regard to GATT itself. Any agreement like the GATT can be emptied of all significance if its letter and not its spirit is adhered to, if everyone does 'what he can get away with'. The establishment of a large free trade area outside Europe itself (and hence with very doubtful offsetting trade-creation effects) is without doubt a breach of the spirit of GATT, of the universalism embodied in the MFN principle. 'Retaliation' by others could take many forms. More specifically, there is a – not so long-term – risk of the emergence of economic blocs. Japan is establishing special links in parts of South-East Asia: with a rigorously centred aid policy (*cum* export promotion), special claims on raw materials, and industrial investments setting up feeder industries for its home economy. The United States' links with South America, in spite of devolution in some areas, are still substantial. All these close economic relationships could gain importance if a reformed monetary system introduced greater flexibility among the industrialised countries. In such an event, the countries of the developing world would in practice have to link their currencies to that of the most important trading partner. The creation of yen, dollar, and 'Europa' areas would thus reinforce the trend towards a world fragmented into economic blocs. There are, however, countervailing forces which work towards the maintenance of a universal economic system. International production, the agent of the second industrial revolution, requires a world setting. The Community, by replacing its preferential zone in the third world through other forms of co-operation, and the Associates, by lowering their tariffs to all countries, could give a decisive push in the right direction.

As to its direct economic effects on the Associates, the first point to make is that the association has not increased the members' exports to the Community relative to other LDCs. The exception is cocoa – at the expense of Ghana and Nigeria, a fact which may pose problems in the future. The reasons for this failure are many. One is that tariff cuts, by themselves, have lost much of their importance. The structure of established economic patterns between the Associates and Europe has changed little. It is now being realised that export promotion may be more important than preferences. Thus, Brazilian coffee, through efficient marketing, has been able to enlarge its share against the 'favoured' African product. One can also ask oneself, why other industrialised countries have not established production facilities in Africa in order to exploit duty-free access to the Community. One reason sometimes cited is the high tariffs levied by the African countries on imports of capital goods from these third countries, tariffs which only protect European industrialists, comfortably installed in a sheltered – and high-price – 'home' market. New possibilities for industrial exports would arise if the United States joined the Generalised Preference scheme (at least as long as the industrialised countries did not make further substantial tariff cuts among themselves); but at present there is talk of the US granting such preferences only to Latin America.

Nothing in the text of the Convention prevents the Associates from lowering their tariffs to third countries. But neither does it encourage them to do so – as an MFN-based, non-preferential trade agreement would have done. If this helps to isolate the Associates from the rest of the world, it also isolates them from each other. For perhaps the most serious fault of the present arrangement is the perpetuation of a relationship, which structurally, as far as trade flows and economic leadership are concerned, resembles the role which used to characterise the Soviet Union in COMECON. That is, relationships run almost exclusively from the centre to the various, much weaker, 'partners', with almost no cross-relationship among the latter. While the encouragement of regional groupings is a stated aim of the Community – efforts in this direction have been and are being made in the Maghreb – the practical effect of the Community arrangements is the opposite.

Part of this is due to the multiple free trade area approach itself, i.e. tariff reductions are only required for Community products, not for those of the other African associates. Thus, no local markets of adequate size develop. Again, Associates are *permitted* to set up free trade areas or customs unions among each other, but they were not encouraged to do so at the beginning – before governments had become dependent on budgetary receipts from border taxes and tariffs, before national pride demanded a steel-mill or major harbour for each; and while the Community still had something to offer in return (duty-free access) which it used instead as a counterpart for its own free access to African markets.

The argument that Africans have nothing to trade with each other is not really convincing. Even if it were true, a general lowering of tariffs would then at least have assured them of cheaper industrial goods from outside. At the same time, intra-African preferences and a dismantling of administrative barriers to trade, coupled with an encouragement to undertake common planning, could have been attempted. Such was indeed the approach chosen towards Europe by the United States: the OEEC, distributor of Marshall funds, and motor of intra-European liberalisation, laid the foundations of European unity and of Europe's ability to become strong and competitive.

A closer parallel is offered by the Alliance for Progress between the United States and Latin America. Not only did total transfers rise much more rapidly than those going to the Yaoundé countries (from $185 million in 1960 to 1206 million in 1970, compared with transfers to Africa of $421 million, rising to 683 million in 1970), but the Alliance has not discouraged the formation of several regional groupings in Latin America. This success is not unrelated to the workings of the Inter-American Development Bank, in contrast with that of the European Development Fund. Whereas the former is a co-operative self-help organisation, a substantial part of whose funds are contributed by the Latin-American governments (who also jointly decide on their use), the EDF deals with each country separately and from the privileged position of a unilateral giver of aid. If, in spite of its merits, the Alliance is considered a failure – it has not achieved most of its stated objectives of social and economic reform – how should one judge the Community's aid effort in Africa?

The Community is proud of the institutions of the Yaoundé

Association. The Association Council and the Parliamentary Conference give parity representation to the Community and the Africans, allowing a constant dialogue between political leaders in government and parliament, which is appreciated by both the Europeans and the Africans. But parity is not the same as equality. Unity, among the Africans, is restricted to issues like the maintenance of advantages over other LDCs. In their bilateral dealings with the Community, the Africans are often competitors for grants, etc.

As to preferential treatment, the Community's ability to accord special favours through tariff concessions has, as we have seen, become more reduced. There is thus a very strong case for combining a qualitative change in the EDF (towards being a true regional bank, or rather several regional banks for co-operation and industrialisation) with a quantitative upgrading of the aid effort. A doubling of the present commitment would – such is the delay caused by the need to study, plan and implement projects – lead to a doubling of actual transfers in perhaps five years. In terms of the structural change of African economies needed to break the post-colonial pattern, this is a modest sum. If by then Community trade liberalisation towards other LDCs had become truly effective, that sum will be a low minimum if African governments are to dispose of the necessary sums to give starting aids to their infant industries.

The Generalised System of Preferences

The Community has had the means of conducting a comprehensive development policy in Africa. The Treaty of Rome has not provided the means with which to conduct a global development policy; its only instrument is commercial policy. It has used this opportunity by introducing in July 1971 (followed by other industrialised countries, but not so far by the United States) the Generalised System of Preferences (GSP) sponsored by UNCTAD.

The Community offers, unilaterally, tariff-free quotas on semi-finished and finished industrial goods to the seventy-seven (now ninety-seven) *bona fide* LDCs. No single LDC may use up more than half of this global quota. For 'sensitive' products

– in practice those which LDCs can actually provide – the quota is allocated in fixed proportion to the member states of the Community. As to textiles, the GSP is only extended to members of the international cotton agreement, i.e. to countries operating restrictions on exports. There are even tighter restrictions on jute and coconut matting, which are vital export products for areas like Bangladesh, Calcutta and Kerala, and until now have been excluded from the Community system. The exclusion of many processed agricultural goods, or the limited margin of preference given to such products is also a major shortcoming, however understandable it may be because of the artificial structure of the market.

This system, as implemented by the Community, is highly complicated; some claim that this prevents its use by LDCs which lack the necessary technical expertise. Furthermore, the GSP in its present form chiefly benefits the so-called 'threshold countries', those that already have fairly sophisticated exports, and for which the Community is only one of many markets. No exporter can afford to rely on the Community as his chief market, if his competitive position can change overnight – i.e. when the quota is filled and tariffs apply again in full.

The value of preferences is in large part determined by the advantage they give over other exporters. This margin has been considerably reduced by tariff-cutting among the developed countries, and may be reduced further. And the total tariff structure (if we except the very partial breach made by the GSP) *de facto* discriminates against the less developed countries.

How is this possible after twenty-five years of applying the most-favoured-nation clause? There are many reasons. First, a quarter of world trade, in 1970, took place within partial or complete free trade areas (EEC, EFTA, US–Canada). The proportion is raised considerably by the end of the EEC/EFTA division in Europe. Furthermore, the tariff reductions which resulted from the Kennedy Round chiefly affected the products which interested the industrialised countries. Also of importance is the fact that these negotiations did not eliminate a distortion in the structure of tariffs: the rate of protection tends to rise with the degree of transformation, of industrial added value, incorporated in the product. The US, for example, puts no duties on animal hides, a 5 per cent duty on leather, and 10 per cent on shoes (plus quantitative restrictions). In the EEC there is a 4 per cent duty on cocoa beans, but 16 per cent on cocoa products. No less important, quotas and other non-tariff barriers apply most frequently to the typical products of the less developed countries: processed agricultural products, petroleum products, cotton and other textiles, jute and leather products, ceramics, etc.

In many areas it should be possible to reverse the process of the last twenty-five years, which has been to negotiate first among industrialised countries, and leave residual benefits to the LDCs.

Thus the next 'round' in GATT should concentrate on products relevant to the LDCs, so as to reverse the past stress on advanced products. Furthermore, progress in the elimination of certain NTBs should not await the conclusion of what promises to become very lengthy negotiations in GATT, but be dealt with among what are often few supplier countries, and a particular market, the Community. A recent trade agreement with Argentina includes a provision for a joint commission to study ways in which health standards for beef exports can be handled more efficiently. This is a step in the right direction, which should be followed by more such agreements.

What can be done?

It may seem hazardous – given the uncertainty reflected in the first part of this chapter, about the goals of development and the best way of achieving them – to make concrete proposals about future policy. But all policy-making takes place in conditions of uncertainty and imperfect knowledge. Furthermore, it is not for the Community and other industrialised countries to 'solve' the problem of development – this remains largely the task of the developing countries themselves. The Community can and should pursue a more limited goal: to develop an economic and political framework which allows the countries of the developing world which so desire to integrate themselves in world economy in socially and politically acceptable conditions.

This means first of all providing market access for the manufactured goods of the developing countries. True, such exports provide only a fraction of the foreign exchange of most developing countries, but it is this sector which more than any other can give dynamic impulses to economic growth. Paradoxically, the best prospect for extending and improving the now narrow limits of the Generalised System of Preferences lies in a general liberalisation of trade between both industrialised and non-industrialised countries. It is in such a more general context that a drastic reduction of quotas has a chance of succeeding, and it is through a joint and mutually enforced commitment by the industrialised countries that safeguard clauses can be kept to a minimum and become less subject to the unilateral discretion of the industrialised countries and more subject to international supervision. It is these most serious obstacles to trade which should have priority in the present GATT negotiations. Equally, a generalised lowering of tariffs on products which are particularly relevant to developing countries would give a more substantial benefit to these countries than a mere tariff-free quota, as at present – especially since this would imply an opening of the US market for such products.[1]

The consumer in the Community would receive substantial economic benefits from a more equitable division of labour extended to the less developed world. In view of these benefits there is every reason to make available the funds needed to ease the burden of adjustment on Community workers, to provide for their retraining and security. Furthermore, since the burden of adjustment will fall unevenly on certain regions and countries, there is much to be said for financial solidarity on the part of the members of the Community in this field, as a natural consequence of having a common commercial policy. But if the Community is going to practise a consistent policy of opening its borders to the products of the third world, something more fundamental than the provision of financial relief for the affected workers is needed: change itself – whether caused by advances in technology or by shifts in international trading patterns – must be seen as an opportunity rather than a threat. An open society, and a just society, are therefore a precondition for an open commercial policy.

[1] See also *Tripartite Report on Reassessing North-South Economic Relations* (The Brookings Institution: Washington, 1972).

At present, however, and in certain countries for many years to come, agricultural exports remain the largest source of revenue for most developing countries. As has been pointed out, this is not the dynamic sector from which significant impulses to growth can be expected. The Community market is highly protected. However, this protection is above all directed against the other producers of the temperate zone. A lowering of barriers in the interest of the developing countries would only need a small change in the agricultural policy, while giving substantial benefits to LDCs, especially as regards sugar (see Chapter 4).

But in the sector of agricultural exports, market stability is often regarded as at least as important as market expansion. Among the member states of the Community there is a debate about the feasibility and long-term viability of commodity agreements. Less ambitiously, and largely in a regional context, the Commission and the European Parliament seem to favour market organisation. This can mean a guarantee by the Community to buy minimum quantities of a product irrespective of annual market fluctuations, while adjusting this minimum to the long-term development of the market. Such a policy, as suggested in the foregoing chapter, could make sense, for example, for citrus fruit and wine from the Mediterranean. More generally, vegetable oil, rice and sugar may lend themselves to a similar form of market organisation. Within such an approach, it would still be possible, on a slowly decreasing scale, to favour traditional suppliers from the associated countries. Experience has shown that such 'regional' forms of market organisation may be easier to operate than global ones, though efforts should be made at least to complement the regional organisation with global arrangements. Thus the Commonwealth Sugar Agreement (for which there will be, according to a Council decision, a Community replacement) has co-existed with the network of arrangements linking especially certain Latin American countries to the US market, while the International Sugar Agreement regulated the remaining 'free' market on which participants in either regional arrangement could sell.

These arrangements, of course, attempt not only to provide a more stable quantitative access to markets, but also to stabilise prices. This opens the possibility of going further and using artificially high prices as a form of transfer. Direct transfers of this sort are perhaps practicable – and this only within a tight system of production control – for goods with a low demand elasticity like coffee and tea. For other goods, high prices would not only encourage overproduction and reduce total consumer demand, but worse, as regards agricultural raw materials, encourage a switch to synthetic substitutes where possible. A financial transfer by means of import prices may be possible through larger use of a Community practice, now used for citrus fruit from the Mediterranean, whereby the Community does not itself raise the levy which normally brings such imports up to the Community price level, but leaves this task, and hence the budgetary receipts, to the exporting country. Again, this is only workable if Community prices are not so high as to incite both the LDC and the Community producer to uneconomic production.

However crucial the importance of trade for development may be, financial transfers from the Community and other industrial countries remain a necessary element of development policy, and especially for those countries which for a long time to come will be unable to initiate growth through their own efforts. The Community as such, of course, only accounts for a small fraction of total transfers by the member states. However, there are a number of things that could be done.

First among these would be an untying of aid among the Community countries, as a first step towards a global untying of aid. This latter step may be difficult to achieve until the international climate in trade relations improves. Within the Community, however, tied aid is in clear contradiction of the Treaty of Rome's general provisions against distortion of competition. Its rapid elimination would be a manifestation of the Community's solidarity while at the same time benefiting the developing countries.

Furthermore, a better co-ordination of the aid efforts of the member states should be high on the agenda of reforms – especially in Africa, where not only these states, but also the EDF, pursue sometimes divergent and unrelated and programmes. Co-ordination, not only within but also among different African states could be achieved by the promotion of regional banks in which the FED would have a share along with the member countries of the Community, and – no less – the African states themselves.

Co-ordinated action by the member countries of the Community is also indicated to deal with what is perhaps the most pressing problem of many developing countries, the growing burden of debt. Already, member countries work together in consortia set up to reschedule such debts, and which in effect often transform the original commercial and semi-commercial short-term debts into long-term, 'soft' loans. Since these debts are in part the result of commercial practices (e.g. export credits) on the part of member states, a joint approach would make it easier both to deal with the effects of past policies, and to design new policies. For this latter purpose, the role of the group attached to the Council of Ministers, which deals with exports credits and guarantees, should be enlarged.

To be really effective, however, the international community at large should monitor its practices and policies in the export credit field much more strictly than has been the case until now. The best way to do this, perhaps, would be for the International Monetary Fund to take responsibility for reviewing flows of export credits to particular countries, evaluating them in relation to domestic economic growth and against the background of the volume of debt assumed. This would be a kind of early warning system through which borrowers and lenders alike could be advised of potential problems ahead. The IMF could discuss its findings confidentially with both lending and borrowing countries in the course of its regular annual consultations. In especially threatening situations, the Fund could recommend more rigorous controls over export credits or even the imposition of temporary ceilings.[1]

Again, this presupposes that for international economic relations in general the present competitive, not to say mercantalist, spirit among the rich countries be replaced by a co-operative approach to the problems of development. This also applies to the opportunity for the most radical means for untying aid, the transfer of a part of international liquidity creation (through SDRs) to the less developed countries. Here,

[1] *Tripartite Report*, op. cit., p. 35.

too, a common Community position is a precondition for, and first step towards, global agreement.

As the Community develops more devices for dealing with the problems of development, its present concern – justified by geography and history – for its Mediterranean and African neighbours should lose its exclusiveness and change its character. Europe, long before the Community existed, fostered a certain economic structure in this part of the world. It cannot simply renounce this responsibility. But to be paid for discharging this responsibility, as is implied by the creation of a privileged market, belittles the efforts made and reduces their economic effectiveness. Furthermore, grateful clients tend to become resentful critics, as future political leaders in these countries begin to pursue political and economic objectives which may well differ from those held by the leaders who, from a position of weakness, and impressed by European 'technical advice', conclude today's bargains.

Great Britain has brought as her 'dowry' special economic links with a great number of additional developing countries. Even taking the restrictive definition of 'associables', i.e. those that are being offered special links with the Community, their population surpasses that of the present members of the Yaoundé Association system. British concern, however, extends beyond these to include, among others, the much larger population of the Indian subcontinent. The renegotiation of the Yaoundé Convention, due to start in 1973, and the host of individual negotiations with the 'associables', therefore provide an opportunity to replace the present and future maintenance of 'special' links with almost fifty developing countries by an approach which is oriented towards problems rather than based on the past. In the short term, the difference between such a policy and the present 'special links' approach is less than one might suppose. Problems are liable to be most serious, and demand most immediate attention, in areas whose economies are linked most closely with that of the Community. But there is a considerable difference between making special efforts to overcome the shortcomings of a situation inherited from history, and considering such inherited situations as something precious and worth perpetuating.

As was pointed out at the beginning of this chapter, the

influence which a major economic power like the Community has on the developing countries goes far beyond specific 'development' policies. The interaction of the Community's industrial, agricultural, commercial, and monetary policies on the process of development is complex but none the less real. In order to increase the Community's 'sensitivity', and to enable it to take a long-term policy view, there is a strong case for establishing an independent advisory council to present an annual report on all aspects of the Community's economic policy as it affects the developing countries.

11 Conclusion

The world in which nine European nations are establishing their union does not allow them to opt out of the tensions and conflicts existing between East and West, North and South. The thirteen British colonies that became the United States could do so: once their existence had been accepted, their foreign policy could simply be to keep aloof from all others, and avoid entangling alliances.

The European Community, however, is not only bound to the whole world by economic links that can neither be severed nor simply left to be governed by an 'invisible hand'. It is also inextricably involved in what remains, however much progress may be made during this decade, an unresolved conflict of power between East and West, sharpened by deep differences of tradition and opinion about basic aspects of the organisation of society.

The Nine have therefore no choice: absorbed in all the problems posed by their progress from what is now a customs union plus an agricultural policy to the economic and monetary union they have decided to form, they must at the same time reach agreement about the foreign policy they want to pursue together: that is, about the place and role of the European Community in the world.

Indeed, an active participation in world affairs is increasingly seen as a major *raison d'être* for the Community. At the same time such participation risks introducing the tensions of the international system into the Community itself, and weakening rather than strengthening its cohesion. This danger should not be underestimated. Monetary and economic union will succeed or fail according to the Community's ability to deal, technically and politically, with the international economy and the international community. The common commercial policy – the major element of joint international action by the Community thus far – required only a limited degree of solidarity on the part of the member states. A common monetary policy requires more fundamental choices; but in the seventies even trade policy will involve much more than harmonising tariffs and economic interests of the member states.

Economic power is a crucial instrument of foreign policy. Therefore no real separation is possible between 'technical' decisions and 'political' decisions, between 'low' policy and 'high' policy. Decisions concerning chickens and oranges, sugar and textiles, development aid or exchange-rate policy are never divorced from considerations of high policy. Even if individual 'minor' acts of policy can sometimes be treated as merely technical issues, their cumulative effect always raises larger questions. This is indeed the danger of divorcing economics from politics: the long-term effects of policy can for a time be ignored, but the consequences cannot be avoided. To deal with economic issues as mere technical matters, and one by one, is to engage in a policy of drift. But taking a long-term view requires a basic agreement by the members of the Community about the direction they want to follow.

In the early fifties, when the process started which led to the European Community of Nine as we know it today, such a common view did exist. The experiences of their thirty years' 'civil war' and the cold war that followed created a consensus about Europe's priorities which did not have to be spelt out and was hardly contested. During the sixties, uncertainty about external priorities played an important part in the slowing-down of progress towards unity in Europe.

Now, enlargement has given a new impetus to the Community. The Paris Summit has taken decisions concerning the Community's internal development and progress towards unity in matters of foreign policy. Such progress is not likely to come from *ad hoc* harmonisation on issues of the moment. Unless a long-term view of external priorities is formed, the decisions of the Summit may well remain a dead letter.

In the preceding chapters, divergences between the member states of the Community have not been ignored. Their approach to the major problems of the international system in the economic, monetary, agricultural and energy fields have been marked by historical experience, national doctrine, and by inevitably particular interests. The same applies in part to relations with our partners in the world. Here, moreover, geographical location has given different member states differing perceptions of reality, however inextricably linked their fate has become.

In spite of these very real differences, we submit as a conclusion to our study that a consensus on the long-term foreign policy goals of the Community is possible, provided a dispassionate analysis of the points of weakness and of strength leads to a common understanding of the limits and the opportunities of joint Community action.

In terms of military power the Nine are weak. Even if they increase the efficiency of their forces through joint efforts, they cannot equal the super-powers. Without a full range of tactical and strategic nuclear weapons no country or group of countries can hope to join this exclusive club. Chapters 1 and 6 of this volume have shown why the construction of such a nuclear arsenal seems impossible for the foreseeable future. This places certain limits on the Community's foreign policy. But military power itself has been devalued through the mutually-imposed discipline of the nuclear powers. In such a world, economic power – if used in ways and for purposes appropriate to it and not as a substitute for military power – takes on a new importance.

But here, too, certain weaknesses of the Community are evident and in all probability long-lasting. Certainly, it is the largest participant in international trade. Certainly, the monetary reserves of the Nine are nearly twice those of the US and Japan put together. But power does not result from a simple addition. The Community still lacks the capacity to focus its economic capacity, to use it jointly for common purposes.

The continuing progress of economic integration will increase the areas of common interest and hence strengthen the basis of joint action by the Nine. Much can and must be done to enable the Community's institutions better to formulate common positions, and defend and promote these positions in discussions and negotiations with others.

To some extent, however, weakness resulting from diversity

is a permanent feature of the Community – unless tragic events change beyond recognition the international climate in which the Community develops. The institutional weakness partly reflects a diversity – of culture, language, and habit – which is and should remain an essential element of our union. Thus the Community will not have a central seat of power like the White House, the Kremlin, or the Japanese Government, and the tasks it sets for itself in foreign policy must take account of this fact.

Taken together, these limitations make it impossible for the Community to become a power like any other – to become a nation writ large. But the Nine can turn the inherent weaknesses of the Community to strength if they conceive of this Community, in François Duchêne's term, as a civilian power, and accept as a guiding concept of their foreign policy that the process which forms the basis of their own union does not stop at the borders of the Community.

At the heart of the Community enterprise lies the realisation that lasting equality between different entities cannot be achieved through balancing power – which creates at best 'armistice', to use the Kantian term, but never peace – but must be sought in submission to common rules. Extending the areas of international life governed by contract – be it with the industrial powers of the West, with Eastern Europe and the Soviet Union, or with the developing countries – should be the first priority of the Community.

Related to this is a further lesson of Community experience: that growing interdependence multiplies rather than reduces opportunity for conflict, as more and more areas of national life are touched by the actions of others. But experience has also shown that it is possible to 'domesticate' conflict: by setting limits to arbitrary action through the acceptance of rules, and by developing a procedural framework in which to deal with inevitable conflicts as they arise.

Certainly, the domestication of economic power – for it is here that the Community's opportunity lies – does not mean the domestication of military power. But if we are correct in assuming that military power is losing some of its value as an instrument of international diplomacy, and that economic power represents the dynamic (but also potentially destructive) element in international politics, and if we furthermore accept that, for the rest of the century perhaps, there will be continual conflicts over the international allocation of resources and economic opportunities, the task of building a global economic order is essential.

This process will certainly not lead to a single set of rules for all states on all matters. Nothing so utopian is suggested here. The willingness of states and groups of states to accept the discipline, assume the obligations, and discharge the responsibilities which the establishment and the maintenance of an international order requires, will differ and vary. The goals of economic policy, and views of how to deal with world social and economic problems, will diverge and conflict. There will be a debate among the industrial countries – just as there was between the Six and the proponents of a pure free-trade approach in the founding days of the Community – about how much 'management' of the international economy is needed, and on the meaning and limits of sovereignty in a world of interdependence. Between the developed and developing world, an even more fundamental debate will continue on the equity of the present international division of labour and the distribution of wealth. It is all the more important to have effective channels for such a debate, and the means to implement such agreement as can be reached. The same is true for the dialogue between East and West, where the search for pragmatic solutions must go hand in hand with the establishment of a durable framework which minimises tensions and creates the basis of confidence without which a genuine mutual opening will not occur.

In all these cases, the Community will find it easier to work together with some countries than others, because their interests converge, or because their links are closer. But it is essential that the area of global agreement be enlarged, and that particular solutions be a complement to and not a substitute for a global approach to the problems of what has rightly been called the 'global village'.

Such an approach is not only best suited to the Community's strength: it also minimises its weaknesses. The Community will always be slow to take decisions. It is ill-equipped to undertake 'crisis management' in an unpredictable world. It can however use its considerable economic weight to influence the ways in which nations behave towards each other, and it can contribute its experience and the civilian values of its society to this task.

Two misunderstandings might stand in the way of a workable consensus about the general context in which the Community must place its foreign policy. The first consists of a conception of independence and interdependence as mutually exclusive. Interdependence cannot exist without independence, without the realisation of one's own personality – in this case Europe's personality. Otherwise, interdependence becomes simply a cover for subjection to others, for the inherently unstable relationship between the dominating and the dominated. But independence, without the readiness to organise interdependence – that is the readiness to accept those disciplines of behaviour others are ready to accept also – cannot be had in today's and, still less, in tomorrow's world.

The Nine cannot act on the world scene unless they develop their Community and their union – that is their 'European personality'. But they cannot develop that personality without accepting the realities of interdependence, and the constraints that interdependence demands if it is to become a creative and not a destructive relationship.

The second misunderstanding lies in a confusion between old fashioned *laissez faire* liberalism, and the use of market forces to regulate certain economic processes.

Today every government is held responsible by all political parties for the economic well-being of the nation. Internally, no government and no nation can accept the result of an uncontrolled play of economic forces. To a large extent, electors judge a government by its capacity to manage the national economy. Nevertheless, today, even centrally planned economics seek, within the framework drawn by a plan, to leave certain tasks to the market mechanism.

Between nations, the economic management function is underdeveloped in relation to the play of the market forces. The European Economic Community is itself the result of the insight that trade liberalisation in our times must be accompanied not only by a number of joint rules and disciplines, but also by certain forms of joint economic management. In this respect the European Community is a denial of pure *laissez-faire* thinking. At the same time, and within the framework set by monetary instruments and by joint economic, social, regional and industrial policies, a large place is left to the market mechanism. As in each country, so within the Community, a political struggle will continue concerning the outline of this framework as well as concerning the limits to be ascribed to the market mechanism within the context set by the disciplines and rules evolved by common institutions.

To opt for an open, one-world economic system means necessarily to begin, together with other countries which are willing to do so, the same process and the same debate. To move towards freer trade in the world without moving at the same time towards a certain amount of joint management is not possible.

The debate about what kind of management is needed, and about what should be left to the market forces will be difficult. In fact, this debate will never end – either within or between our nations. It is the essence of modern political life. But the progress made during recent years in the discussions concerning world monetary management, although leaving many and important divergences of opinion, shows that it is not illusory to think that agreement about the scope and methods of economic management between participants in the world economic system is feasible. Just as within the Community itself the debate is not between pure *laissez-faire*, pure market mechanism, and total joint economic management, but concerns how and how much to manage, and how much to leave to market forces.

Internationally, as internally, it is impossible to return to management by an 'invisible hand'. Free trade and joint management have become inseparable: the first cannot progress without the latter. And the Nine cannot really influence the debate about what kind of management and how it should be organised, unless they speak with one voice and establish their own 'personality'.

Finally, a few remarks about the institutional aspects of Community foreign policy making. For two reasons these aspects have been neglected in this volume. At the present stage of European unity it is first necessary to build a working consensus on the role of the Community in the world. Only when this debate has produced results can the discussion about institutions for foreign policy be fruitfully resumed.

Secondly, the present institutional structure, although far from perfect, leaves scope for considerable progress if full use is made of the possibilities of the Treaty of Rome. The European Parliament does, and should even more often and thoroughly, discuss the general direction of Community foreign policy. For, although at the present time it is for the Ministers and, when necessary, the Summit, to decide on the direction of this policy, a broad public debate on the issues is essential. Such a debate would also help the Commission to reflect and interpret European opinion. The Commission's power to propose remains a formidable power, though it is circumscribed by a far too restrictive interpretation of the Treaty articles dealing with foreign economic policy. No treaty revision is necessary to change this situation. At least for the moment, a larger interpretation of these articles combined with, where needed, recourse to Article 235 of the Rome Treaty, as envisaged by the Paris Summit, will suffice. It would be illusionary to think that if on this basis no agreement were possible, a treaty revision would alter the differences of opinion which such disagreement would reflect.

Nor should one make too much of the dangers of an 'Economic Community' policy worked out in isolation from an intergovernmental 'high policy' worked out by the so-called Davignon Committee. In logic, little can be said for the existence of two parallel systems, both dealing with foreign policy matters. But in practice the Ministers forming the Council of the Community are the same men who direct and bear responsibility for the work of the Davignon Committee. And, just as important, the inclusion of the Commission in the work of the Davignon Committee in practice is proceeding satisfactorily. A look at the agenda for the next few years – the reform of the world monetary system, the new round of GATT negotiations, the Conference on Security and Co-operation in Europe, the renegotiations of the Yaoundé and Arusha Conventions, together with the negotiations with those eligible for association – makes it clear that any separation between 'low' and 'high' policy in practice will prove to be impossible.

One further observation must be made about the instruments of foreign policy. Whichever aspect of the external relations of the Community one studies, it becomes obvious that every constructive move, every step in the direction of an open, one-world economy with the common disciplines and the joint management that this requires, implies changes in the industrial as well as the agricultural structures of the Community. It is no exaggeration to say that its capacity for constructive action depends on the capacity to deal internally with the problems of structural change. Within the Community the instruments for adjustment are thus essential instruments of foreign policy.

Satisfactory adjustment, however, involves much more than reasonable severance payments and retraining policies for those in agriculture or in industry who are the victims of change. It means a social policy where change becomes not a threat but a source of hope. Adjustment, seen in this way, involves the educational system and progress towards equality of opportunity; it involves the entire quality of life of our society. If the direction this volume indicates for the Community's foreign policy is the right one, then the Community's capacity to act constructively in the world depends in the last resort on its success in establishing within its boundaries a more united and more just society.

MAX KOHNSTAMM
WOLFGANG HAGER

Notes on Contributors

SIR BERNARD BURROWS
Former British Permanent Representative at NATO and Deputy Under-Secretary at the Foreign Office. Co-author (with Christopher Irwin) of *The Security of Western Europe: Towards a Common Defense Policy* (Charles Knight, 1972).

FRANÇOIS DUCHÊNE
Director of the International Institute for Strategic Studies, London. Author of *The Endless Crisis* (Simon & Schuster, 1970).

EMANUELE GAZZO
Director, Agence Europe, Brussels. Author of *Un secolo di storia dell'Ansaldo* and other works.

WOLFGANG HAGER
Formerly on the staff of the Foreign Policy Research Institute, Philadelphia. Now Project Director, European Community Institute for University Studies.

JACK HARTSHORN
Consultant on oil and energy questions, with Walter Levy S. A. Author of *Oil Companies and Governments* (Faber & Faber, 1967).

ALBERT KERVYN DE LETTENHOVE
Professor of Economics, University of Louvain; Chairman, Advisory Committee on Medium Term Economic Policy, European Community.

MAX KOHNSTAMM
Formerly Secretary of the European Coal and Steel Community. President of the European Community Institute for

University Studies and Vice-President of the Action Committee for the United States of Europe.

THEO PEETERS
Professor of Economics, Louvain University. Consultant on trade problems for the European Community and the Belgian Foreign Ministry.

HENRI PERROY, S.J.
Professor of International Economics in Paris. Now on the staff of the European Community Institute for University Studies. He is the author of *L'Europe devant le Tiers Monde* (Aubier, 1969).

MICHEL TATU
For many years Moscow corespondent of *Le Monde*, now its Foreign Editor. He is the author of *Le Pouvoir en URSS* (Grasset, 1967), and *Le Triangle Moscou, Pékin et les deux Europes* (Casterman, 1972).

ADRIEN ZELLER
An agricultural economist living in Brussels. Author of *L'Imbroglio agricole du Marché Commun* (Calmann-Lévy, 1972).

The following, in private or group discussion with the authors, took part in the study project which led to this volume.

ROBERTO ALIBONI Secretary General, Istituto Affari Internazionali, Rome

GIORGIO BASEVI Professor of International Economics, University of Bologna and Louvain

OLAV BORGAN Director, Norwegian Federation of Agriculture, Oslo

GEORGES BRONDEL Commission of the European Community, Brussels

FRÉDÉRIC BOYER DE LA GIRODAY Commission of the European Community, Brussels

ALASTAIR BUCHAN Professor of International Relations, Oxford.

PAOLO CALZINI   Professor, Johns Hopkins University School of Advanced International Studies, European Center of American Studies, Bologna

KARL CARSTENS   Director, Forschungsinstitut der Deutschen Gesellschaft für Auswärtige Politik, Bonn

GUY DE CARMOY   Professor, INSEAD, Fontainebleau

CARLO M. CIPOLLA   Professor of Economic History, University of Pavia and Berkeley, California

RONALD CLAPHAM   Professor, Institut für Wirtschaftspolitik, Universität Köln

ROBERT FLOWER   British Delegation to NATO, Brussels

CURT GASTEYGER   Director of Studies, Atlantic Institute, Paris

JULIAN GRENFELL   Head of Information and Public Affairs, Europe, World Bank, Paris

PIERRE HASSNER   Professor, Centre d'Études des Relations Internationales, Fondation Nationale des Sciences Politiques, Paris

W. G. C. M. HAACK   Economist, Europa Institute, Amsterdam

RAINER HELLMANN   Head of the Brussels Office, Vereinigte Wirtschaftsdienste, Brussels

STANLEY HENIG   Civil Service College, London

M. J. 'T HOOFT-WELVAARS   Professor, Economic and Social Institute, University of Amsterdam

J. F. JANSES   Esso–Belgium, Antwerp

TIM JOSLING   Senior Lecturer, London School of Economics

KARL KAISER   Director, Institut für Theorie und Soziologie der Politik, University of Saarbrücken

ALEXANDER KING   Director for Scientific Affairs, OECD, Paris

NORBERT KLOTEN   Chairman, German Council of Economic Advisers, University of Tübingen

DIETER KÖNIG   Commission of the European Community, Brussels

BEATE KOHLER   Professor, Darmstadt University

NORBERT KOHLHASE Director, Press and Information Office of the European Community, Geneva

JEAN LALOY Ministry of Foreign Affairs, Paris

CHRISTOPHER LAYTON Commission of the European Community, Brussels

ARRIGIO LEVI Journalist, *La Stampa*, Turin

HERIBERT MAIER International Confederation of Free Trade Unions, Brussels

RICHARD MAYNE Director, Federal Trust, London

CESARE MERLINI Director, Istituto Affari Internazionali, Rome

ROGER MORGAN Deputy Director of Studies, Chatham House, Royal Institute of International Affairs, London

PETER ODELL Director, Economisch-Geografisch Instituut, Nederlandse Economische Hogeschool, Rotterdam

MICHAEL PALMER Director, Committee Services, European Parliament, Luxembourg

JOHN PINDER Director, Political and Economic Planning, London

GIAN CARLO PAPPALARDO ENI, Rome

DANIEL PEPY Director, Institut de Recherches agronomiques et tropicales, Paris

UGO PICCIONE Journalist, *Il Sole/24 ore*

HARTMUT ROENNEKE Consultant, Arnsberg

JEAN ROYER Former Assistant General Secretary, GATT. Consultant to International Chamber of Commerce, Paris

PIERRE SALIN Professor, Centre Universitaire Dauphine, Paris

ROBERT SCHAETZEL Former Head of the US Mission to the EEC

EBERHARD SCHULZ Forschungsinstitut der Deutschen Gesellschaft für Auswärtige Politik, Bonn

HENRI SCHWAMM Professor, Institut Universitaire d'Études Européennes, Geneva

ANDREW SHONFIELD Director, Royal Institute of International Affairs, Chatham House, London

JEAN SIOTIS Professor, Institut Universitaire des Hautes Études Internationales, Geneva

STEFANO SILVESTRI Istituto Affari Internazionali, Rome

ROLAND TAVITIAN Commission of the European Community, Brussels

PETER TULLOCH Overseas Development Institute, London

MARC ULLMANN Foreign Editor, *L'Express*, Paris

RAYMOND VERNON Professor, Centre for Industrial Studies, Geneva

GERHARD WETTIG Professor Bundesinstitut für Osteuropäische und Internationale Studien, Köln

JOHN WILLIAMSON Former Professor of Economics, University of Warwick. Senior Adviser to the IMF

HERMAN WORTMANN Commission of the European Community, Brussels

ROBERT WOOD Director of Studies, Overseas Development Institute, London

Glossary

ALLIANCE FOR PROGRESS
Its Charter, signed in 1961 at Punta del Este between 20 American States, gave a more comprehensive institutional expression to the attempt by the US, begun with the Inter-American Development Bank in 1958, to stimulate economic co-operation in Latin America through multilateral aid. Neither of its main objectives, a 2.5 per cent per capita growth rate and social reform, was met, partly because aid had to be used to finance external debts.

BRETTON WOODS
An international conference held at Bretton Woods, New Hampshire, in 1944, which discussed the post-war international payments system and led to the creation of the IMF (q.v.) and the World Bank (see International Bank).

COMMON AGRICULTURAL POLICY (CAP)
System of agricultural market organisation applied by the EEC, involving common minimum prices for major products, financial solidarity, and Community preference over outside suppliers.

COMECON
(COUNCIL FOR MUTUAL ECONOMIC ASSISTANCE)
Founded in 1949. Membership identical with that of the Warsaw Part (q.v.) plus the Mongolian People's Republic and Cuba. Strictly intergovernmental, COMECON's main goals – co-ordination of national plans, specialisation of production, and expansion of interregional trade – have often been frustrated by the rigidity of national central plans, the tradition of autarky, and the absence of multilateral means of settlement. With the adoption of the Complex Programme (q.v.) and the renewed interest in integration in Eastern Europe, COMECON may be entering a more active phase.

COMPLEX PROGRAMME

Adopted in July 1971 at Bucharest, the Complex Programme for Further Co-operation and Integration develops long-term goals for COMECON (*q.v.*), to be implemented in the next two decades. Though internally inconsistent, reflecting the divergent economic philosophies of the member states, the Complex Programme seeks to extend COMECON activity beyond the harmonisation of investment plans towards creating conditions for multilateral trade through the introduction of true exchange rates, alignment of domestic and foreign trade prices, and credits to finance payments disequilibria.

CONFERENCE ON SECURITY AND CO-OPERATION IN EUROPE (CSCE)

First proposed by the members of the Warsaw Pact (*q.v.*) in 1966, the CSCE reached the stage of preparatory talks in November 1972. Including all European states, the United States and Canada, it is meant to deal with the political aspects of security (the military aspects are to be discussed in the MBFR (*q.v.*) negotiations), economic co-operation, freer movement of persons and ideas between East and West, etc.

EURO-DOLLAR

Claims on US banks held by individuals or institutions outside the United States. The possibility of trading these claims outside normal exchange and interest-rate restrictions has led to the creation of an international capital market largely denominated in Euro-dollars.

EUROGROUP

Informal caucus of ten European countries within NATO (*q.v.*), founded in 1968 on British initiative. It aims to increase European solidarity in defence matters. After a cautious start, it now discusses common problems before full NATO meetings, seeks common arguments, including financial incentives, to keep present US troop levels in Europe, and has begun (with French participation) to discuss joint production of military equipment.

EUROPEAN DEFENCE COMMUNITY (EDC)
An ambitious project initiated by the French government in 1950 to permit German rearmament by integrating national armed forces down to brigade level in a European army, with institutions on the model of the European Coal and Steel Community (ECSC). Treaty signed in May 1952 by the six members of ECSC and ratified by all except France and Italy. It was rejected by the French Assembly in June 1954. (*See also* WEU.)

EUROPEAN DEVELOPMENT FUND (EDF)
An agency for the allocation of grants and soft loans to the members of the Yaoundé Convention (*q.v.*). Its resources ($730 for Yaoundé I, and $900 for Yaoundé II) represent only a fraction of total aid transfers by Community member states. It is managed by a committee of experts from the member states with the Commission presiding, and is administered by the Commission.

EUROPEAN FREE TRADE ASSOCIATION (EFTA)
A free trade area between seven West European states created in 1959. It virtually ceased to exist with the accession of Great Britain and Denmark to the European Community and the conclusion of industrial free trade agreements between the Community and the remaining EFTA members.

FLEXIBLE RESPONSE
NATO strategic doctrine providing defence proportionate to the size of the attack; developed as alternative to the earlier massive retaliation doctrine involving immediate use of strategic nuclear deterrent.

GATT
(THE GENERAL AGREEMENT ON TARIFFS AND TRADE)
In operation since 1948, with a membership now approaching eighty countries. From its secretariat in Geneva, and through a number of major rounds of tariff-cutting, the GATT has been an important instrument for the dismantling of tariffs and other barriers to trade among its members. Its major principle is the MFN (*q.v.*) clause.

GENERALISED SYSTEM OF PREFERENCES (GSP)

Approved in principle by UNCTAD (*q.v.*) at New Delhi in 1968, GSP was introduced first by the EEC in 1971, followed by other industrialised countries but not the US and Canada. It grants unilaterally, and on a non-reciprocal basis, a partial or total suppression of tariffs on manufactured and semi-manufactured goods, with important exceptions, *a priori* safe-guard clauses and/or tariff-quotas, to the Group of 77 (now 96) among the developing countries.

GROUP OF TEN

The ten richest members of the IMF (*q.v.*), US, Netherlands, UK, Sweden, France, Japan, Germany, Italy, Belgium, Canada. With Switzerland, under the 1962 General Agreement to Borrow it makes available to the IMF (*q.v.*) additional funds with which to finance temporary balance-of-payments deficits.

INTERNATIONAL BANK FOR RECONSTRUCTION AND DEVELOPMENT (IBRD OR WORLD BANK)

A specialised agency of the UN, the Bank, whose membership and voting rights are those of the IMF (*q.v.*), provides loans on commercial terms for development purposes, and acts as a financial adviser to LDCs. It acquires its fund from subscriptions by member states and by floating bonds on the international capital market. The International Finance Corporation, which participates in private investment in LDCs, and since 1960, the International Development Association which provides soft loans, complement World Bank activities.

INTERNATIONAL MONETARY FUND (IMF)

Set up under the 1944 Bretton Woods (*q.v.*) agreement, the IMF became important with the introduction of general currency convertibility in the late 1950s. Principal world forum for monetary policy discussion. Its articles of agreement set limits to permissible exchange rate fluctuations, provide for a gold-exchange standard, fix quotas paid by each member into the 'Fund' which finances balance-of-payments disequilibria.

INTERNATIONAL SUGAR AGREEMENT

The present agreement, in force since 1969, attempts to maintain stable and remunerative export prices by means of export quotas for that part of the international market (about half) not covered by the US Sugar Act, the Commonwealth Sugar Agreement, and Soviet–Cuban purchase arrangements. The European Community is not a member.

KENNEDY ROUND
A major GATT (*q.v.*) negotiation (1964–7) made possible by the US Trade Expansion Act (1962), which achieved substantial cuts in industrial, but not in agricultural tariffs. The European Community negotiated as a unit.

MBFR
(MUTUAL AND BALANCED FORCE REDUCTIONS)
First proposed by NATO in 1968, MBFR negotiations are meant to maintain the present balance of NATO and Warsaw Pact (*q.v.*) armed forces in Europe at a lower level. These negotiations are parallel to, but not formally linked to the Conference on Security and Co-operation in Europe (*q.v.*).

MOST-FAVOURED NATION CLAUSE (MFN)
Part of many bilateral trade agreements in the nineteenth century, MFN became the central element of post-war trade liberalisation through GATT (*q.v.*) Article 1 of which reads: 'With respect to customs duties and charges of any kind imposed on or in connection with importation or exportation . . . any advantage, favour, privilege or immunity granted by any contracting party to any product originating in or destined for any other country shall be accorded immediately and unconditionally to the like product originating in or destined for the territories of all other contracting parties.'

NON-PROLIFERATION TREATY (NPT)
Signed in 1968 by the UK, USA, USSR and 60 other states, the NPT seeks to curb the spread of nuclear weapons, by forbidding their transfer from one state to another. France and China did not accede.

NORTH ATLANTIC ALLIANCE
Set up by the Treaty of 1949 by the US, Canada, and eight European states, later joined by the Federal Republic of

Germany, Greece, and Turkey. Members are pledged to consider attack on one of them as an attack on all, and in the event of such an attack to help by 'such action as it deems necessary'. The Alliance has found its institutional expression in the (civilian) North Atlantic Treaty Organisation (NATO), which integrates part (in Germany's case all) of the military efforts of the members of the organisation under a unified command (Supreme Headquarters Allied Powers Europe – SHAPE). France left the organisation in 1965, though it continues to adhere to the Treaty.

NUCLEAR PLANNING GROUP (NPG)
Composed of four permanent, and four or five rotating members of NATO, the NPG, since 1967, works out a doctrine for the use of (US held) tactical nuclear weapons in the event of an aggresion.

OECD (ORGANISATION FOR ECONOMIC CO-OPERATION AND DEVELOPMENT)
Successor organisation to OEEC (*q.v.*) with expanded membership (the US, Canada, Spain, and in 1964 Japan) and changed functions: to promote growth, high employment and financial stability among the member states by means of joint reviews of their economic policies in a wide range of fields; the coordination and encouragement of development aid.

OEEC (ORGANISATION FOR EUROPEAN ECONOMIC CO-OPERATION)
Established in 1948 by 16 European countries plus allied representatives for Germany, OEEC's immediate purpose was to present a plan for the efficient distribution of American aid under the European Recovery Programme (Marshall Aid). Progressively, the liberalisation of trade, payments, and capital in Europe became its primary task. It was replaced by the OECD (*q.v.*) in 1961.

OPEC (ORGANISATION OF PETROLEUM EXPORTING COUNTRIES)
The organisation represents the interests of Venezuela, Indonesia, and Middle Eastern and North African oil-exporting

countries *vis-à-vis* the international oil companies. It pursues the twin goals of securing a greater share of revenues for its members, where its first major success was the Teheran Agreement of 1971, and of achieving greater control by its members over the ownership and management of their oil resouces, as regards both production and marketing (participation issue).

OSTPOLITIK

A German term used with particular reference to Chancellor Willy Brandt's efforts to improve relations with Eastern Europe, including the Moscow agreement of 1970, the Berlin agreement and the Basic Treaty with the German Democratic Republic of 1972, and the resumption of diplomatic relations with Poland and Czechoslovakia. Ostpolitik essentially exchanges West German recognition of the territorial *status quo* for improved diplomatic relations with the East.

SALT (STRATEGIC ARMS LIMITATION TALKS)

The first SALT agreement between the US and the USSR was signed in Moscow in May 1972. It can be said to have institutionalised deterrence, since it allows for only limited expansion of ABM (anti-ballistic missile) systems. There was also an Interim Agreement on limiting ICBM (inter-continental ballistic missile) launcher construction, which however risks provoking a qualitative arms race. The new round of talks, SALT II, deals with qualitative limitations.

SDRs (SPECIAL DRAWING RIGHTS)

Since 1969, a low-interest-bearing issue of reserve assets by the IMF (*q.v.*). The creation of artificial (but gold-backed) international liquidity is intended to make a global money supply independent of the size of the US balance-of-payments deficit and international gold production.

SMITHSONIAN AGREEMENT

An agreement in December 1971 by the Group of Ten (*q.v.*) setting new par values for the dollar (10 per cent devaluation), and raising permissible margins of exchange rate fluctuation from ± 1 per cent to ± 2.25 per cent.

UNCTAD (United Nations Conference on Trade and Development)

Conference with permanent secretariat in Geneva convened three times since 1964 to seek solutions to the trade problems of developing countries. It has concentrated on such problems as the deterioration of the terms of trade, has achieved special financing of balance-of-payments difficulties caused by fluctuating commodity prices, and most importantly, obtained agreement from GATT that the MFN (*q.v.*) clause need not apply to LDCs (*see also* Generalised System . . .).

Warsaw Pact

The Eastern European Mutual Assistance Treaty (1955) between the USSR, Bulgaria, Czechoslovakia, the GDR, Hungary, Poland, and Roumania (Albania was excluded in 1961); Warsaw Pact forces are under a unified command.

WEU (Western European Union)

Created in 1955 to allow German rearmament after failure of EDC (*q.v.*) project. Successor to the Brussels Treaty (1948). Its defence functions are carried out by NATO. Its main operational task has been armaments control. It also provides a forum in its Assembly for discussion of foreign policy and defence. Members: Benelux, France, Germany, Italy and the UK.

World Bank *see* International Bank

Yaoundé Convention

The first (1964) Convention replaced Part IV of the Rome Treaty, and provided for association with the EEC of the former dependencies of Italy, Belgium and France. Of the 18 Associates, 14 are the countries in West and Central Africa which had been French (excluding Guinea) and Madagascar. The others are the former Belgian Congo (now Zaire), Burundi and Ruanda; and Somalia, formerly Italian. The Convention establishes free trade areas between each Associate and the Community, and provides for financial and technical co-

operation (*see* European Development Fund), and Institutions
– a Council (EEC Council plus representatives from Associates) and a Parliamentary Conference. A second agreement
(Yaoundé II) was initialled in June 1969 and expires on
January 31, 1975.

Index